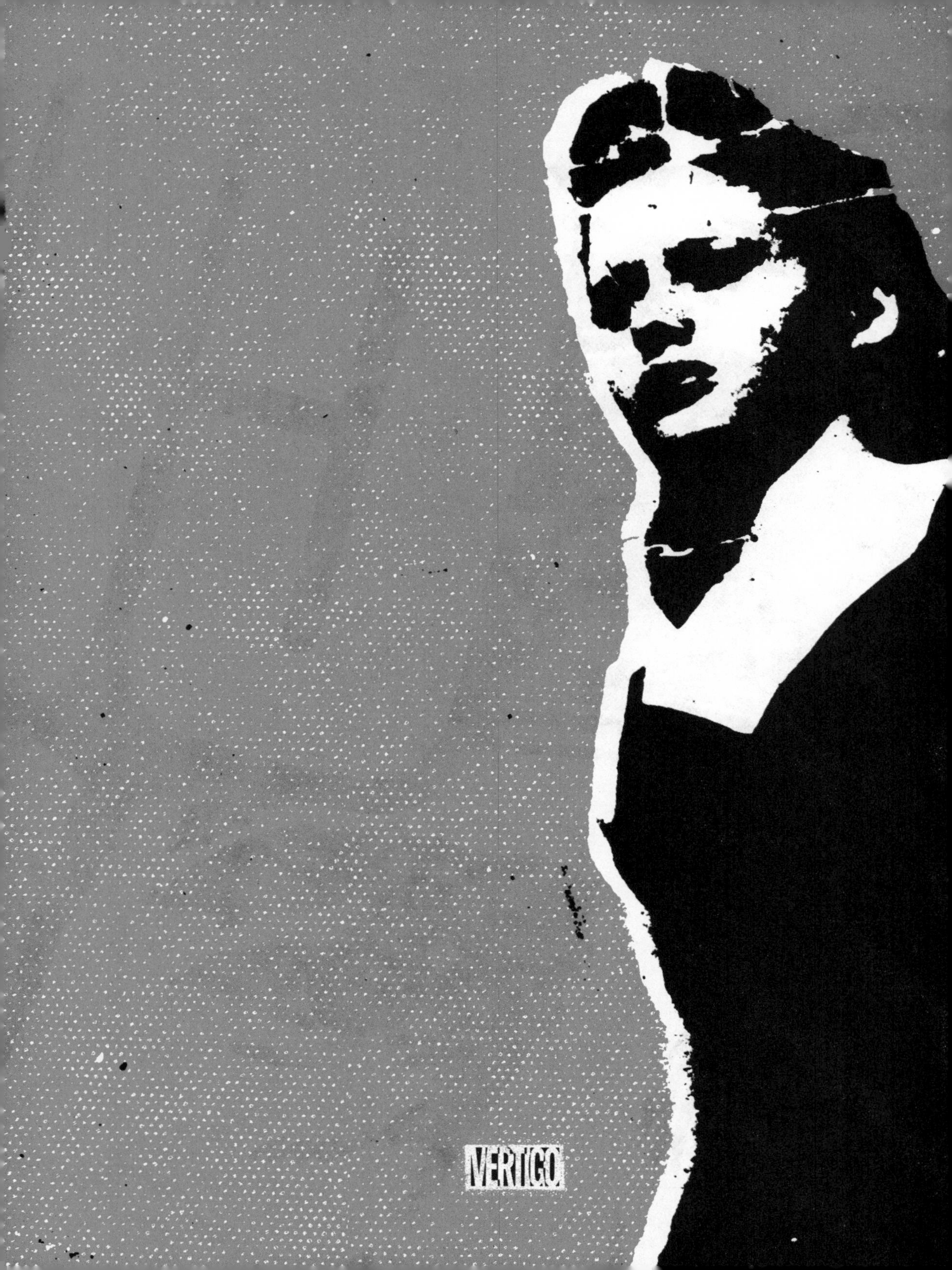
VERTIGO

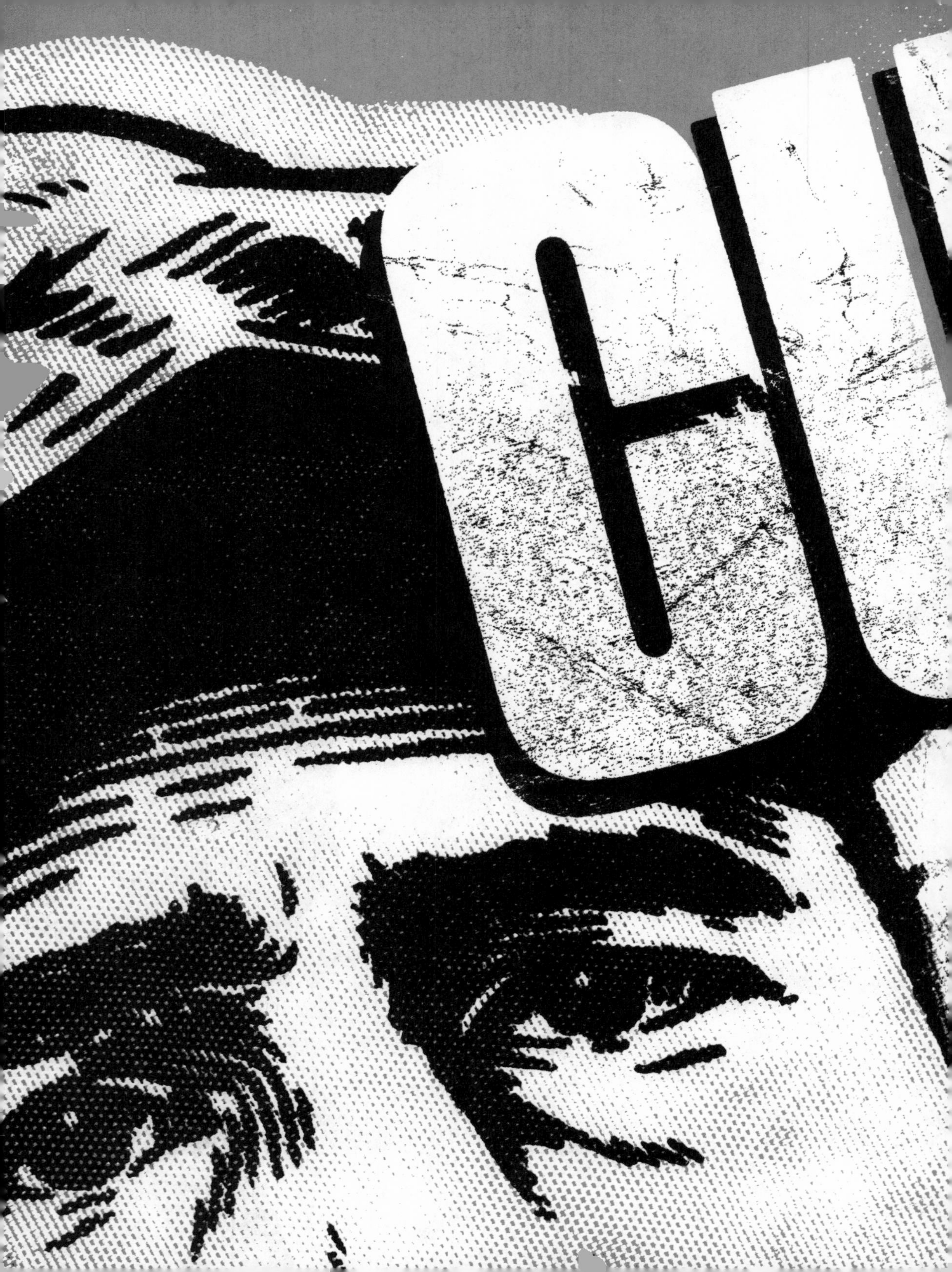

BA

my revolution

writer **INVERNA LOCKPEZ**

artist **DEAN HASPIEL**

colorist **JOSÉ VILLARRUBIA**   letterer **PAT BROSSEAU**

Author's Note

There were aspects of my life I preferred to forget because they were too painful to remember. In spite of myself, flashes of past experiences appeared, and in the process of reconstructing them I learned that testimony is important to the ideals and endurance of the human spirit, as well as to my own.

This book is for the people of Cuba everywhere who have not been heard, who have endured economic hardship, who long to express themselves through art without the fear of imprisonment, and who still fight for the return of freedom once enjoyed.

—Inverna Lockpez

DEDICATIONS

I want to thank Dean Haspiel for encouraging me to tell my story and for an incredibly inspiring and challenging collaboration; my editor, Joan Hilty, for her insightful guidance; Jose Villarrubia for making me love pink again; and my friends who read the manuscript and gave valuable suggestions: Lisa Rainwater, Andy Mele, and Wendy Kesselman. Special thanks to my partner Ali, for working with me on this project with patience and understanding.

—Inverna Lockpez

I'd like to thank my beautiful mother, Barbara Haspiel, for introducing me to Inverna Lockpez, who, over the past two decades, became my second mother and bravely divulged her personal experiences of Cuba. I'm luckier than most human beings to have these two women help shape my life.

I'd like to thank Joan Hilty for being the best editor I've ever worked with. This book could not have happened without her commitment and sensitivity to storytelling and detail. I'd like to give Jose Villarrubia a big bear hug for helping me realize a highly romanticized yet tragic era with the mastery of his colors and painting.

I'd also like to acknowledge the wisdom and support of Michel Fiffe, Jen Ferguson, and DEEP6 Studios.

—Dean Haspiel

Karen Berger SVP - Executive Editor **Joan Hilty** Editor **Sarah Litt** Assistant Editor
Robbin Brosterman Design Director - Books **Louis Prandi** Art Director

DC COMICS
Diane Nelson President, **Dan DiDio** and **Jim Lee** Co-Publishers **Geoff Johns** Chief Creative Officer
John Rood Executive Vice President, Sales, Marketing and Business Development **Amy Genkins** Senior VP Business and Legal Affairs
Patrick Caldon Executive Vice President, Finance and Administration **John Cunningham** VP Marketing
Steve Rotterdam Senior VP-Sales and Marketing **Alison Gill** VP-Manufacturing **David Hyde** VP Publicity
Terri Cunningham VP-Managing Editor **Alysse Soll** VP-Advertising and Custom Publishing
Sue Pohja VP-Book Trade Sales **Mark Chiarello** Art Director
Bob Wayne VP-Sales

Cover Artist: **Dean Haspiel**
CUBA: MY REVOLUTION Published by DC Comics, 1700 Broadway, New York, NY 10019. Copyright © 2010 by Inverna Lockpez and Dean Haspiel. Artwork on pages 6, 38 and 94 by and © Inverna Lockpez, graphite on paper, Cuba, 1960s. All rights reserved. VERTIGO is a trademark of DC Comics. Printed in the USA. First Printing. DC Comics, a Warner Bros. Entertainment Company.
HC ISBN: 978-1-4012-2217-8   SC ISBN: 978-1-4012-2218-5

SUSTAINABLE FORESTRY INITIATIVE
Certified Fiber Sourcing
www.sfiprogram.org
Fiber used in this product line meets the sourcing requirements of the SFI program.
www.sfiprogram.org NFS-SPICOC-C0001801

PART ONE

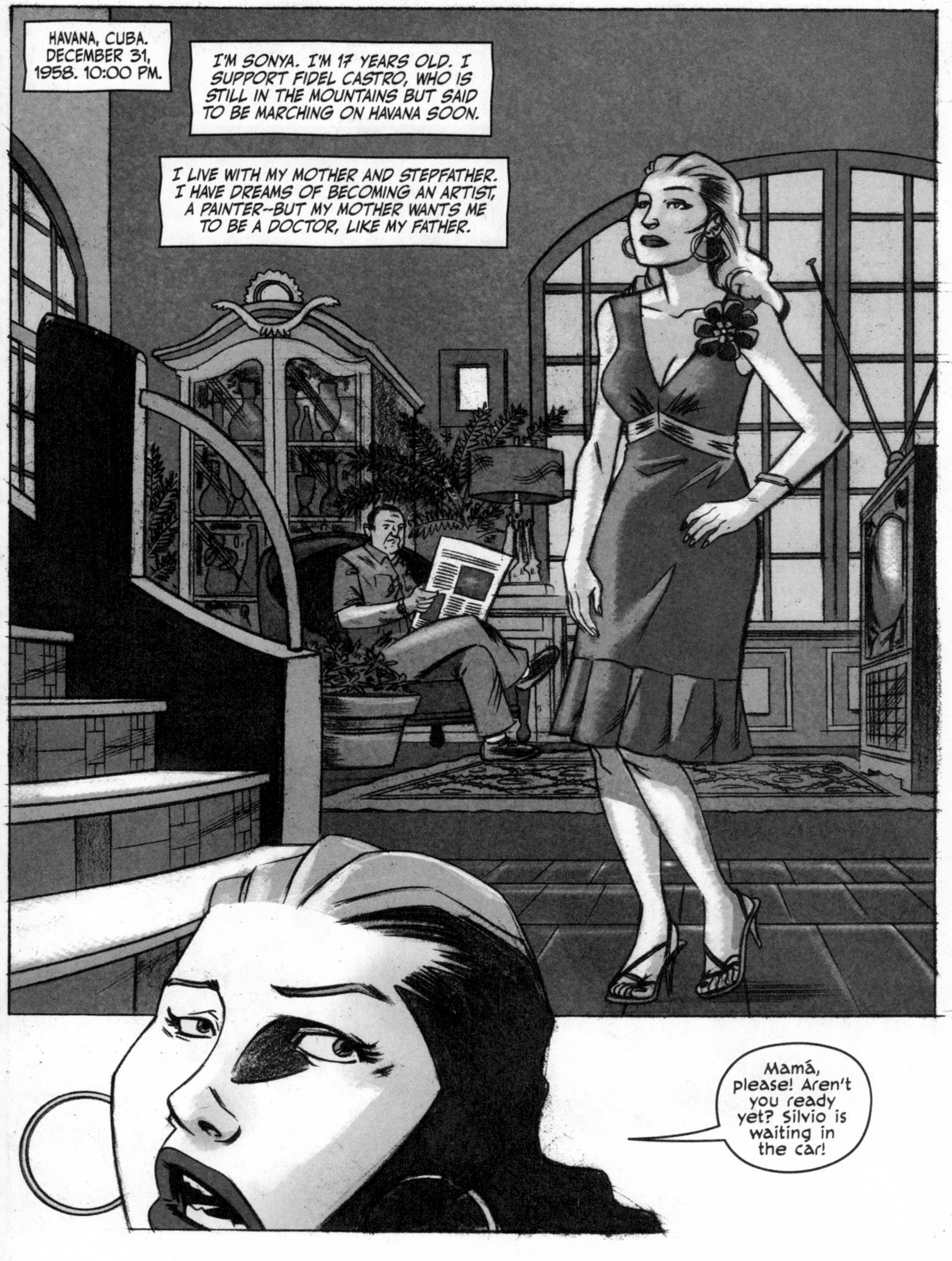
HAVANA, CUBA. DECEMBER 31, 1958. 10:00 PM.
I'M SONYA. I'M 17 YEARS OLD. I SUPPORT FIDEL CASTRO, WHO IS STILL IN THE MOUNTAINS BUT SAID TO BE MARCHING ON HAVANA SOON.
I LIVE WITH MY MOTHER AND STEPFATHER. I HAVE DREAMS OF BECOMING AN ARTIST, A PAINTER--BUT MY MOTHER WANTS ME TO BE A DOCTOR, LIKE MY FATHER.
Mamá, please! Aren't you ready yet? Silvio is waiting in the car!

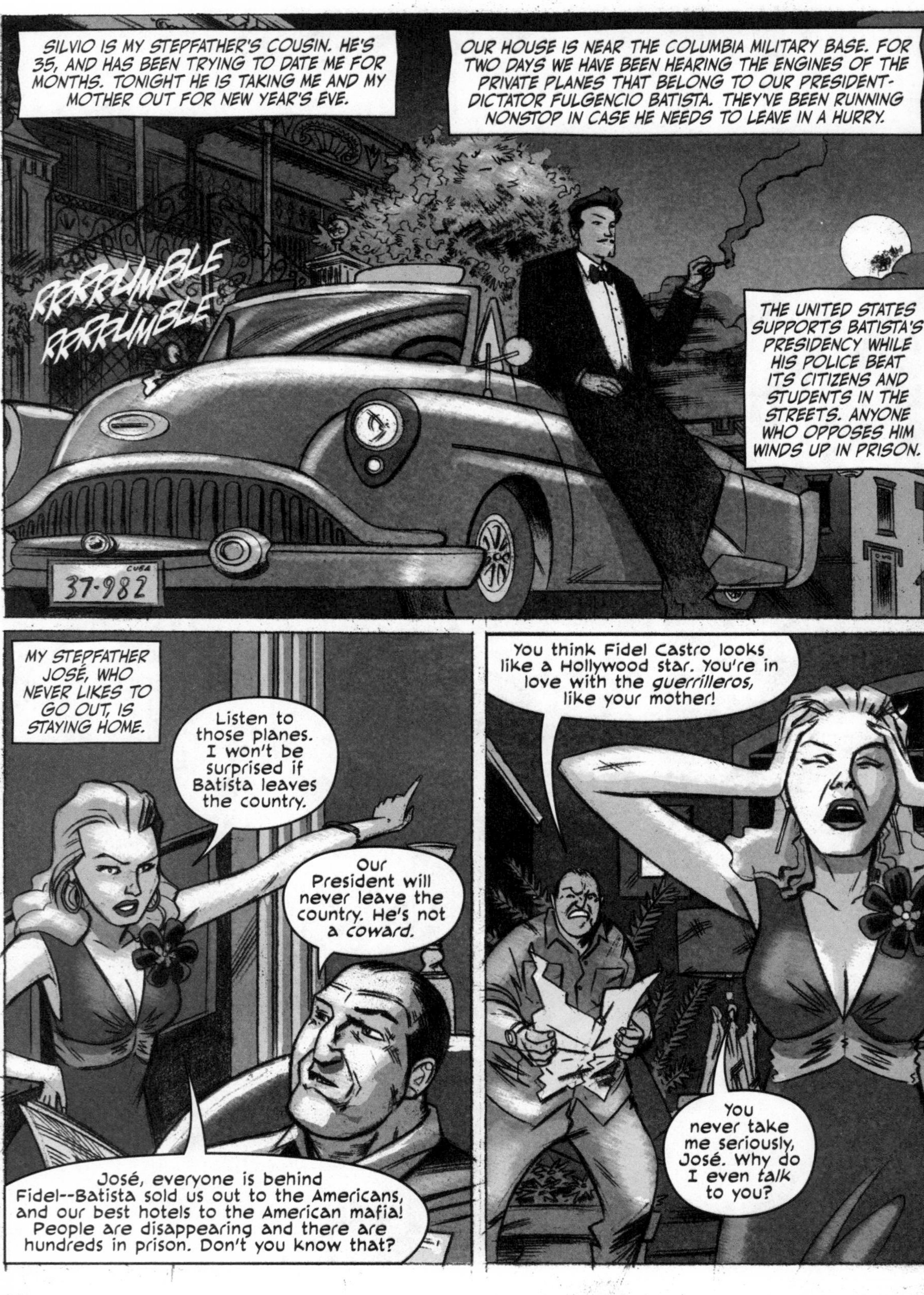
SILVIO IS MY STEPFATHER'S COUSIN. HE'S 35, AND HAS BEEN TRYING TO DATE ME FOR MONTHS. TONIGHT HE IS TAKING ME AND MY MOTHER OUT FOR NEW YEAR'S EVE.
OUR HOUSE IS NEAR THE COLUMBIA MILITARY BASE. FOR TWO DAYS WE HAVE BEEN HEARING THE ENGINES OF THE PRIVATE PLANES THAT BELONG TO OUR PRESIDENT-DICTATOR FULGENCIO BATISTA. THEY'VE BEEN RUNNING NONSTOP IN CASE HE NEEDS TO LEAVE IN A HURRY.
RRRRUMBLE
RRRRUMBLE
THE UNITED STATES SUPPORTS BATISTA'S PRESIDENCY WHILE HIS POLICE BEAT ITS CITIZENS AND STUDENTS IN THE STREETS. ANYONE WHO OPPOSES HIM WINDS UP IN PRISON.
CUBA
37-982
MY STEPFATHER JOSÉ, WHO NEVER LIKES TO GO OUT, IS STAYING HOME.
Listen to those planes. I won't be surprised if Batista leaves the country.
Our President will never leave the country. He's not a *coward.*
José, everyone is behind Fidel--Batista sold us out to the Americans, and our best hotels to the American mafia! People are disappearing and there are hundreds in prison. Don't you know that?
You think Fidel Castro looks like a Hollywood star. You're in love with the *guerrilleros,* like your mother!
You never take me seriously, José. Why do I even *talk* to you?

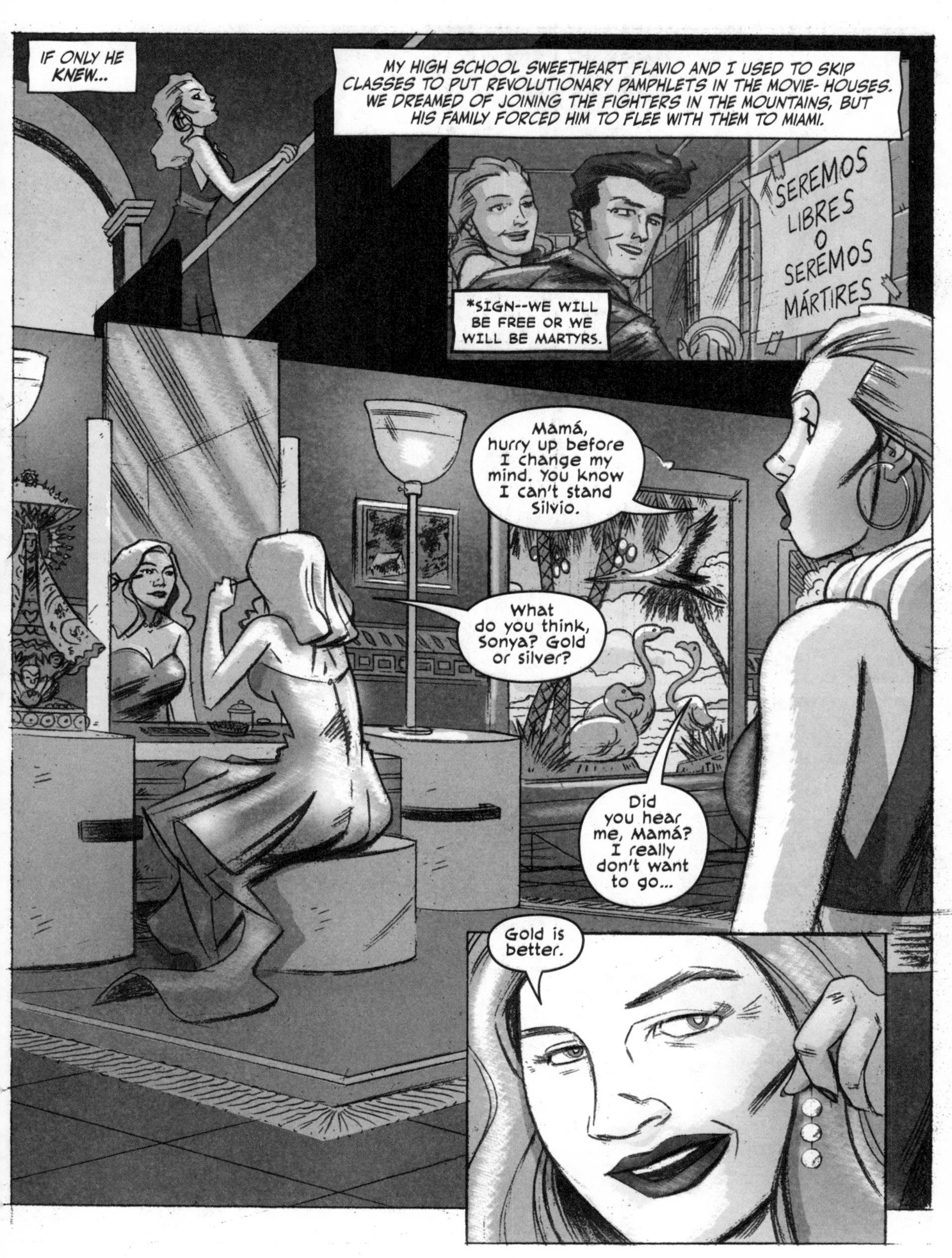
IF ONLY HE KNEW...
MY HIGH SCHOOL SWEETHEART FLAVIO AND I USED TO SKIP CLASSES TO PUT REVOLUTIONARY PAMPHLETS IN THE MOVIE- HOUSES. WE DREAMED OF JOINING THE FIGHTERS IN THE MOUNTAINS, BUT HIS FAMILY FORCED HIM TO FLEE WITH THEM TO MIAMI.
SEREMOS LIBRES O SEREMOS MÁRTIRES
*SIGN--WE WILL BE FREE OR WE WILL BE MARTYRS.
Mamá, hurry up before I change my mind. You know I can't stand Silvio.
What do you think, Sonya? Gold or silver?
Did you hear me, Mamá? I really don't want to go...
Gold is better.

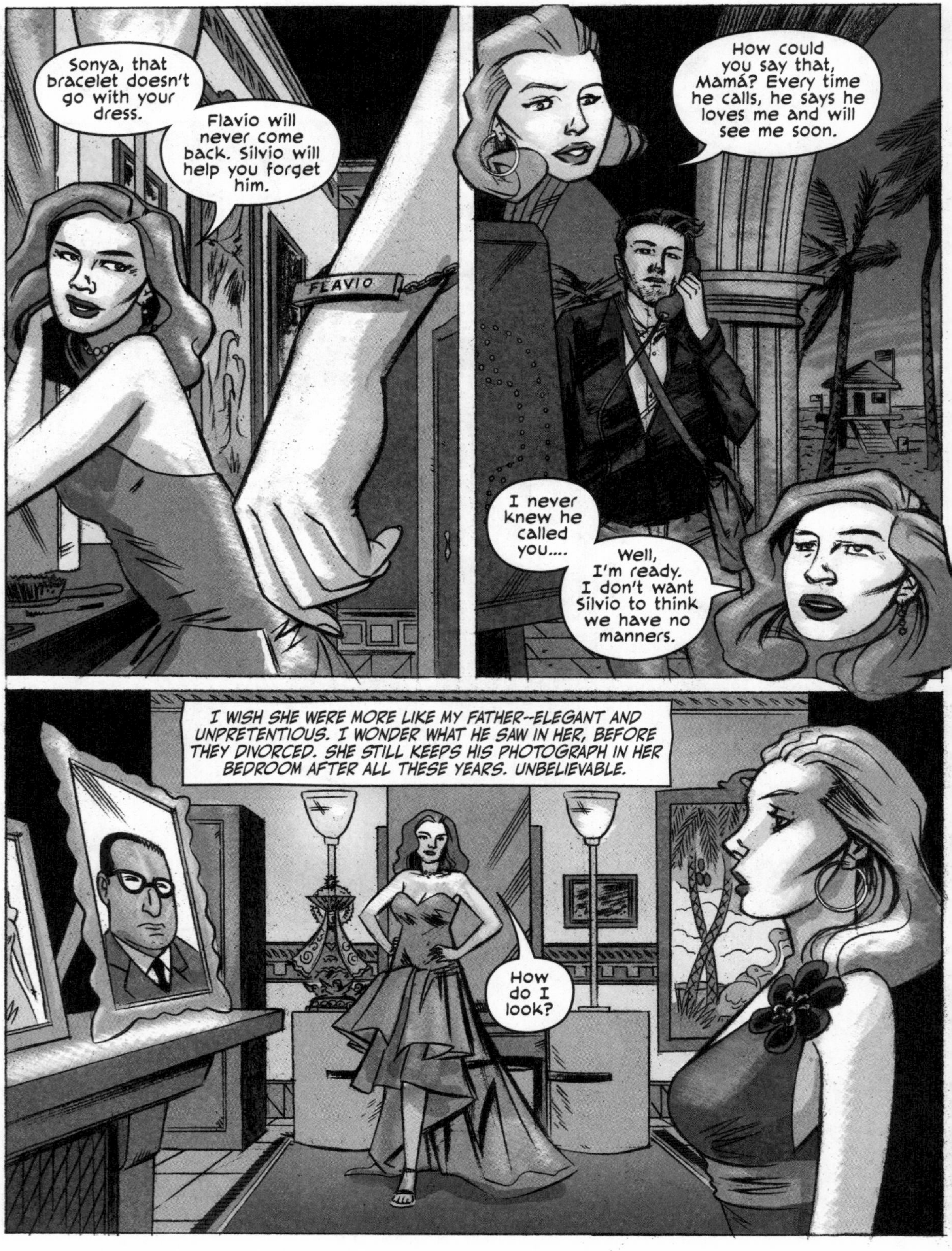
Sonya, that bracelet doesn't go with your dress.
Flavio will never come back. Silvio will help you forget him.
FLAVIO
How could you say that, Mamá? Every time he calls, he says he loves me and will see me soon.
I never knew he called you....
Well, I'm ready. I don't want Silvio to think we have no manners.
I WISH SHE WERE MORE LIKE MY FATHER--ELEGANT AND UNPRETENTIOUS. I WONDER WHAT HE SAW IN HER, BEFORE THEY DIVORCED. SHE STILL KEEPS HIS PHOTOGRAPH IN HER BEDROOM AFTER ALL THESE YEARS. UNBELIEVABLE.
How do I look?

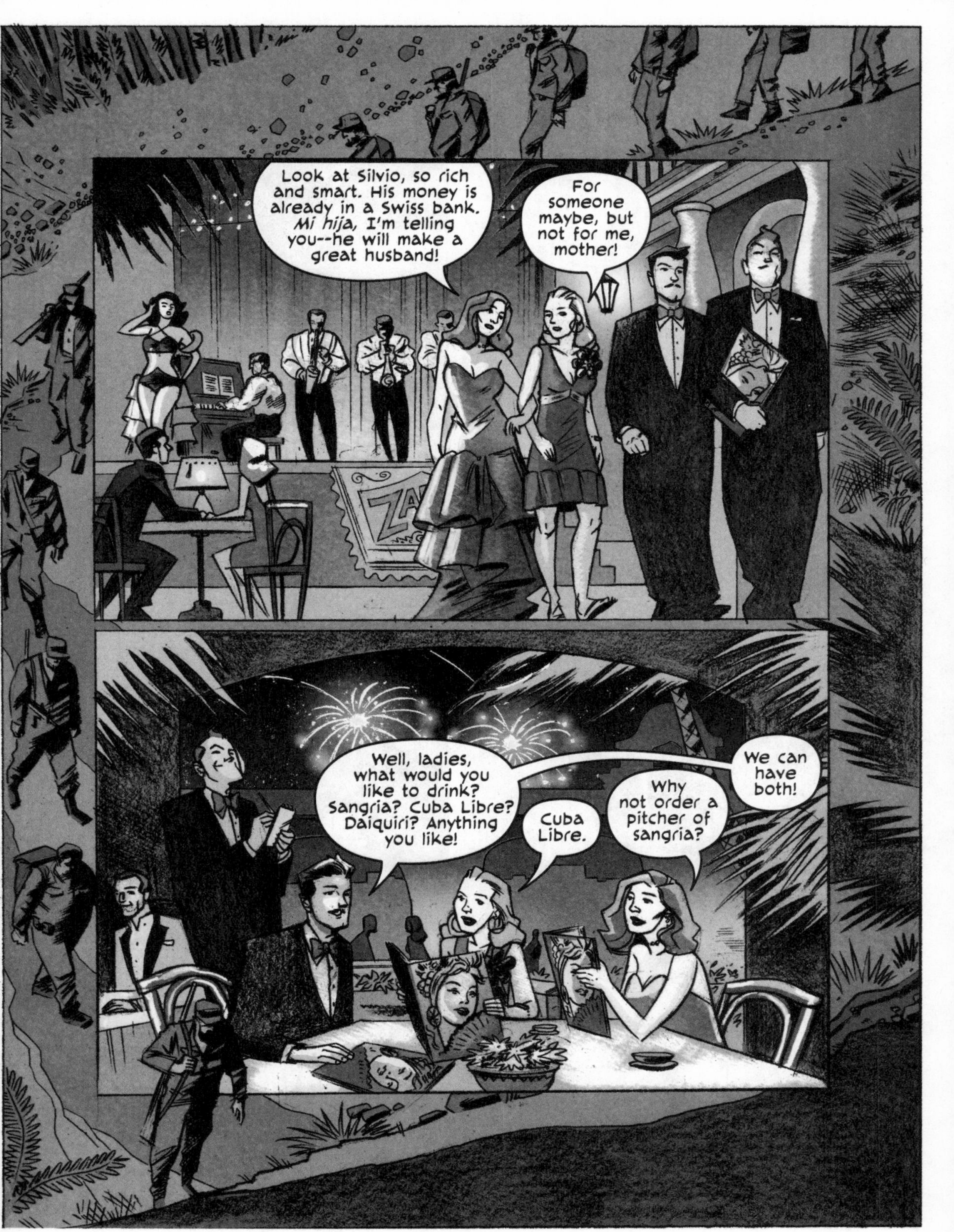

Look at Silvio, so rich and smart. His money is already in a Swiss bank. *Mi hija,* I'm telling you--he will make a great husband!
For someone maybe, but not for me, mother!
Well, ladies, what would you like to drink? Sangria? Cuba Libre? Daiquiri? Anything you like!
Cuba Libre.
Why not order a pitcher of sangria?
We can have both!

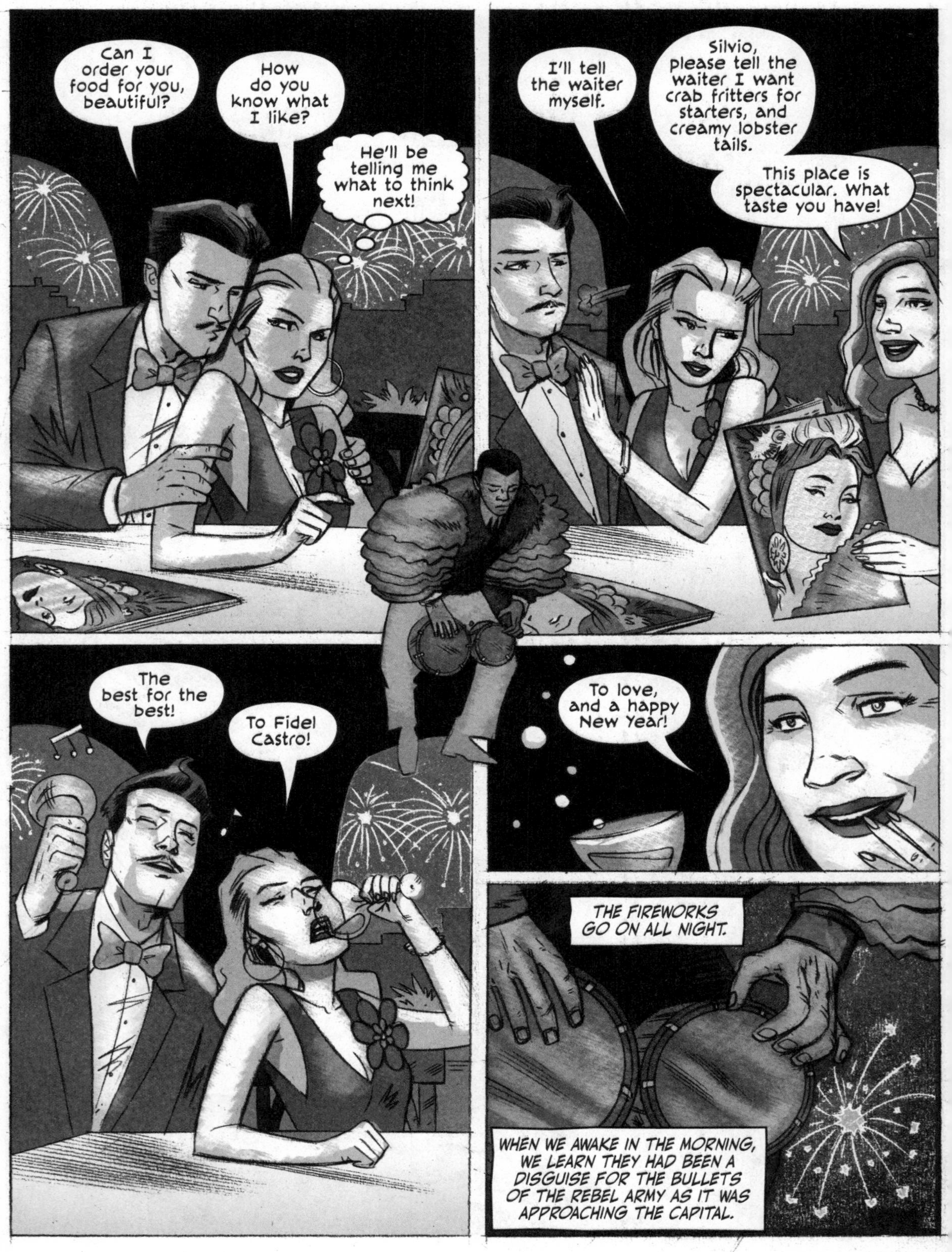
Can I order your food for you, beautiful?
How do you know what I like?
He'll be telling me what to think next!
I'll tell the waiter myself.
Silvio, please tell the waiter I want crab fritters for starters, and creamy lobster tails.
This place is spectacular. What taste you have!
The best for the best!
To Fidel Castro!
To love, and a happy New Year!
THE FIREWORKS GO ON ALL NIGHT.
WHEN WE AWAKE IN THE MORNING, WE LEARN THEY HAD BEEN A DISGUISE FOR THE BULLETS OF THE REBEL ARMY AS IT WAS APPROACHING THE CAPITAL.

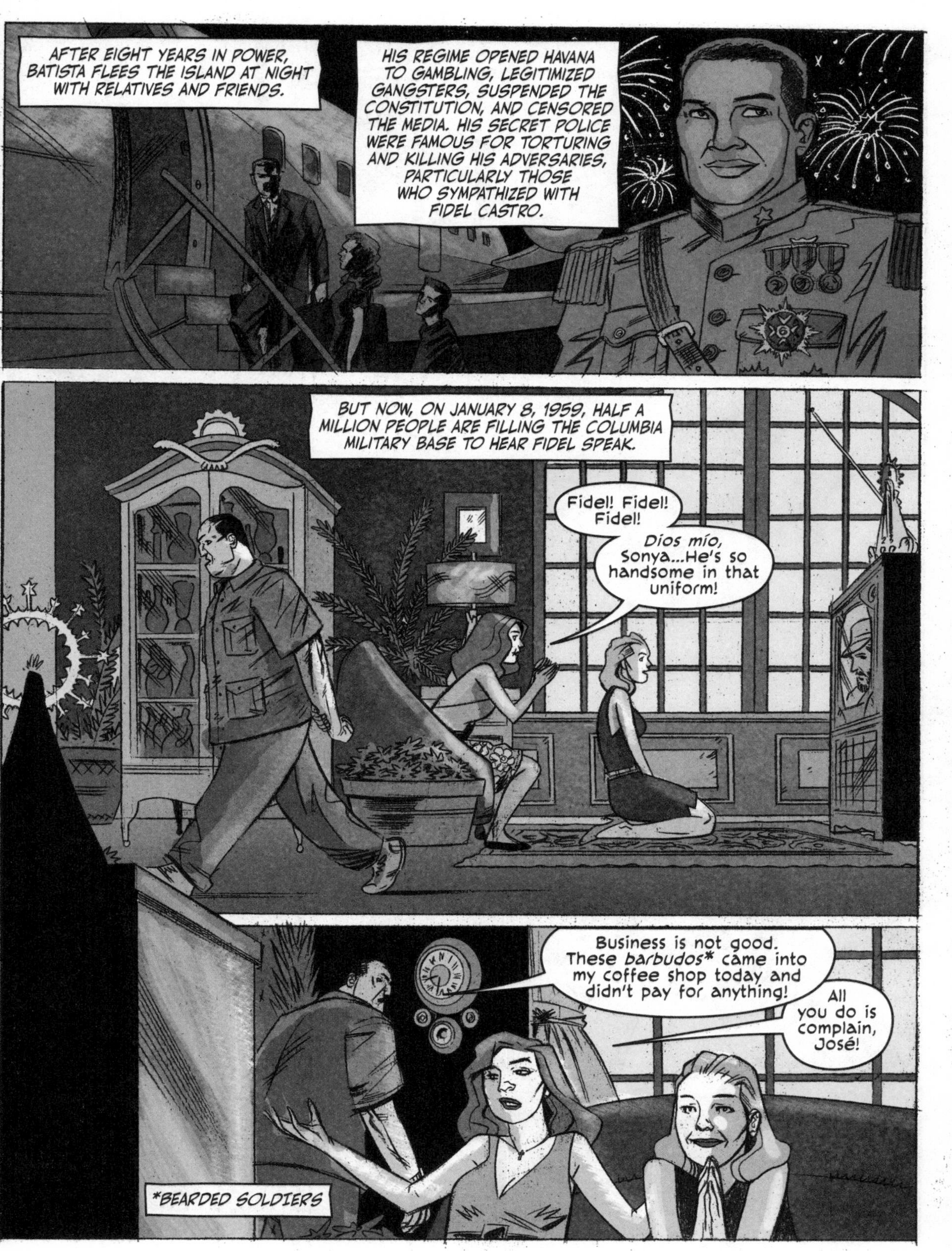
AFTER EIGHT YEARS IN POWER, BATISTA FLEES THE ISLAND AT NIGHT WITH RELATIVES AND FRIENDS.
HIS REGIME OPENED HAVANA TO GAMBLING, LEGITIMIZED GANGSTERS, SUSPENDED THE CONSTITUTION, AND CENSORED THE MEDIA. HIS SECRET POLICE WERE FAMOUS FOR TORTURING AND KILLING HIS ADVERSARIES, PARTICULARLY THOSE WHO SYMPATHIZED WITH FIDEL CASTRO.
BUT NOW, ON JANUARY 8, 1959, HALF A MILLION PEOPLE ARE FILLING THE COLUMBIA MILITARY BASE TO HEAR FIDEL SPEAK.
Fidel! Fidel! Fidel!
Dios mío, Sonya...He's so handsome in that uniform!
Business is not good. These *barbudos** came into my coffee shop today and didn't pay for anything!
All you do is complain, José!
*BEARDED SOLDIERS

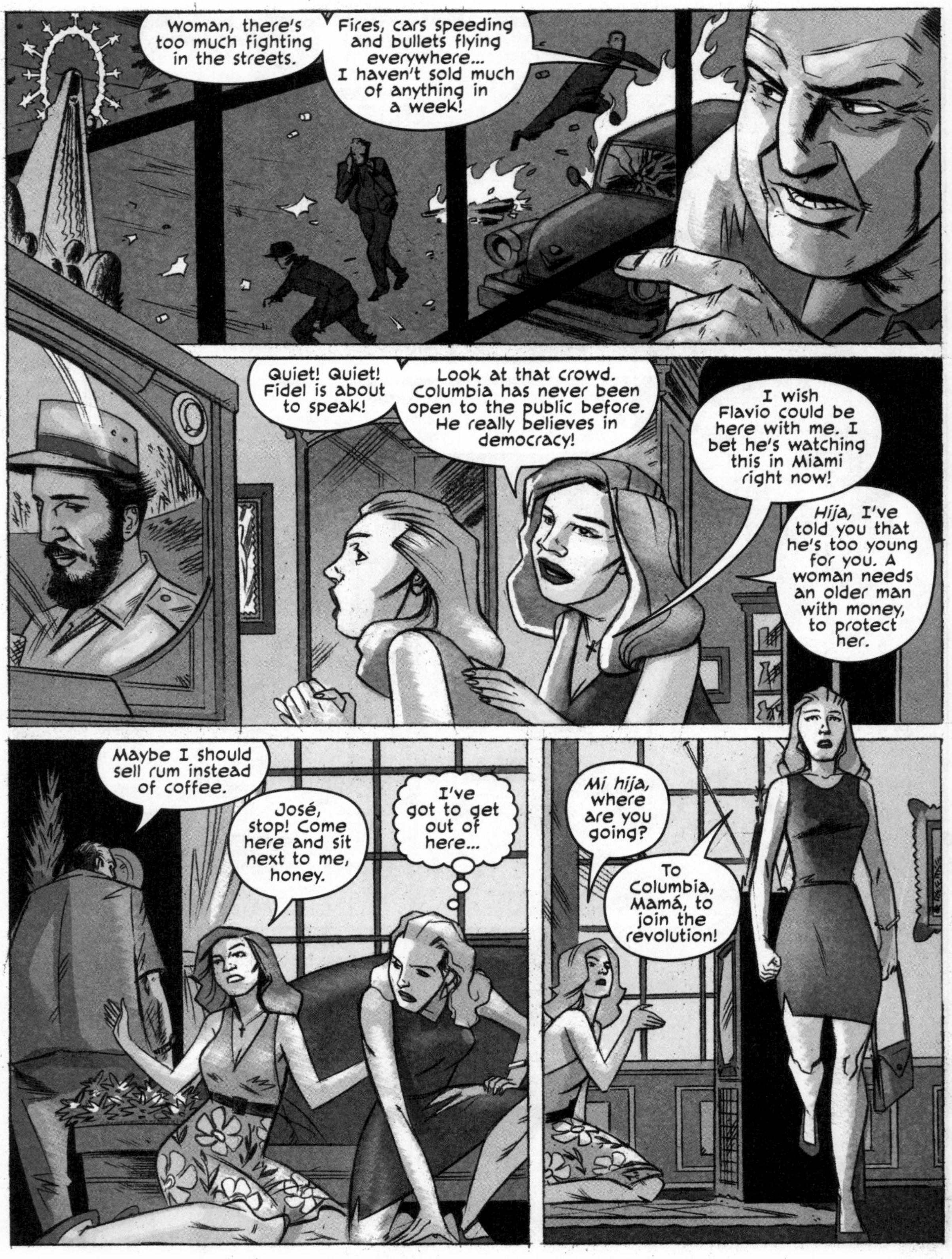

Woman, there's too much fighting in the streets.
Fires, cars speeding and bullets flying everywhere... I haven't sold much of anything in a week!
Quiet! Quiet! Fidel is about to speak!
Look at that crowd. Columbia has never been open to the public before. He really believes in democracy!
I wish Flavio could be here with me. I bet he's watching this in Miami right now!
Hija, I've told you that he's too young for you. A woman needs an older man with money, to protect her.
Maybe I should sell rum instead of coffee.
José, stop! Come here and sit next to me, honey.
I've got to get out of here...
Mi hija, where are you going?
To Columbia, Mamá, to join the revolution!

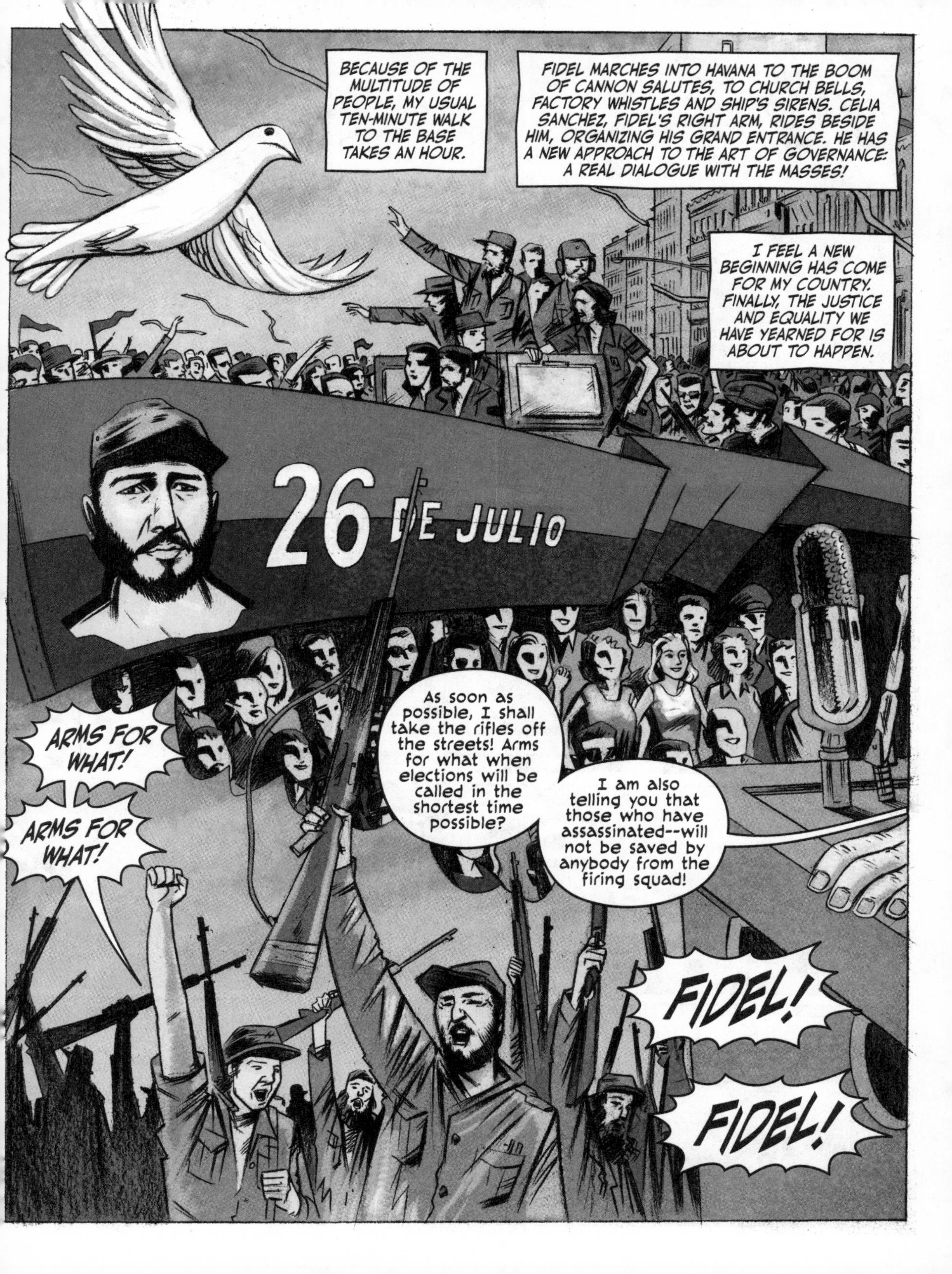
BECAUSE OF THE MULTITUDE OF PEOPLE, MY USUAL TEN-MINUTE WALK TO THE BASE TAKES AN HOUR.
FIDEL MARCHES INTO HAVANA TO THE BOOM OF CANNON SALUTES, TO CHURCH BELLS, FACTORY WHISTLES AND SHIP'S SIRENS. CELIA SANCHEZ, FIDEL'S RIGHT ARM, RIDES BESIDE HIM, ORGANIZING HIS GRAND ENTRANCE. HE HAS A NEW APPROACH TO THE ART OF GOVERNANCE: A REAL DIALOGUE WITH THE MASSES!
I FEEL A NEW BEGINNING HAS COME FOR MY COUNTRY. FINALLY, THE JUSTICE AND EQUALITY WE HAVE YEARNED FOR IS ABOUT TO HAPPEN.
26 DE JULIO
As soon as possible, I shall take the rifles off the streets! Arms for what when elections will be called in the shortest time possible?
ARMS FOR WHAT!
ARMS FOR WHAT!
I am also telling you that those who have assassinated--will not be saved by anybody from the firing squad!
FIDEL!
FIDEL!

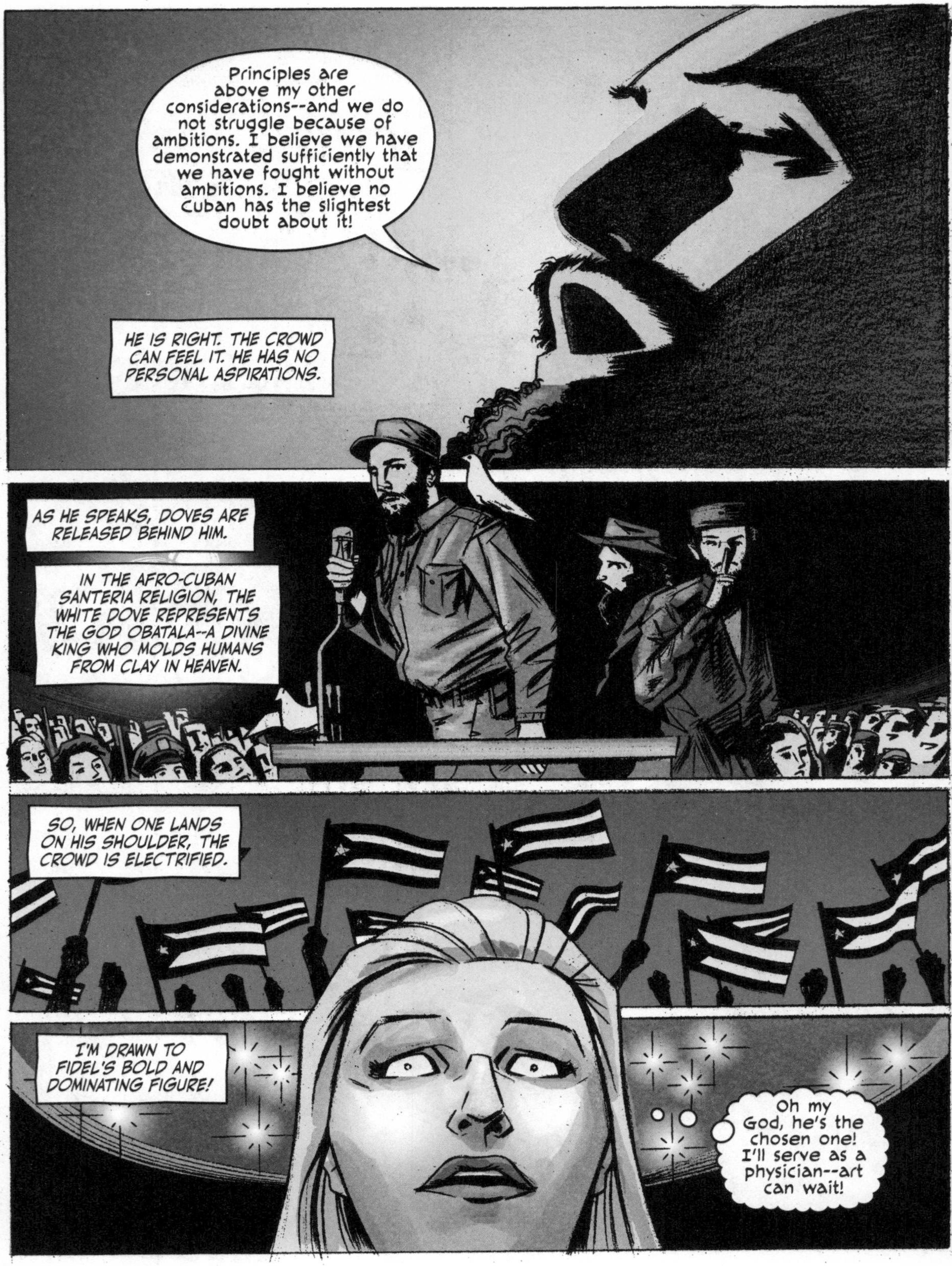
Principles are above my other considerations--and we do not struggle because of ambitions. I believe we have demonstrated sufficiently that we have fought without ambitions. I believe no Cuban has the slightest doubt about it!
HE IS RIGHT. THE CROWD CAN FEEL IT. HE HAS NO PERSONAL ASPIRATIONS.
AS HE SPEAKS, DOVES ARE RELEASED BEHIND HIM.
IN THE AFRO-CUBAN SANTERIA RELIGION, THE WHITE DOVE REPRESENTS THE GOD OBATALA--A DIVINE KING WHO MOLDS HUMANS FROM CLAY IN HEAVEN.
SO, WHEN ONE LANDS ON HIS SHOULDER, THE CROWD IS ELECTRIFIED.
I'M DRAWN TO FIDEL'S BOLD AND DOMINATING FIGURE!
Oh my God, he's the chosen one! I'll serve as a physician--art can wait!

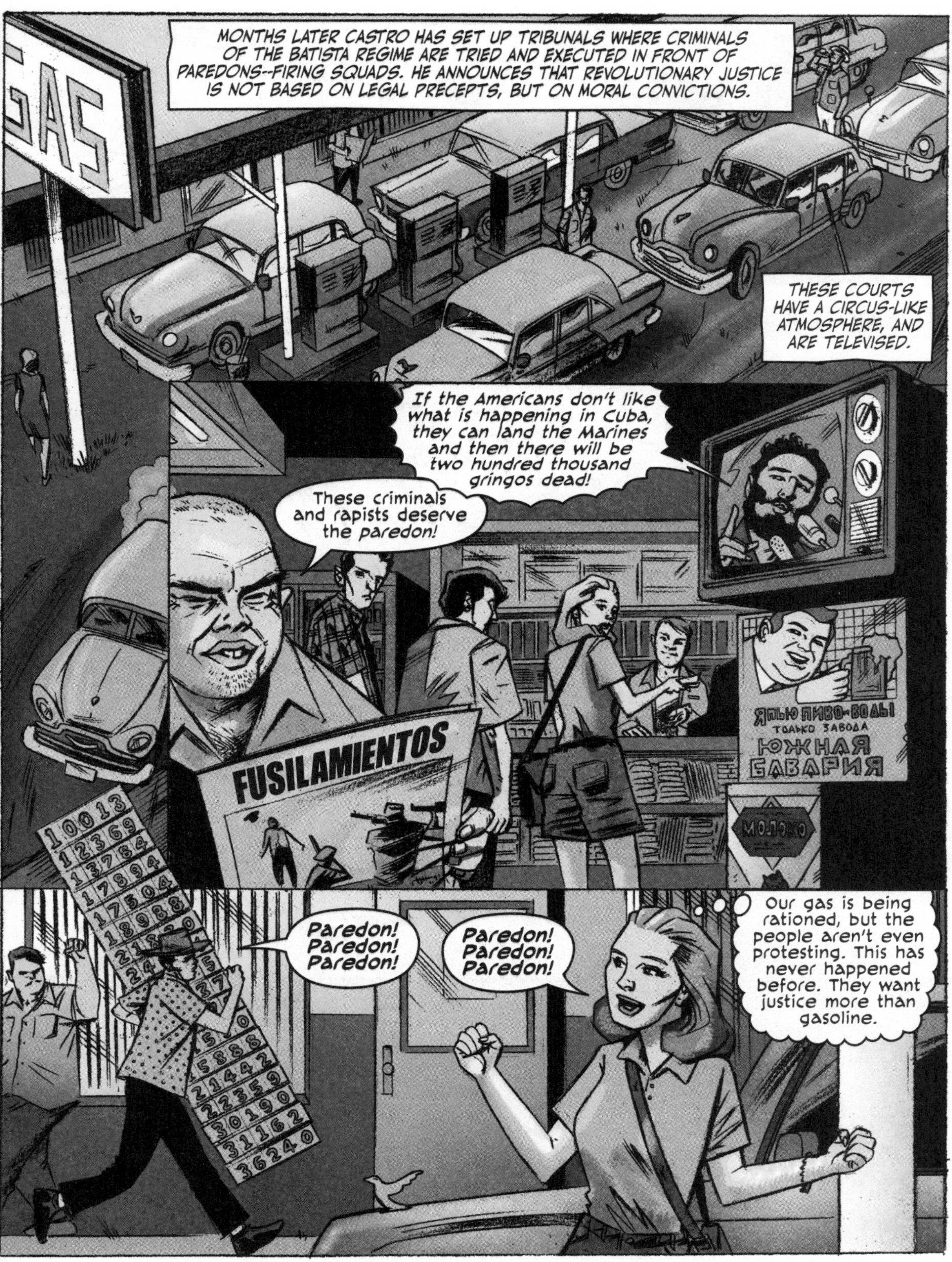
MONTHS LATER CASTRO HAS SET UP TRIBUNALS WHERE CRIMINALS OF THE BATISTA REGIME ARE TRIED AND EXECUTED IN FRONT OF PAREDONS--FIRING SQUADS. HE ANNOUNCES THAT REVOLUTIONARY JUSTICE IS NOT BASED ON LEGAL PRECEPTS, BUT ON MORAL CONVICTIONS.
GAS
THESE COURTS HAVE A CIRCUS-LIKE ATMOSPHERE, AND ARE TELEVISED.
If the Americans don't like what is happening in Cuba, they can land the Marines and then there will be two hundred thousand gringos dead!
These criminals and rapists deserve the *paredon!*
FUSILAMIENTOS
ЯПЬЮ ПИВО-ВОДЫ
ТОЛЬКО ЗАВОДА
ЮЖНАЯ
БАВАРИЯ
Paredon! Paredon! Paredon!
Paredon! Paredon! Paredon!
Our gas is being rationed, but the people aren't even protesting. This has never happened before. They want justice more than gasoline.

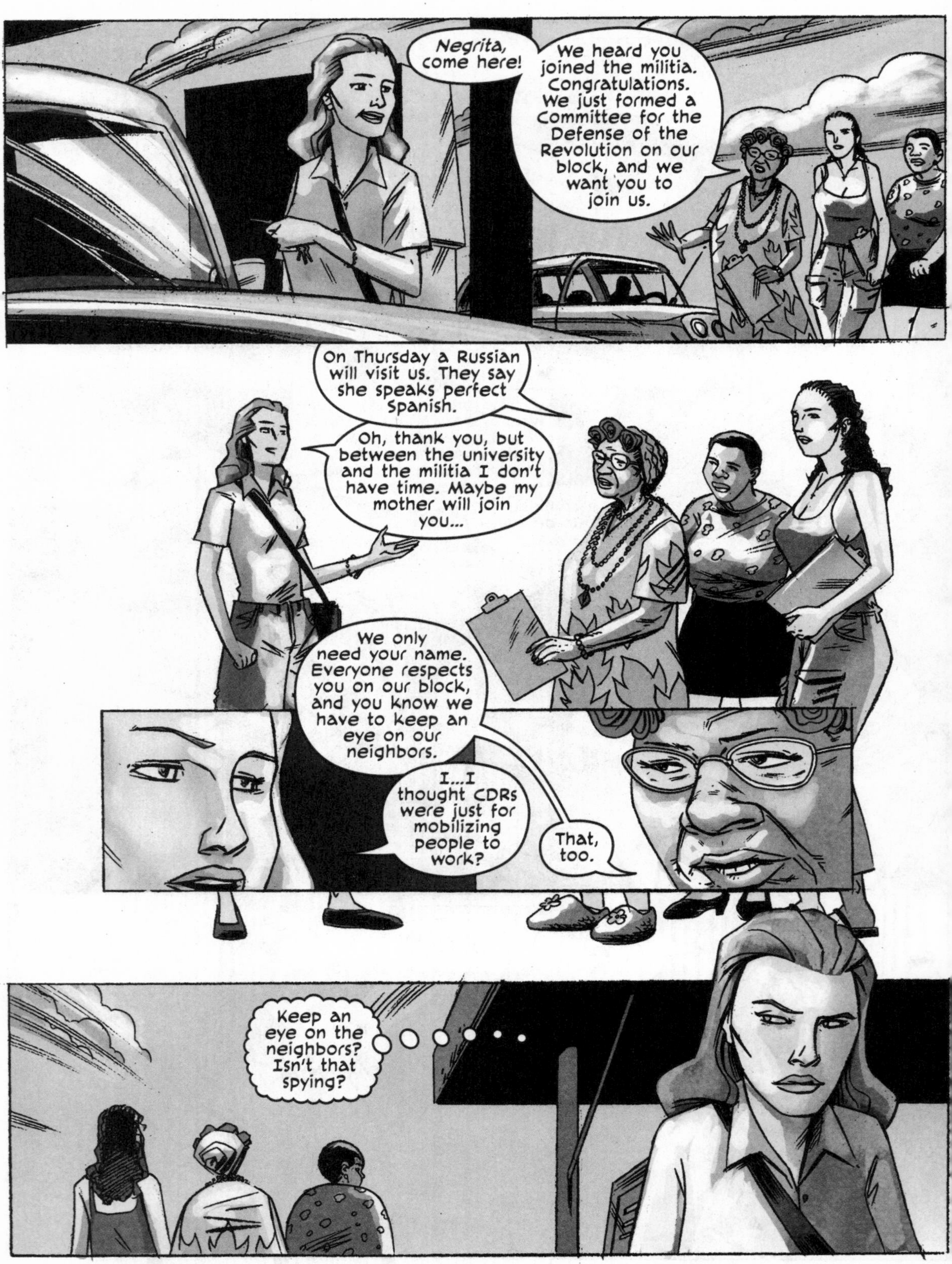

Negrita, come here!
We heard you joined the militia. Congratulations. We just formed a Committee for the Defense of the Revolution on our block, and we want you to join us.
On Thursday a Russian will visit us. They say she speaks perfect Spanish.
Oh, thank you, but between the university and the militia I don't have time. Maybe my mother will join you...
We only need your name. Everyone respects you on our block, and you know we have to keep an eye on our neighbors.
I...I thought CDRs were just for mobilizing people to work?
That, too.
Keep an eye on the neighbors? Isn't that spying?

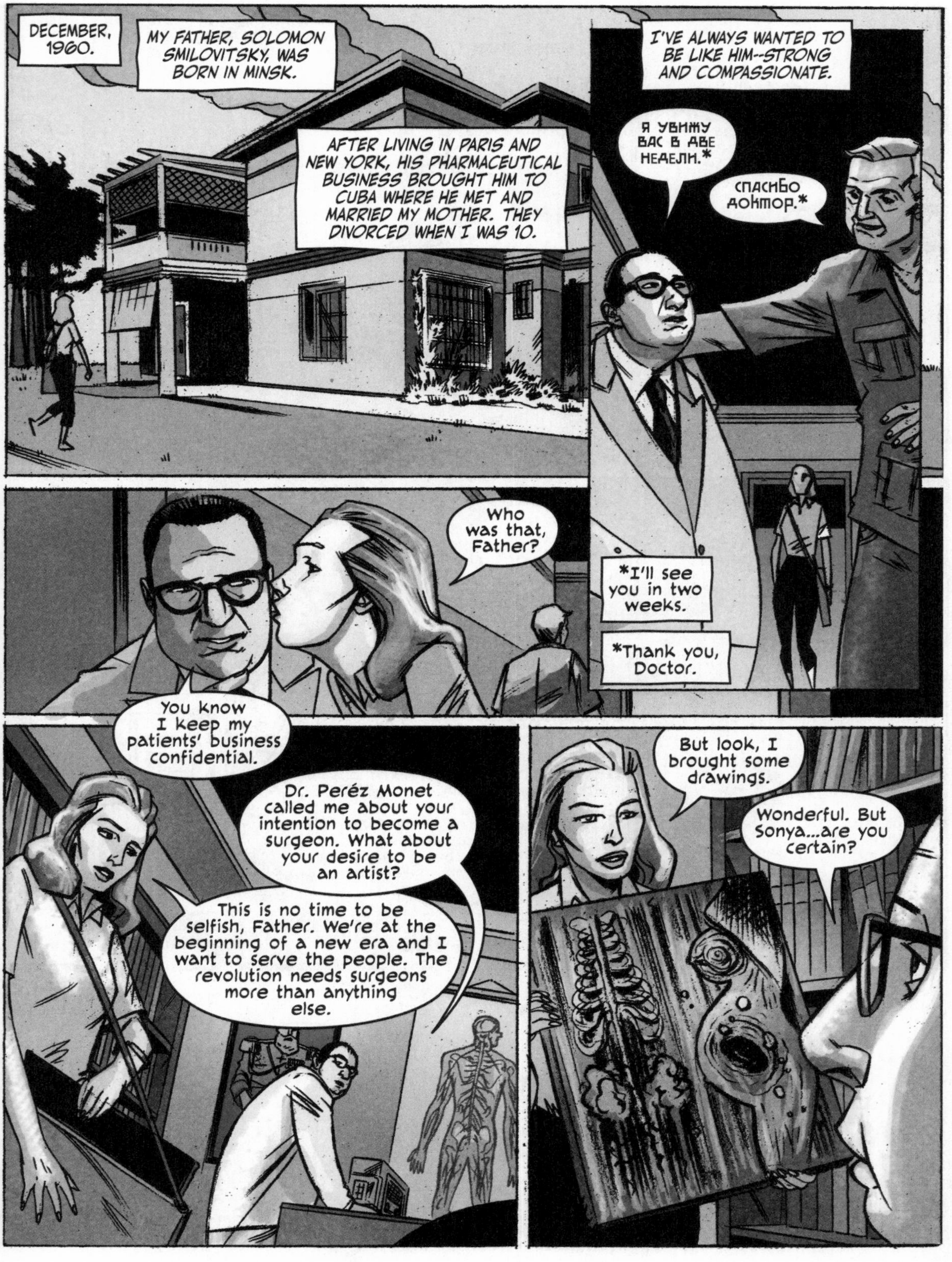

DECEMBER, 1960.
MY FATHER, SOLOMON SMILOVITSKY, WAS BORN IN MINSK.
AFTER LIVING IN PARIS AND NEW YORK, HIS PHARMACEUTICAL BUSINESS BROUGHT HIM TO CUBA WHERE HE MET AND MARRIED MY MOTHER. THEY DIVORCED WHEN I WAS 10.
I'VE ALWAYS WANTED TO BE LIKE HIM--STRONG AND COMPASSIONATE.
Я УВИЖУ ВАС В ДВЕ НЕДЕЛИ.*
спасибо доктор.*
*I'll see you in two weeks.
*Thank you, Doctor.
Who was that, Father?
You know I keep my patients' business confidential.
Dr. Peréz Monet called me about your intention to become a surgeon. What about your desire to be an artist?
This is no time to be selfish, Father. We're at the beginning of a new era and I want to serve the people. The revolution needs surgeons more than anything else.
But look, I brought some drawings.
Wonderful. But Sonya...are you certain?

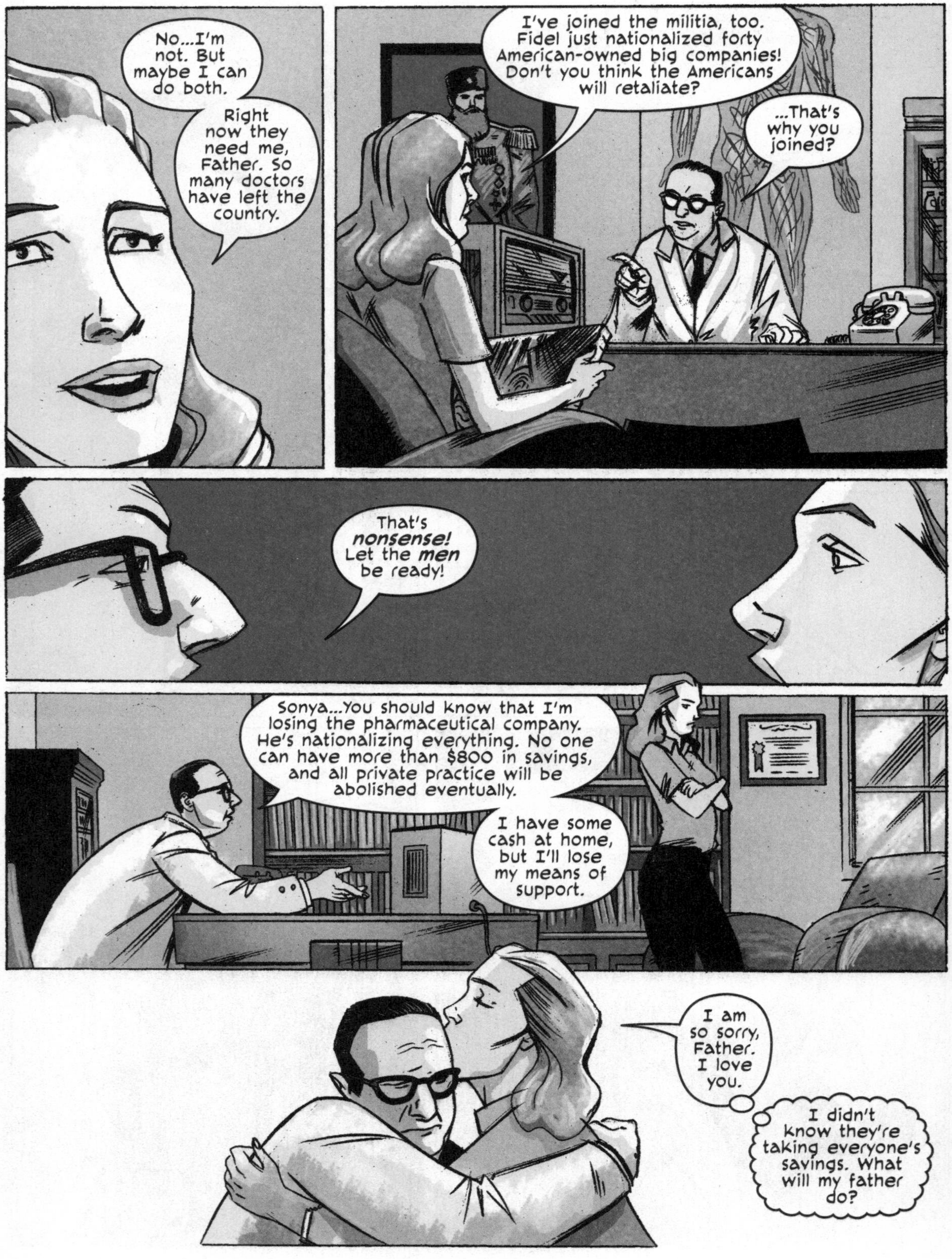
No...I'm not. But maybe I can do both.
Right now they need me, Father. So many doctors have left the country.
I've joined the militia, too. Fidel just nationalized forty American-owned big companies! Don't you think the Americans will retaliate?
...That's why you joined?
That's *nonsense!* Let the *men* be ready!
Sonya...You should know that I'm losing the pharmaceutical company. He's nationalizing everything. No one can have more than $800 in savings, and all private practice will be abolished eventually.
I have some cash at home, but I'll lose my means of support.
I am so sorry, Father. I love you.
I didn't know they're taking everyone's savings. What will my father do?

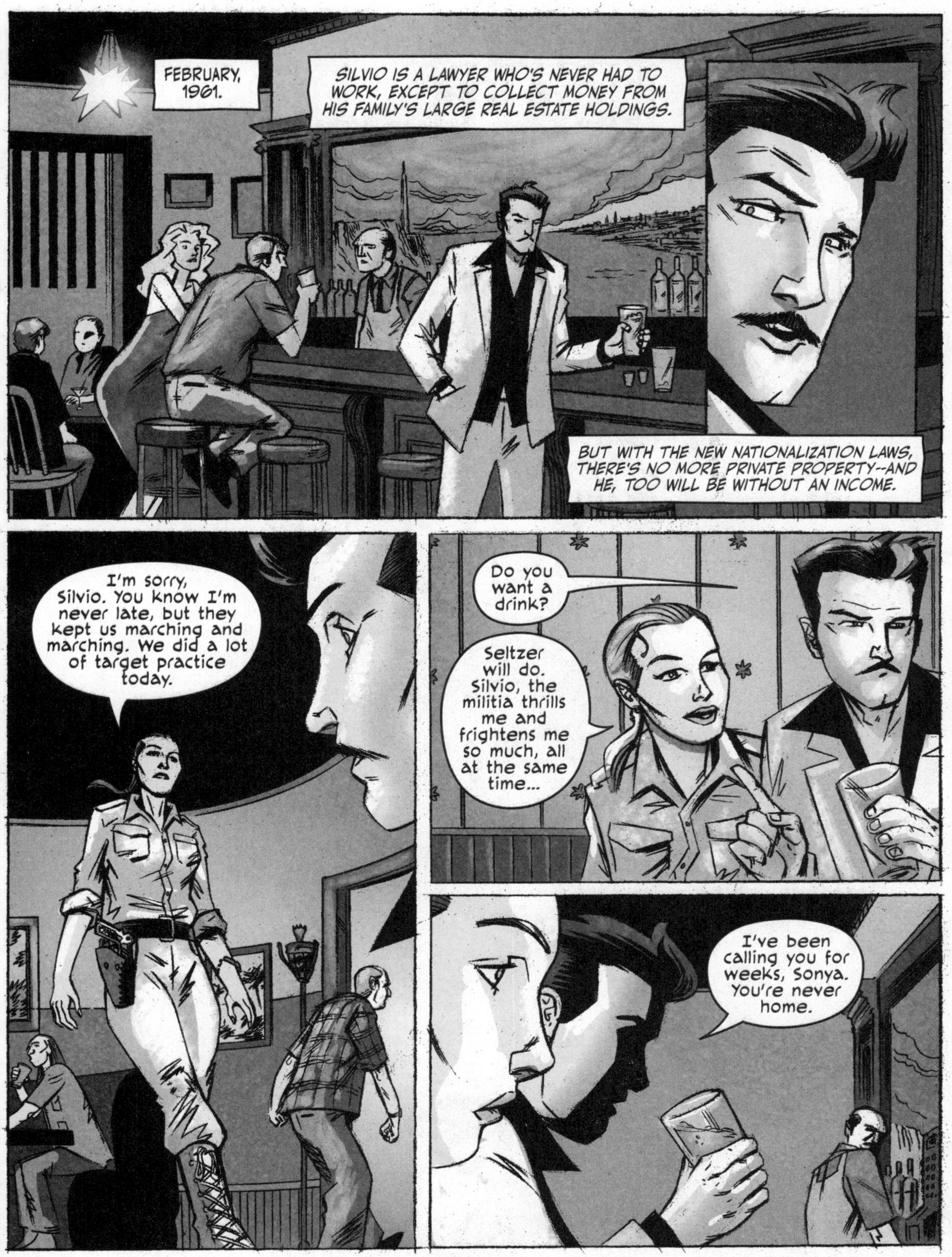
FEBRUARY, 1961.
SILVIO IS A LAWYER WHO'S NEVER HAD TO WORK, EXCEPT TO COLLECT MONEY FROM HIS FAMILY'S LARGE REAL ESTATE HOLDINGS.
BUT WITH THE NEW NATIONALIZATION LAWS, THERE'S NO MORE PRIVATE PROPERTY--AND HE, TOO WILL BE WITHOUT AN INCOME.
I'm sorry, Silvio. You know I'm never late, but they kept us marching and marching. We did a lot of target practice today.
Do you want a drink?
Seltzer will do. Silvio, the militia thrills me and frightens me so much, all at the same time...
I've been calling you for weeks, Sonya. You're never home.

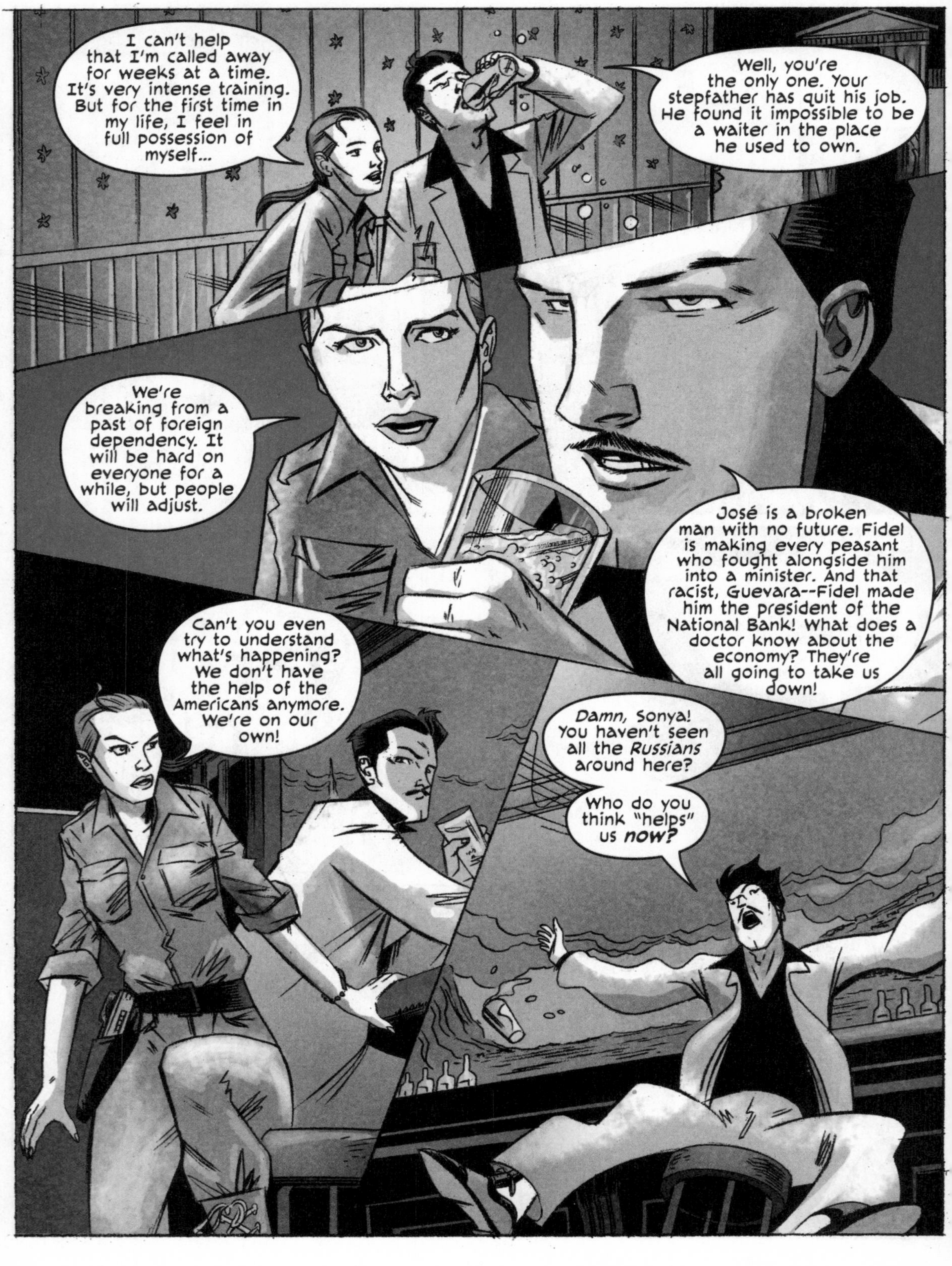
I can't help that I'm called away for weeks at a time. It's very intense training. But for the first time in my life, I feel in full possession of myself...
Well, you're the only one. Your stepfather has quit his job. He found it impossible to be a waiter in the place he used to own.
We're breaking from a past of foreign dependency. It will be hard on everyone for a while, but people will adjust.
José is a broken man with no future. Fidel is making every peasant who fought alongside him into a minister. And that racist, Guevara--Fidel made him the president of the National Bank! What does a doctor know about the economy? They're all going to take us down!
Can't you even try to understand what's happening? We don't have the help of the Americans anymore. We're on our own!
Damn, Sonya! You haven't seen all the Russians around here?
Who do you think "helps" us now?

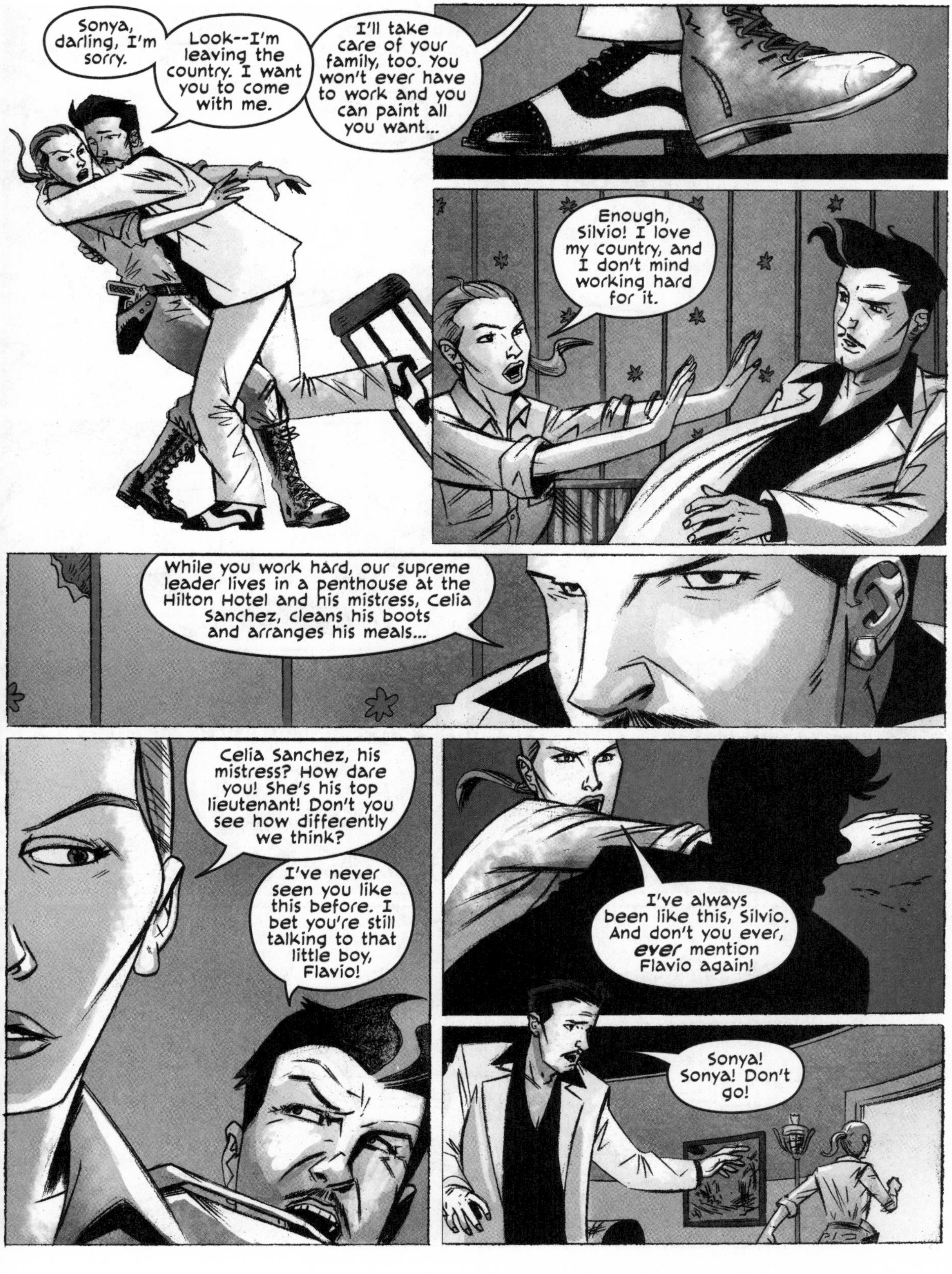

Sonya, darling, I'm sorry.
Look--I'm leaving the country. I want you to come with me.
I'll take care of your family, too. You won't ever have to work and you can paint all you want...
Enough, Silvio! I love my country, and I don't mind working hard for it.
While you work hard, our supreme leader lives in a penthouse at the Hilton Hotel and his mistress, Celia Sanchez, cleans his boots and arranges his meals...
Celia Sanchez, his mistress? How dare you! She's his top lieutenant! Don't you see how differently we think?
I've never seen you like this before. I bet you're still talking to that little boy, Flavio!
I've always been like this, Silvio. And don't you ever, *ever* mention Flavio again!
Sonya! Sonya! Don't go!

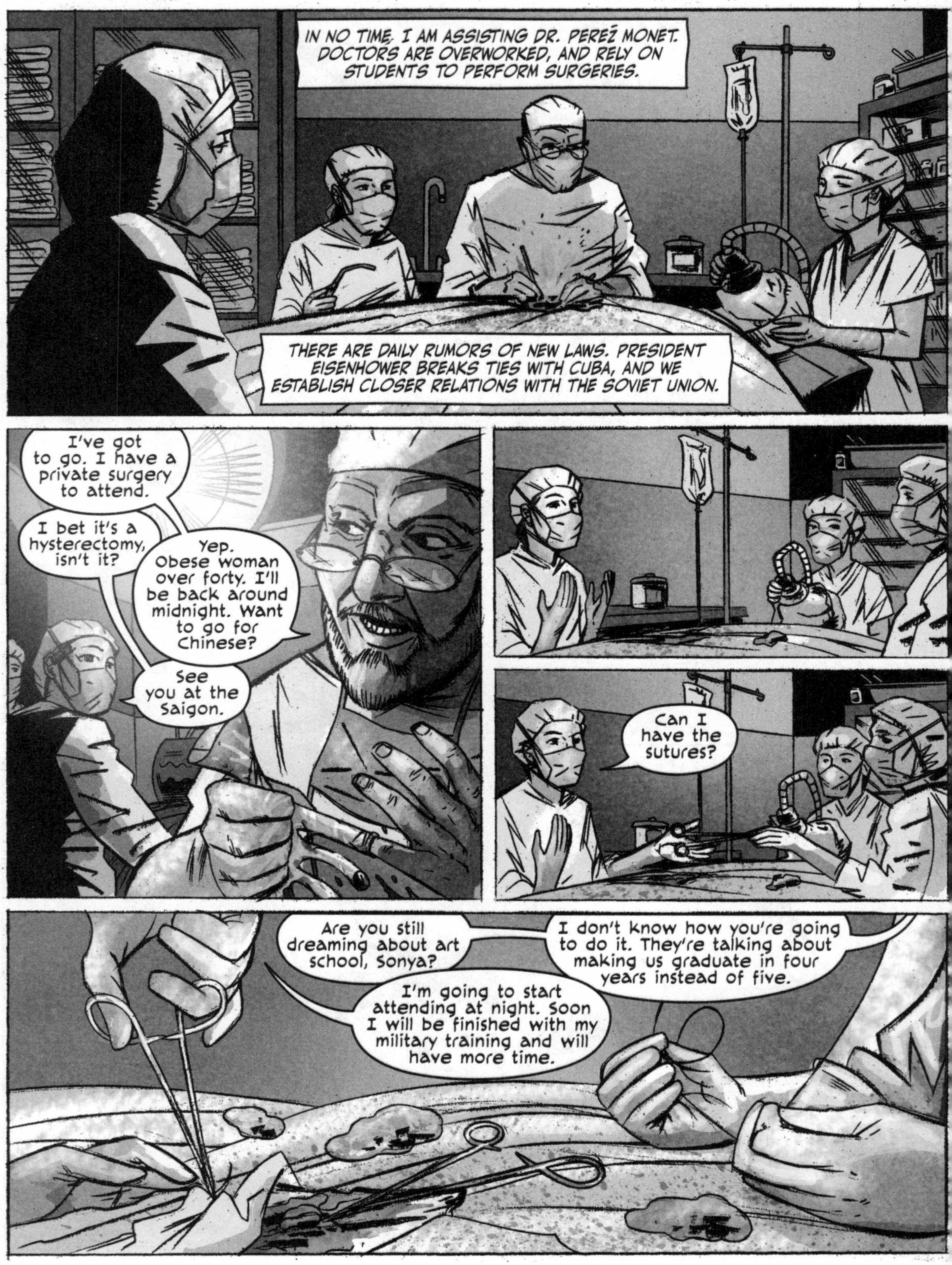
IN NO TIME, I AM ASSISTING DR. PERÉZ MONET. DOCTORS ARE OVERWORKED, AND RELY ON STUDENTS TO PERFORM SURGERIES.
THERE ARE DAILY RUMORS OF NEW LAWS. PRESIDENT EISENHOWER BREAKS TIES WITH CUBA, AND WE ESTABLISH CLOSER RELATIONS WITH THE SOVIET UNION.
I've got to go. I have a private surgery to attend.
I bet it's a hysterectomy, isn't it?
Yep. Obese woman over forty. I'll be back around midnight. Want to go for Chinese?
See you at the Saigon.
Can I have the sutures?
Are you still dreaming about art school, Sonya?
I'm going to start attending at night. Soon I will be finished with my military training and will have more time.
I don't know how you're going to do it. They're talking about making us graduate in four years instead of five.

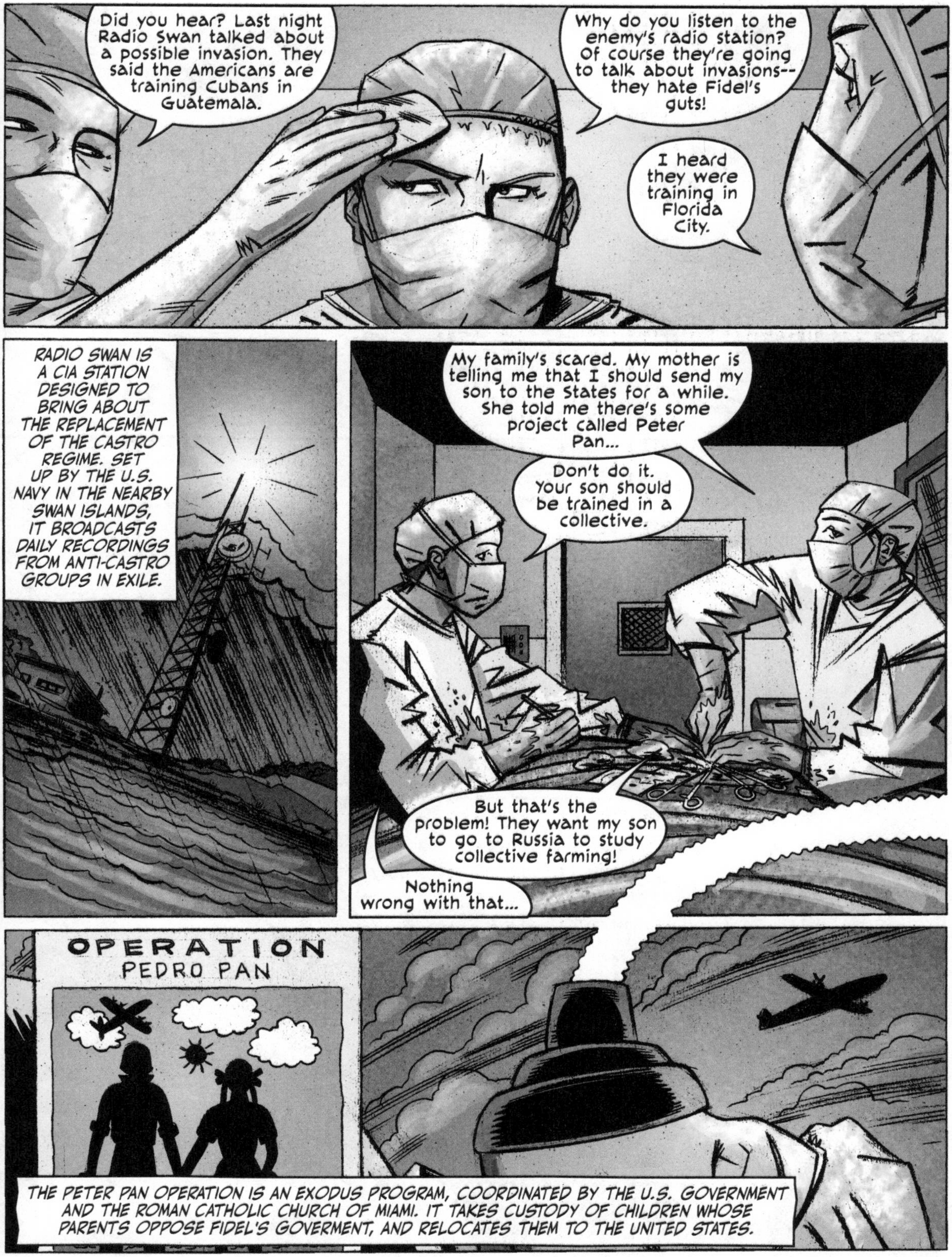

Did you hear? Last night Radio Swan talked about a possible invasion. They said the Americans are training Cubans in Guatemala.
Why do you listen to the enemy's radio station? Of course they're going to talk about invasions--they hate Fidel's guts!
I heard they were training in Florida City.
RADIO SWAN IS A CIA STATION DESIGNED TO BRING ABOUT THE REPLACEMENT OF THE CASTRO REGIME. SET UP BY THE U.S. NAVY IN THE NEARBY SWAN ISLANDS, IT BROADCASTS DAILY RECORDINGS FROM ANTI-CASTRO GROUPS IN EXILE.
My family's scared. My mother is telling me that I should send my son to the States for a while. She told me there's some project called Peter Pan...
Don't do it. Your son should be trained in a collective.
But that's the problem! They want my son to go to Russia to study collective farming!
Nothing wrong with that...
OPERATION
PEDRO PAN
THE PETER PAN OPERATION IS AN EXODUS PROGRAM, COORDINATED BY THE U.S. GOVERNMENT AND THE ROMAN CATHOLIC CHURCH OF MIAMI. IT TAKES CUSTODY OF CHILDREN WHOSE PARENTS OPPOSE FIDEL'S GOVERMENT, AND RELOCATES THEM TO THE UNITED STATES.

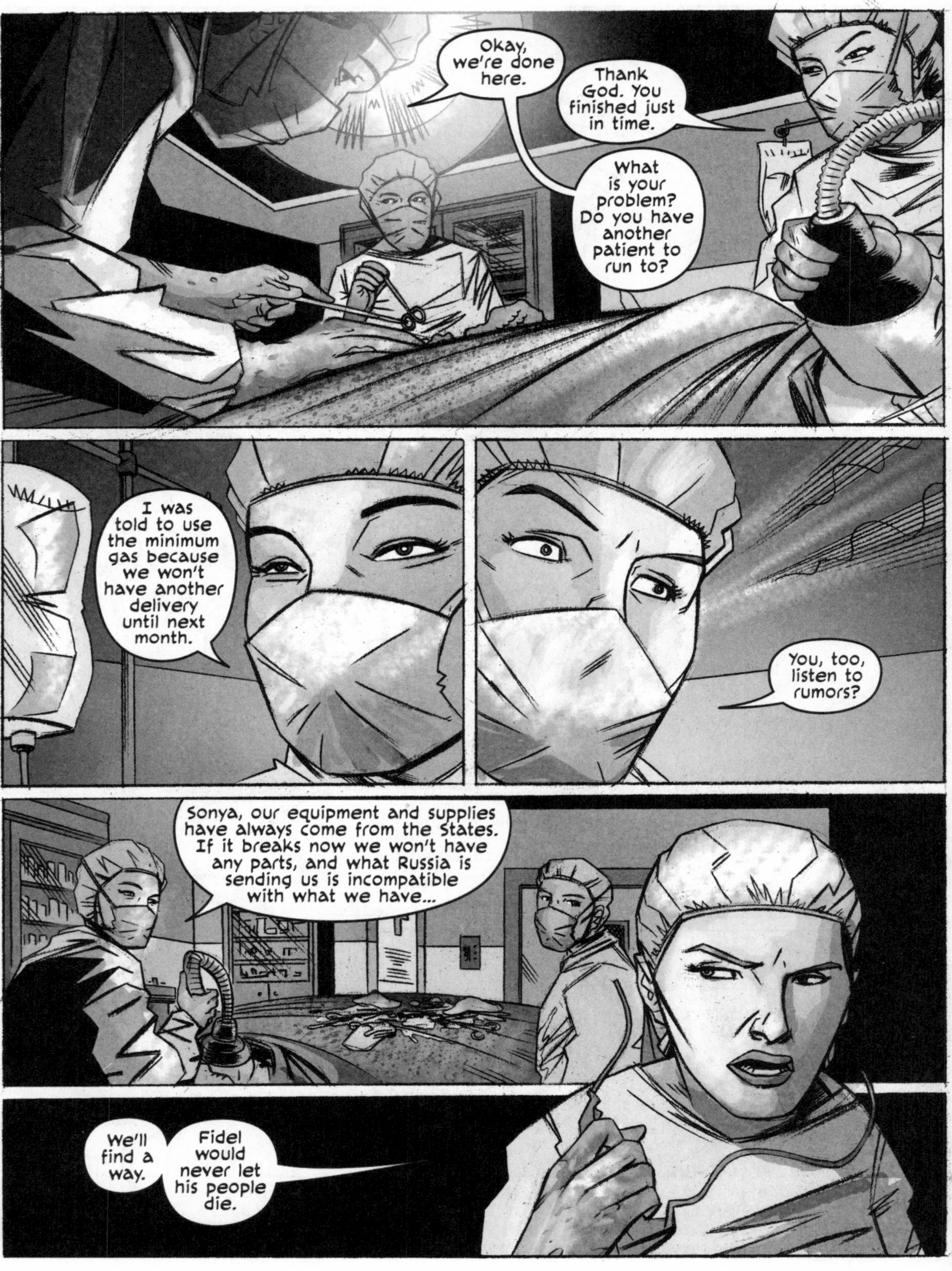
Okay, we're done here.
Thank God. You finished just in time.
What is your problem? Do you have another patient to run to?
I was told to use the minimum gas because we won't have another delivery until next month.
You, too, listen to rumors?
Sonya, our equipment and supplies have always come from the States. If it breaks now we won't have any parts, and what Russia is sending us is incompatible with what we have...
We'll find a way.
Fidel would never let his people die.

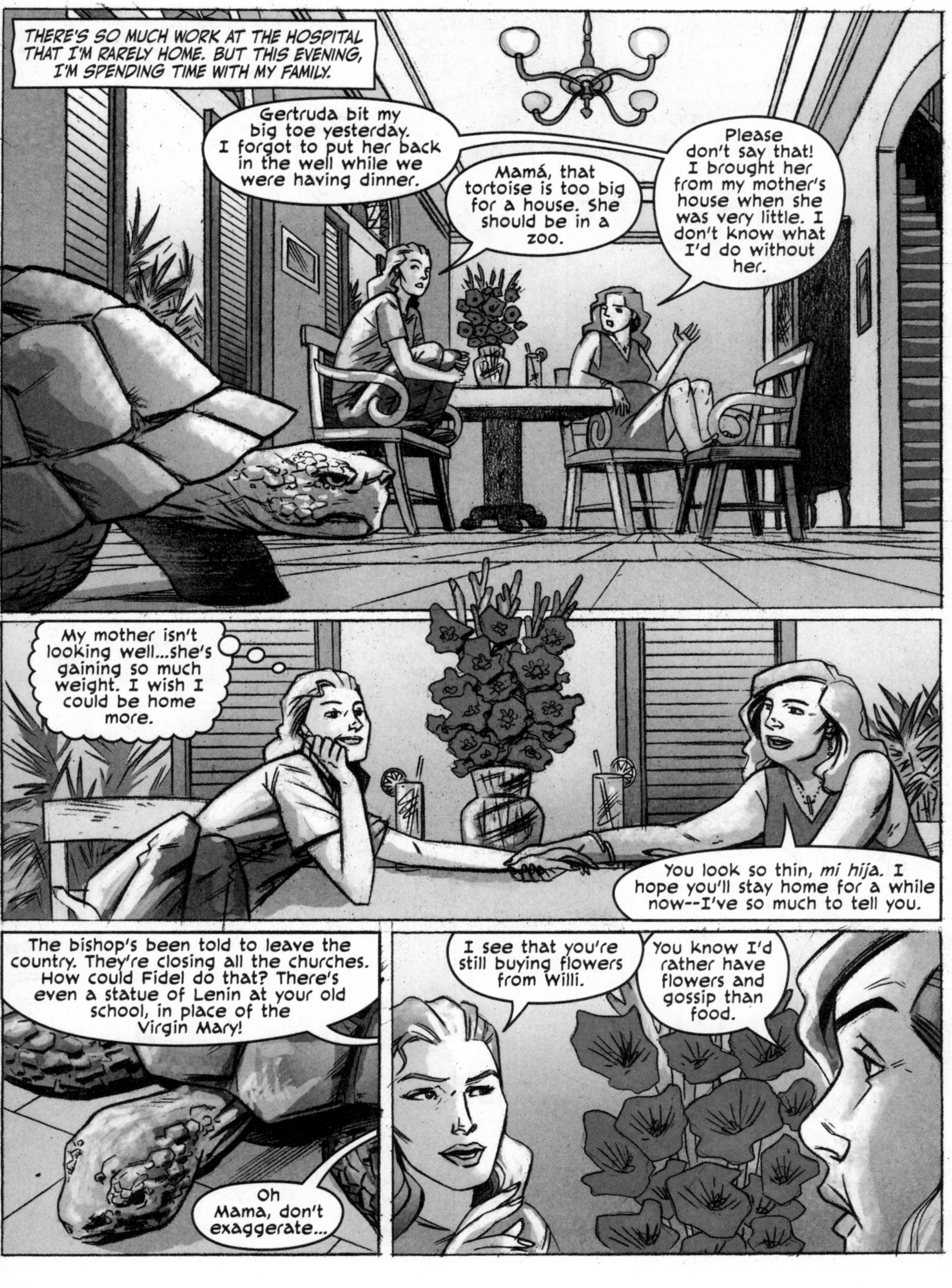
THERE'S SO MUCH WORK AT THE HOSPITAL THAT I'M RARELY HOME. BUT THIS EVENING, I'M SPENDING TIME WITH MY FAMILY.
Gertruda bit my big toe yesterday. I forgot to put her back in the well while we were having dinner.
Mamá, that tortoise is too big for a house. She should be in a zoo.
Please don't say that! I brought her from my mother's house when she was very little. I don't know what I'd do without her.
My mother isn't looking well...she's gaining so much weight. I wish I could be home more.
You look so thin, *mi hija.* I hope you'll stay home for a while now--I've so much to tell you.
The bishop's been told to leave the country. They're closing all the churches. How could Fidel do that? There's even a statue of Lenin at your old school, in place of the Virgin Mary!
Oh Mama, don't exaggerate...
I see that you're still buying flowers from Willi.
You know I'd rather have flowers and gossip than food.

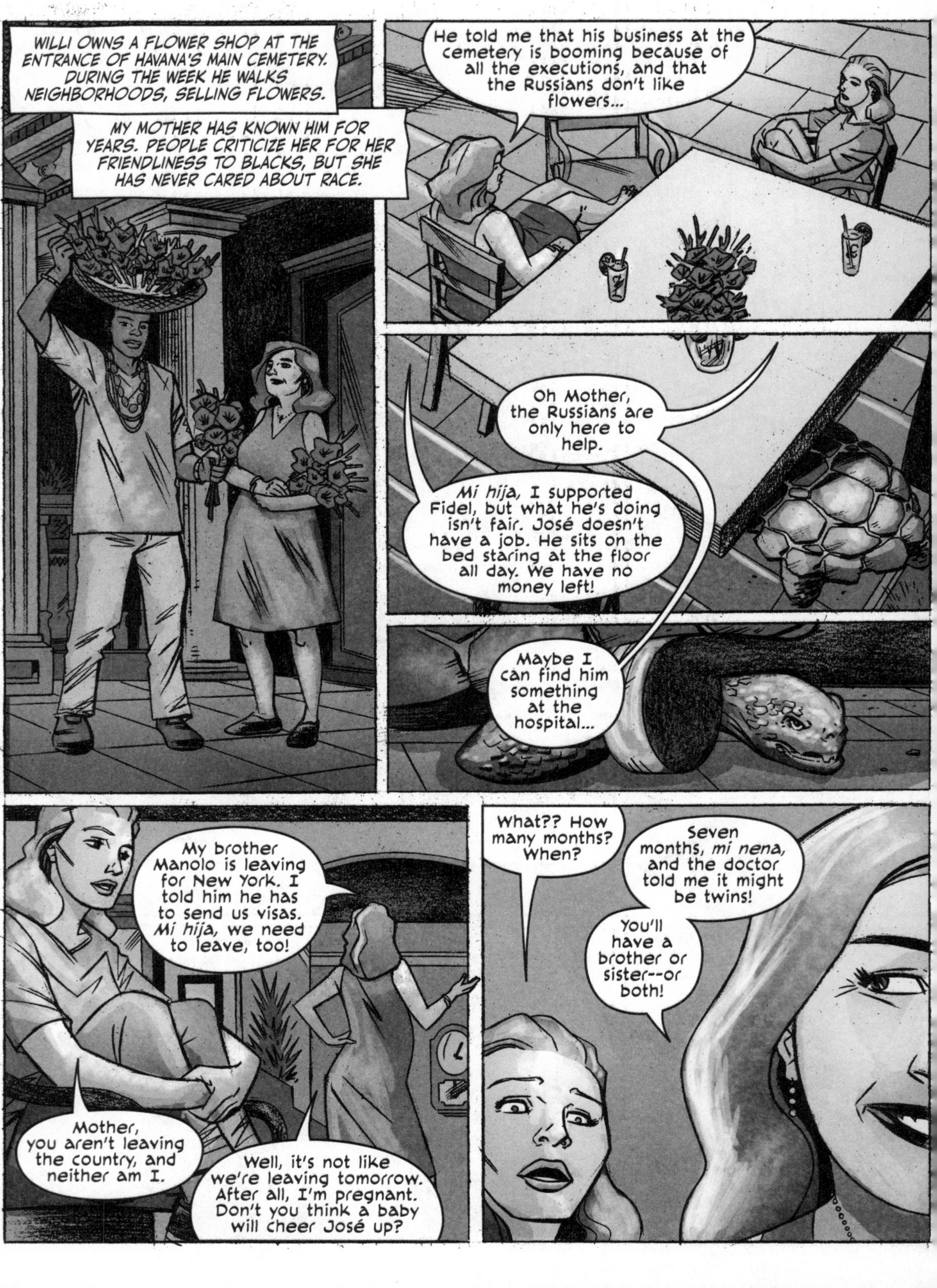
WILLI OWNS A FLOWER SHOP AT THE ENTRANCE OF HAVANA'S MAIN CEMETERY. DURING THE WEEK HE WALKS NEIGHBORHOODS, SELLING FLOWERS.
MY MOTHER HAS KNOWN HIM FOR YEARS. PEOPLE CRITICIZE HER FOR HER FRIENDLINESS TO BLACKS, BUT SHE HAS NEVER CARED ABOUT RACE.
He told me that his business at the cemetery is booming because of all the executions, and that the Russians don't like flowers...
Oh Mother, the Russians are only here to help.
Mi hija, I supported Fidel, but what he's doing isn't fair. José doesn't have a job. He sits on the bed staring at the floor all day. We have no money left!
Maybe I can find him something at the hospital...
My brother Manolo is leaving for New York. I told him he has to send us visas. Mi hija, we need to leave, too!
Mother, you aren't leaving the country, and neither am I.
Well, it's not like we're leaving tomorrow. After all, I'm pregnant. Don't you think a baby will cheer José up?
What?? How many months? When?
Seven months, mi nena, and the doctor told me it might be twins!
You'll have a brother or sister--or both!

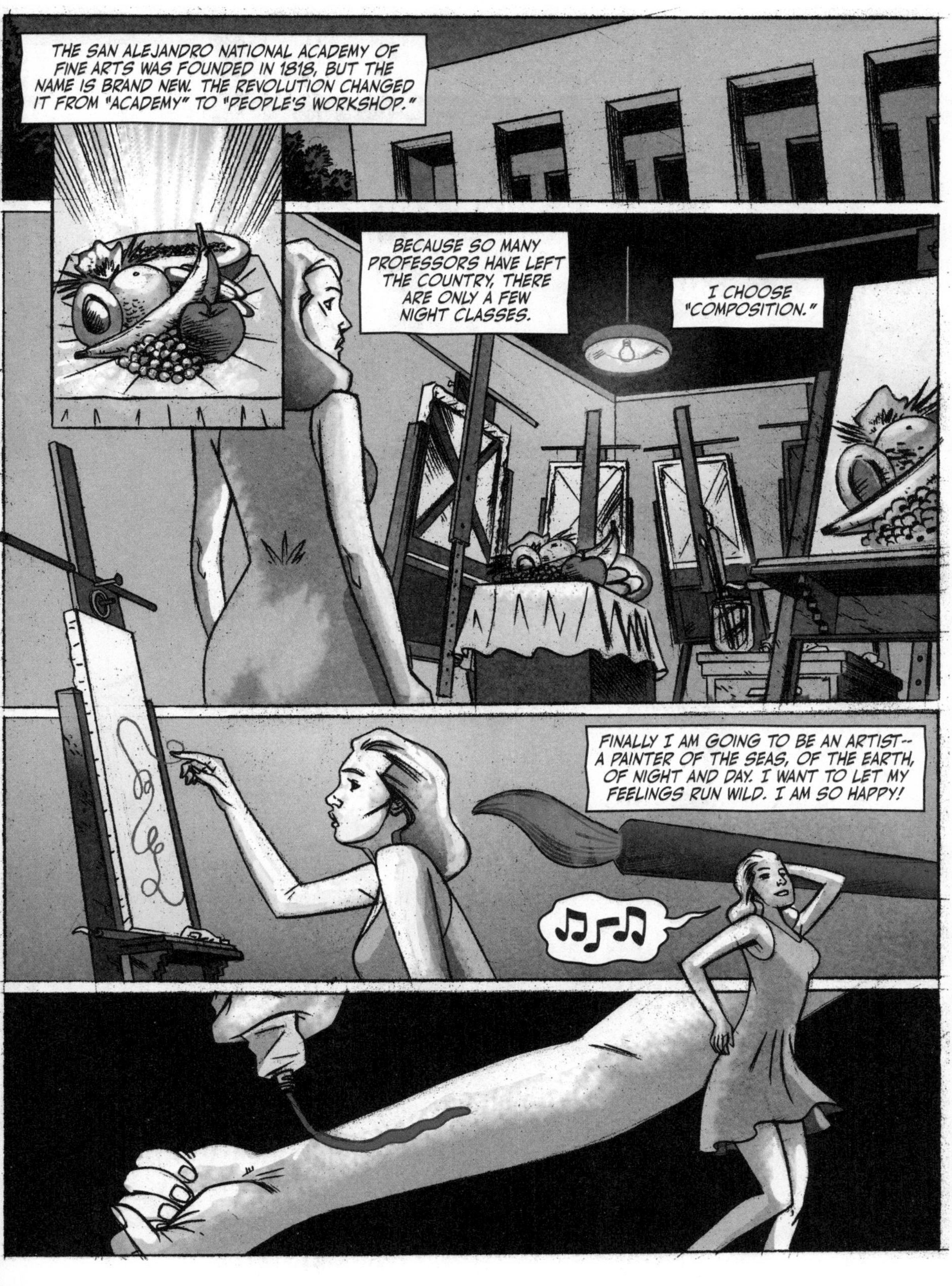
THE SAN ALEJANDRO NATIONAL ACADEMY OF FINE ARTS WAS FOUNDED IN 1818, BUT THE NAME IS BRAND NEW. THE REVOLUTION CHANGED IT FROM "ACADEMY" TO "PEOPLE'S WORKSHOP."
BECAUSE SO MANY PROFESSORS HAVE LEFT THE COUNTRY, THERE ARE ONLY A FEW NIGHT CLASSES.
I CHOOSE "COMPOSITION."
FINALLY I AM GOING TO BE AN ARTIST-- A PAINTER OF THE SEAS, OF THE EARTH, OF NIGHT AND DAY. I WANT TO LET MY FEELINGS RUN WILD. I AM SO HAPPY!

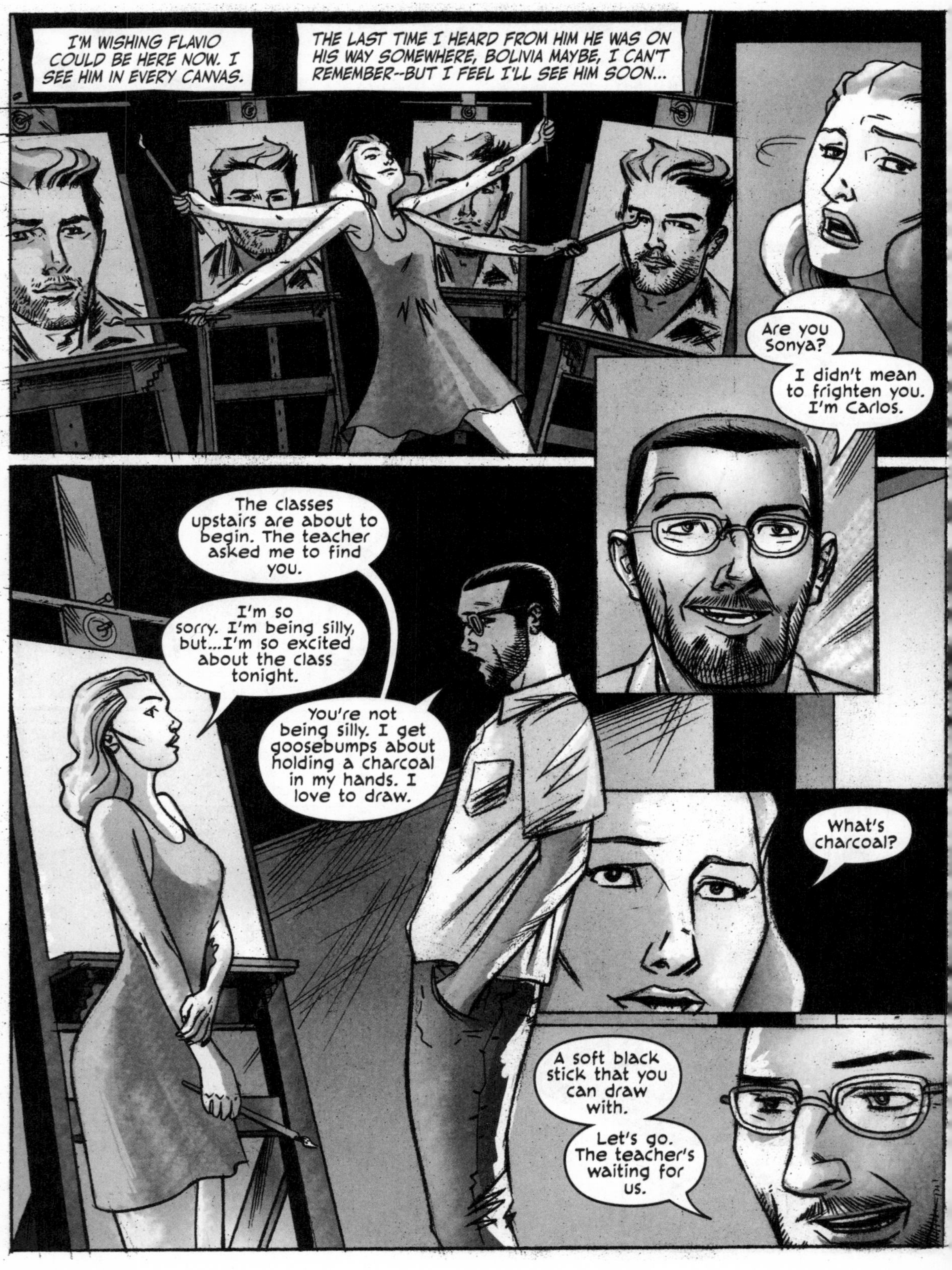
I'M WISHING FLAVIO COULD BE HERE NOW. I SEE HIM IN EVERY CANVAS.
THE LAST TIME I HEARD FROM HIM HE WAS ON HIS WAY SOMEWHERE, BOLIVIA MAYBE, I CAN'T REMEMBER--BUT I FEEL I'LL SEE HIM SOON...
Are you Sonya?
I didn't mean to frighten you. I'm Carlos.
The classes upstairs are about to begin. The teacher asked me to find you.
I'm so sorry. I'm being silly, but...I'm so excited about the class tonight.
You're not being silly. I get goosebumps about holding a charcoal in my hands. I love to draw.
What's charcoal?
A soft black stick that you can draw with.
Let's go. The teacher's waiting for us.

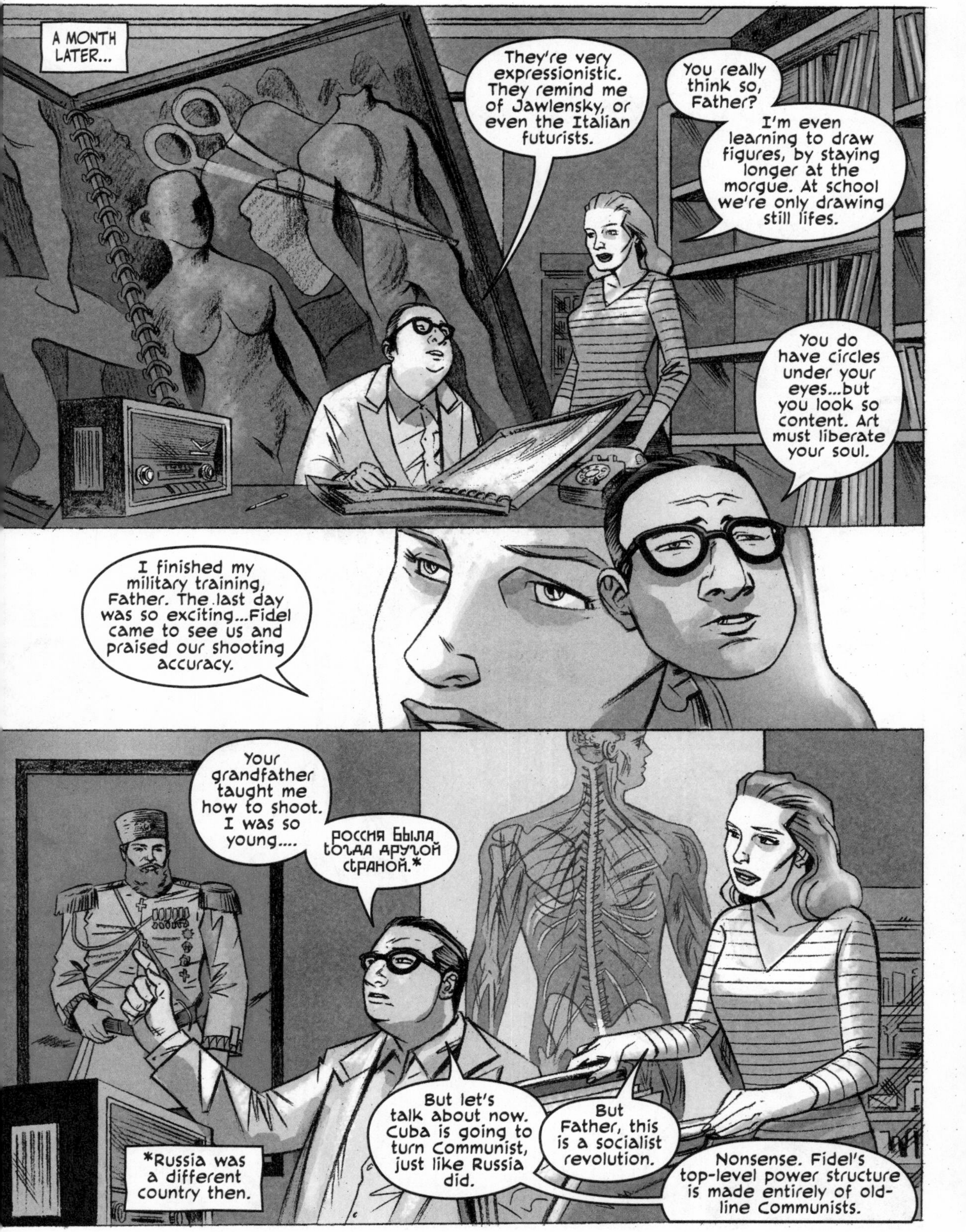
A MONTH LATER...
They're very expressionistic. They remind me of Jawlensky, or even the Italian futurists.
You really think so, Father?
I'm even learning to draw figures, by staying longer at the morgue. At school we're only drawing still lifes.
You do have circles under your eyes...but you look so content. Art must liberate your soul.
I finished my military training, Father. The last day was so exciting...Fidel came to see us and praised our shooting accuracy.
Your grandfather taught me how to shoot. I was so young....
россия была тогда другой страной.*
But let's talk about now. Cuba is going to turn Communist, just like Russia did.
But Father, this is a socialist revolution.
Nonsense. Fidel's top-level power structure is made entirely of old-line Communists.
*Russia was a different country then.

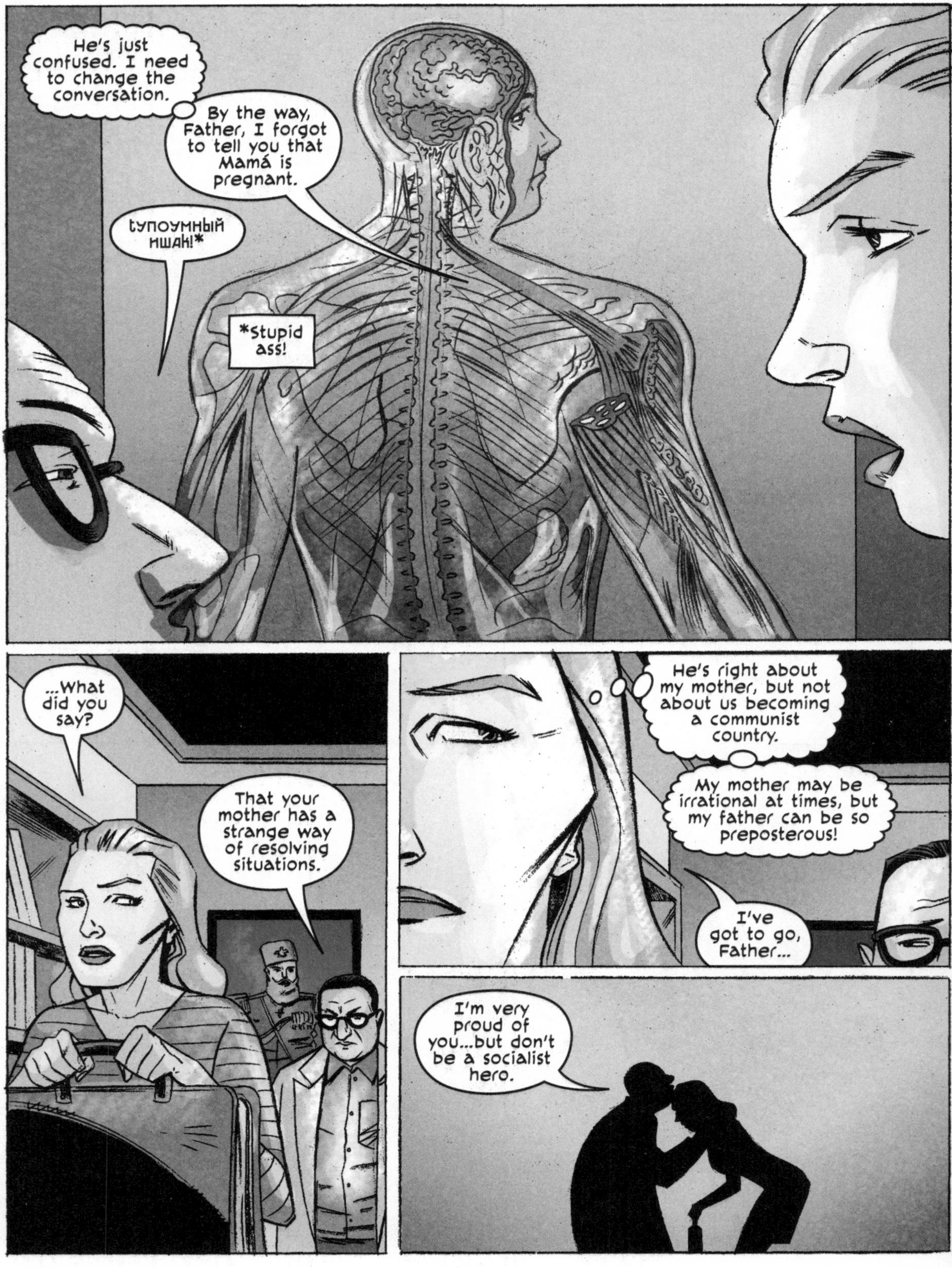
He's just confused. I need to change the conversation.
By the way, Father, I forgot to tell you that Mamá is pregnant.
тупоумный ишак!*
*Stupid ass!
...What did you say?
That your mother has a strange way of resolving situations.
He's right about my mother, but not about us becoming a communist country.
My mother may be irrational at times, but my father can be so preposterous!
I've got to go, Father...
I'm very proud of you...but don't be a socialist hero.

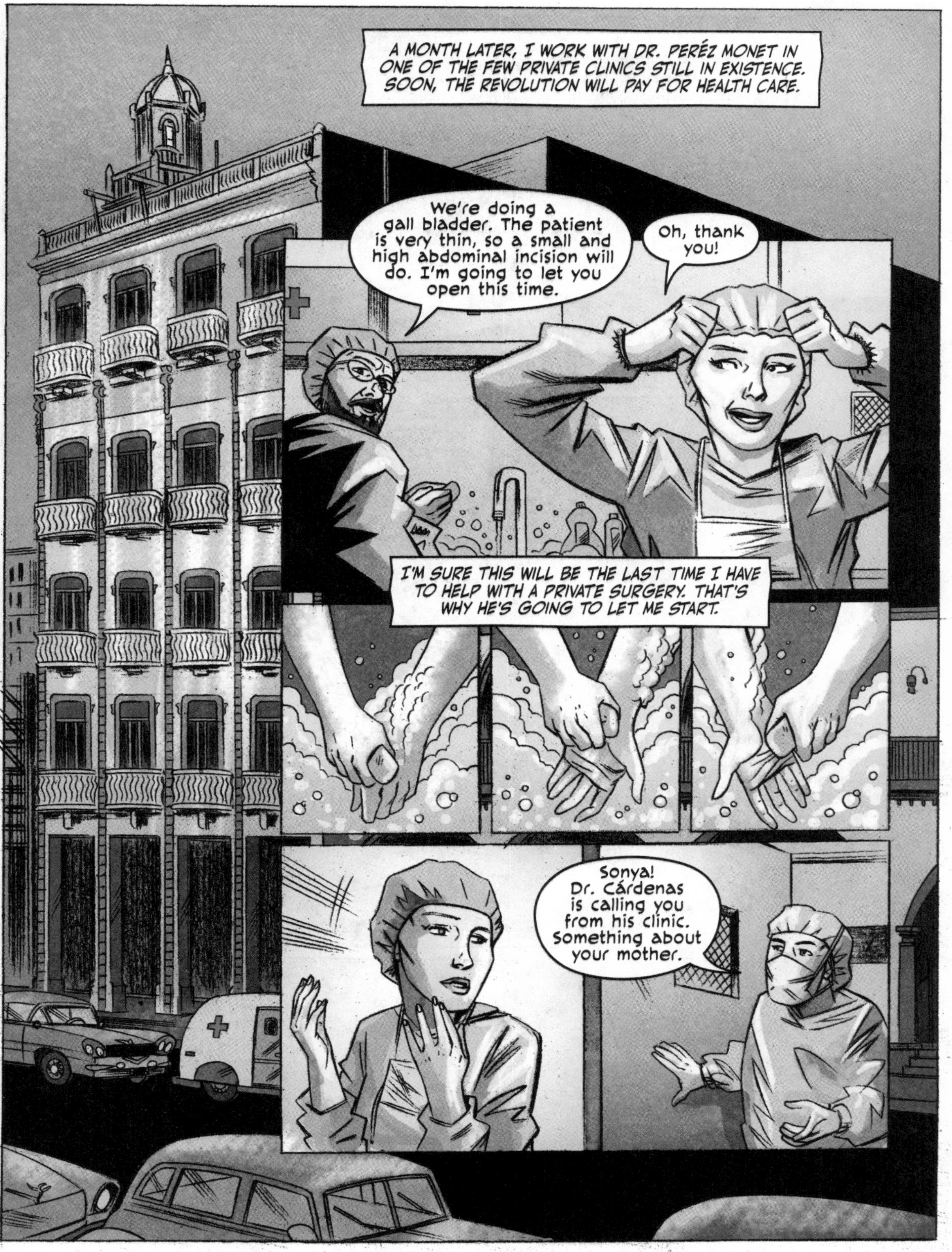
A MONTH LATER, I WORK WITH DR. PERÉZ MONET IN ONE OF THE FEW PRIVATE CLINICS STILL IN EXISTENCE. SOON, THE REVOLUTION WILL PAY FOR HEALTH CARE.
We're doing a gall bladder. The patient is very thin, so a small and high abdominal incision will do. I'm going to let you open this time.
Oh, thank you!
I'M SURE THIS WILL BE THE LAST TIME I HAVE TO HELP WITH A PRIVATE SURGERY. THAT'S WHY HE'S GOING TO LET ME START.
Sonya! Dr. Cárdenas is calling you from his clinic. Something about your mother.

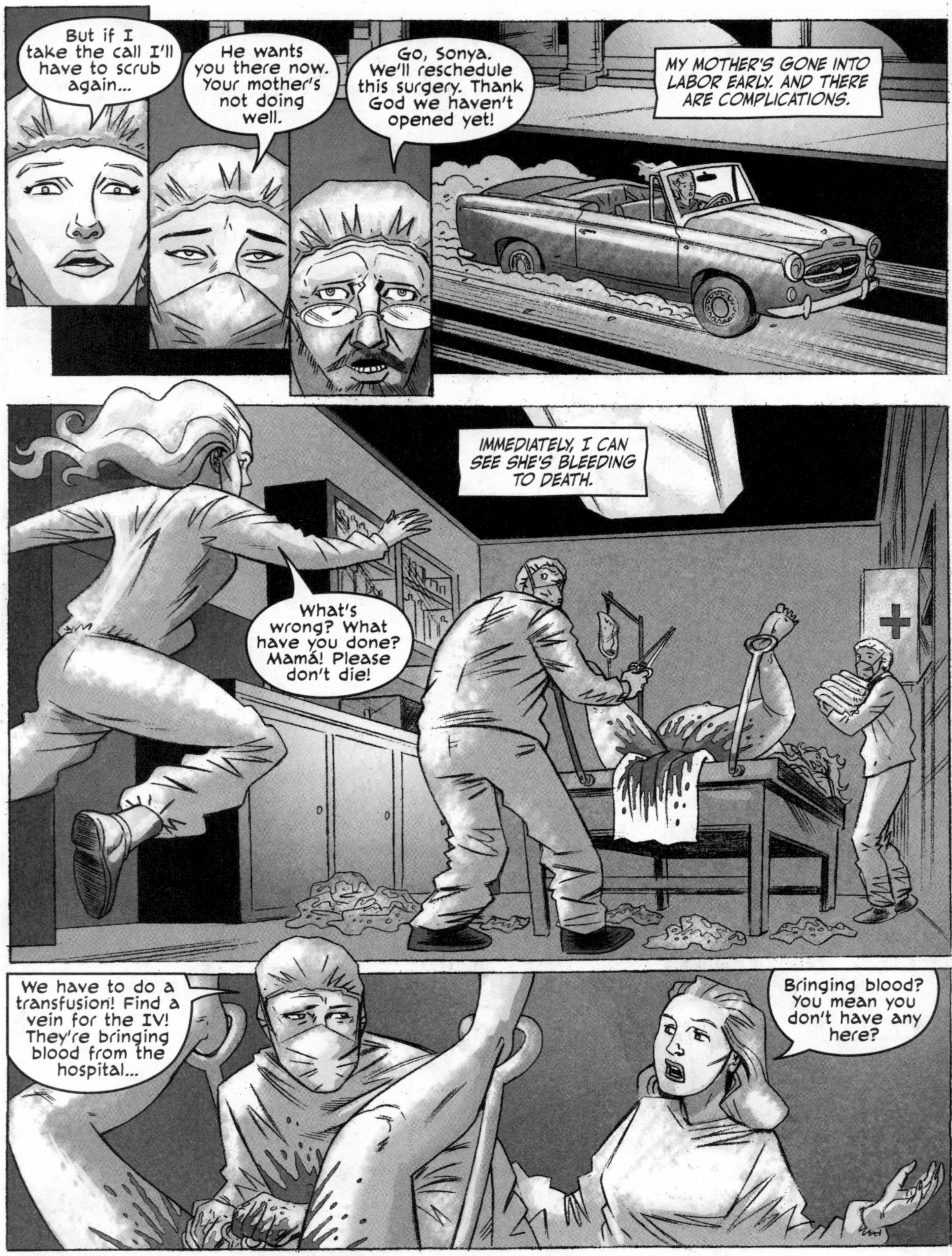

But if I take the call I'll have to scrub again...
He wants you there now. Your mother's not doing well.
Go, Sonya. We'll reschedule this surgery. Thank God we haven't opened yet!
MY MOTHER'S GONE INTO LABOR EARLY. AND THERE ARE COMPLICATIONS.
IMMEDIATELY, I CAN SEE SHE'S BLEEDING TO DEATH.
What's wrong? What have you done? Mamá! Please don't die!
We have to do a transfusion! Find a vein for the IV! They're bringing blood from the hospital...
Bringing blood? You mean you don't have any here?

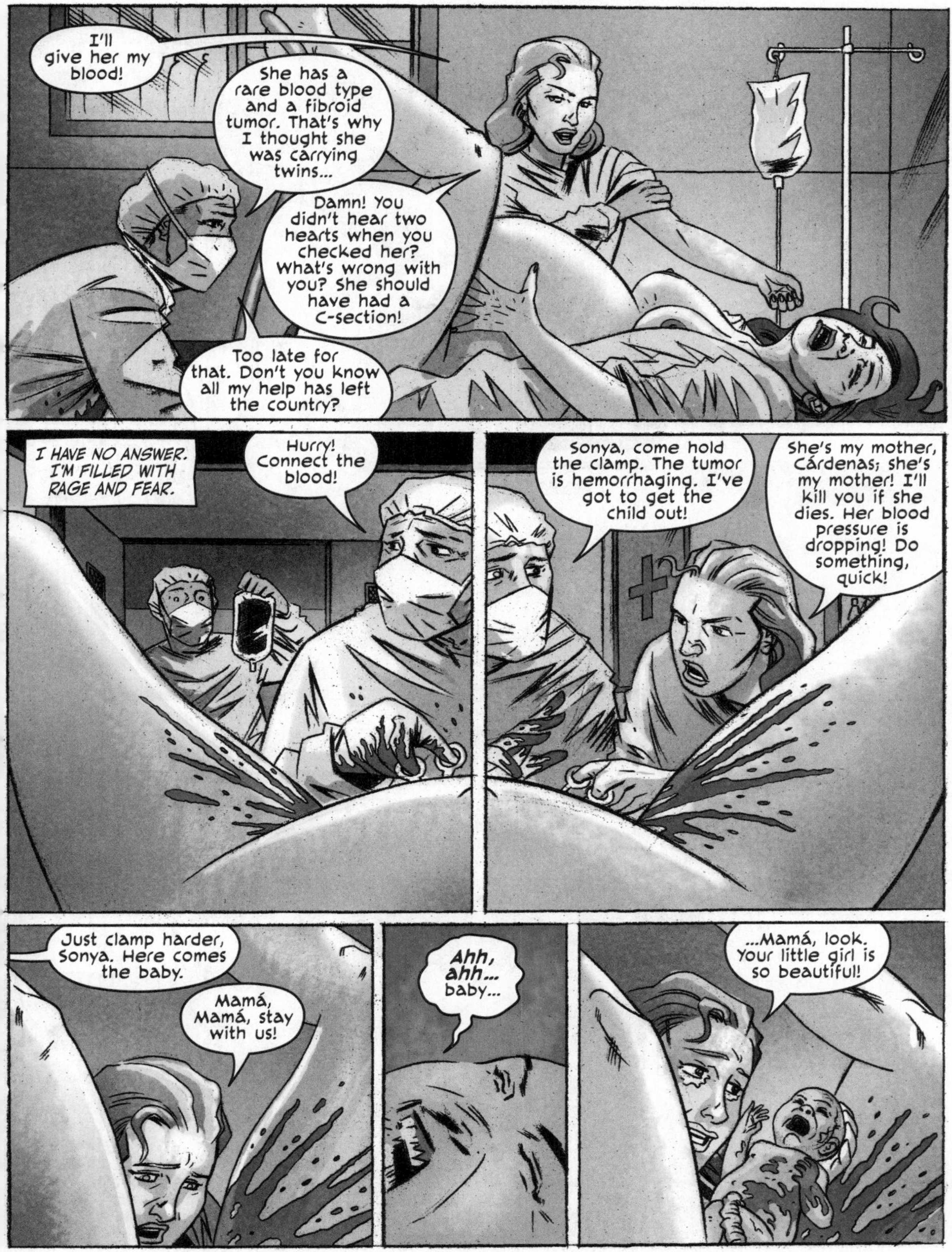

I'll give her my blood!
She has a rare blood type and a fibroid tumor. That's why I thought she was carrying twins...
Damn! You didn't hear two hearts when you checked her? What's wrong with you? She should have had a C-section!
Too late for that. Don't you know all my help has left the country?
I HAVE NO ANSWER. I'M FILLED WITH RAGE AND FEAR.
Hurry! Connect the blood!
Sonya, come hold the clamp. The tumor is hemorrhaging. I've got to get the child out!
She's my mother, Cárdenas; she's my mother! I'll kill you if she dies. Her blood pressure is dropping! Do something, quick!
Just clamp harder, Sonya. Here comes the baby.
Mamá, Mamá, stay with us!
Ahh, ahh... baby...
...Mamá, look. Your little girl is so beautiful!

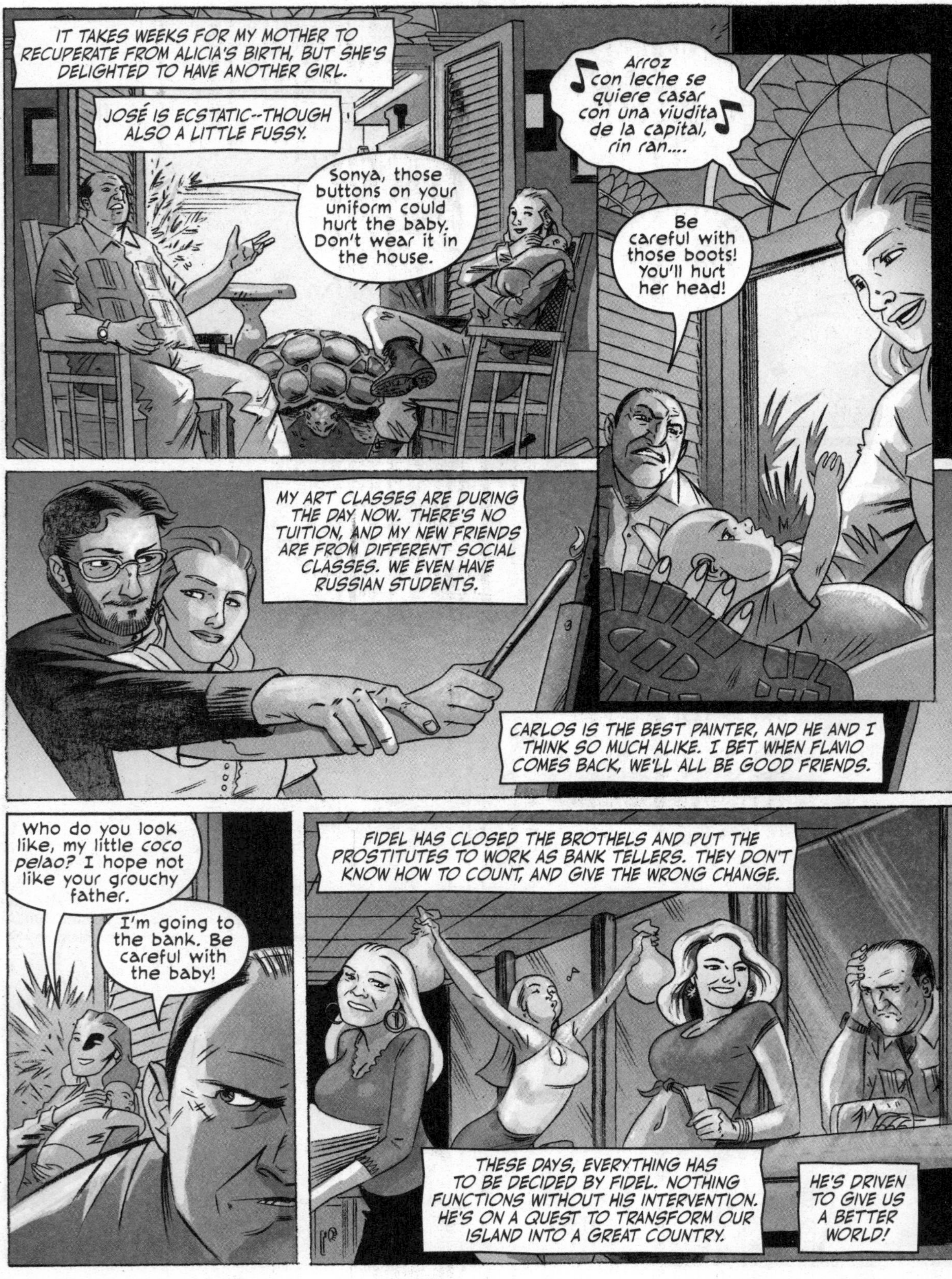
IT TAKES WEEKS FOR MY MOTHER TO RECUPERATE FROM ALICIA'S BIRTH, BUT SHE'S DELIGHTED TO HAVE ANOTHER GIRL.
JOSÉ IS ECSTATIC--THOUGH ALSO A LITTLE FUSSY.
Sonya, those buttons on your uniform could hurt the baby. Don't wear it in the house.
Arroz con leche se quiere casar con una viudita de la capital, rin ran....
Be careful with those boots! You'll hurt her head!
MY ART CLASSES ARE DURING THE DAY NOW. THERE'S NO TUITION, AND MY NEW FRIENDS ARE FROM DIFFERENT SOCIAL CLASSES. WE EVEN HAVE RUSSIAN STUDENTS.
CARLOS IS THE BEST PAINTER, AND HE AND I THINK SO MUCH ALIKE. I BET WHEN FLAVIO COMES BACK, WE'LL ALL BE GOOD FRIENDS.
Who do you look like, my little *coco pelao*? I hope not like your grouchy father.
I'm going to the bank. Be careful with the baby!
FIDEL HAS CLOSED THE BROTHELS AND PUT THE PROSTITUTES TO WORK AS BANK TELLERS. THEY DON'T KNOW HOW TO COUNT, AND GIVE THE WRONG CHANGE.
THESE DAYS, EVERYTHING HAS TO BE DECIDED BY FIDEL. NOTHING FUNCTIONS WITHOUT HIS INTERVENTION. HE'S ON A QUEST TO TRANSFORM OUR ISLAND INTO A GREAT COUNTRY.
HE'S DRIVEN TO GIVE US A BETTER WORLD!

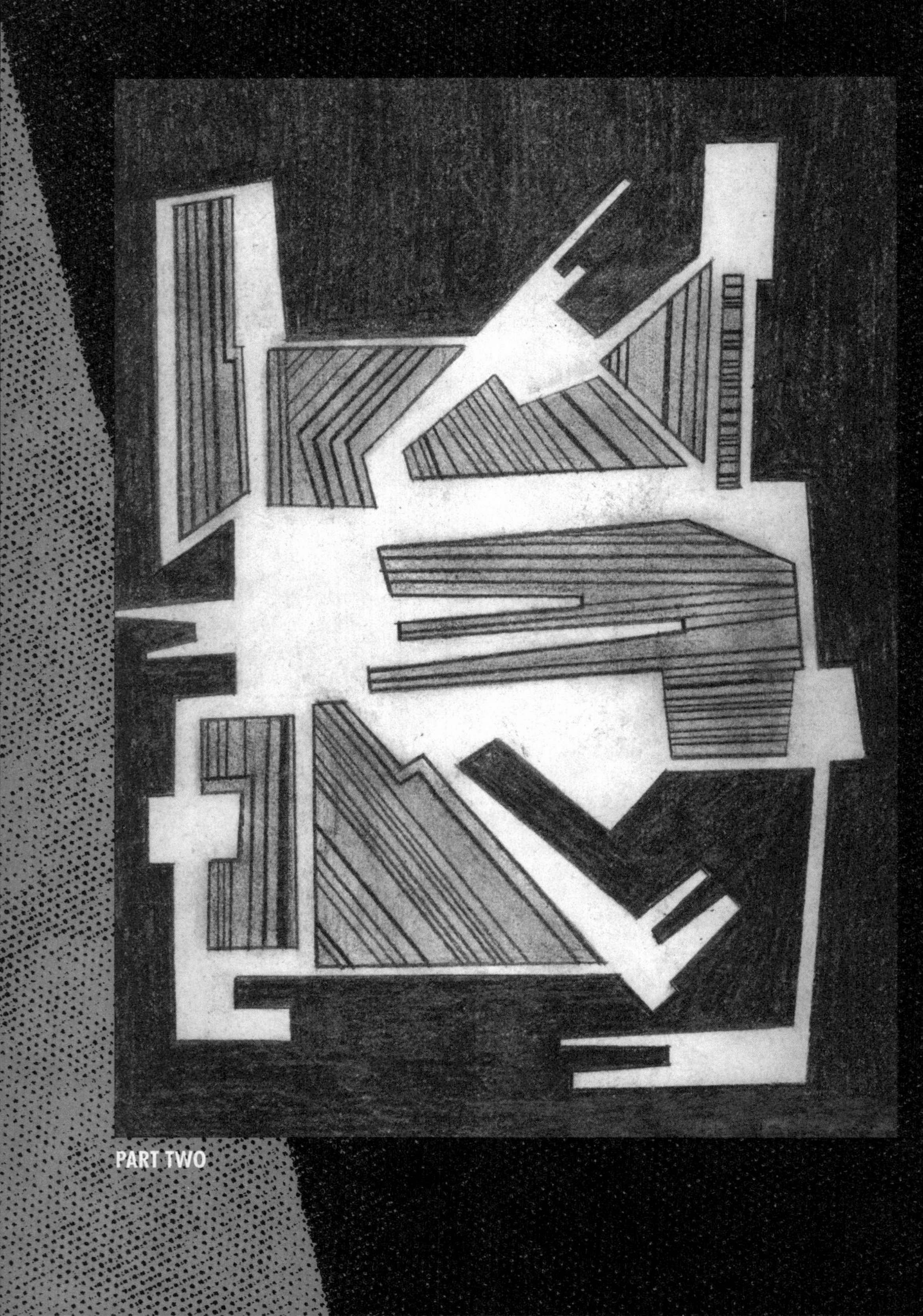

PART TWO

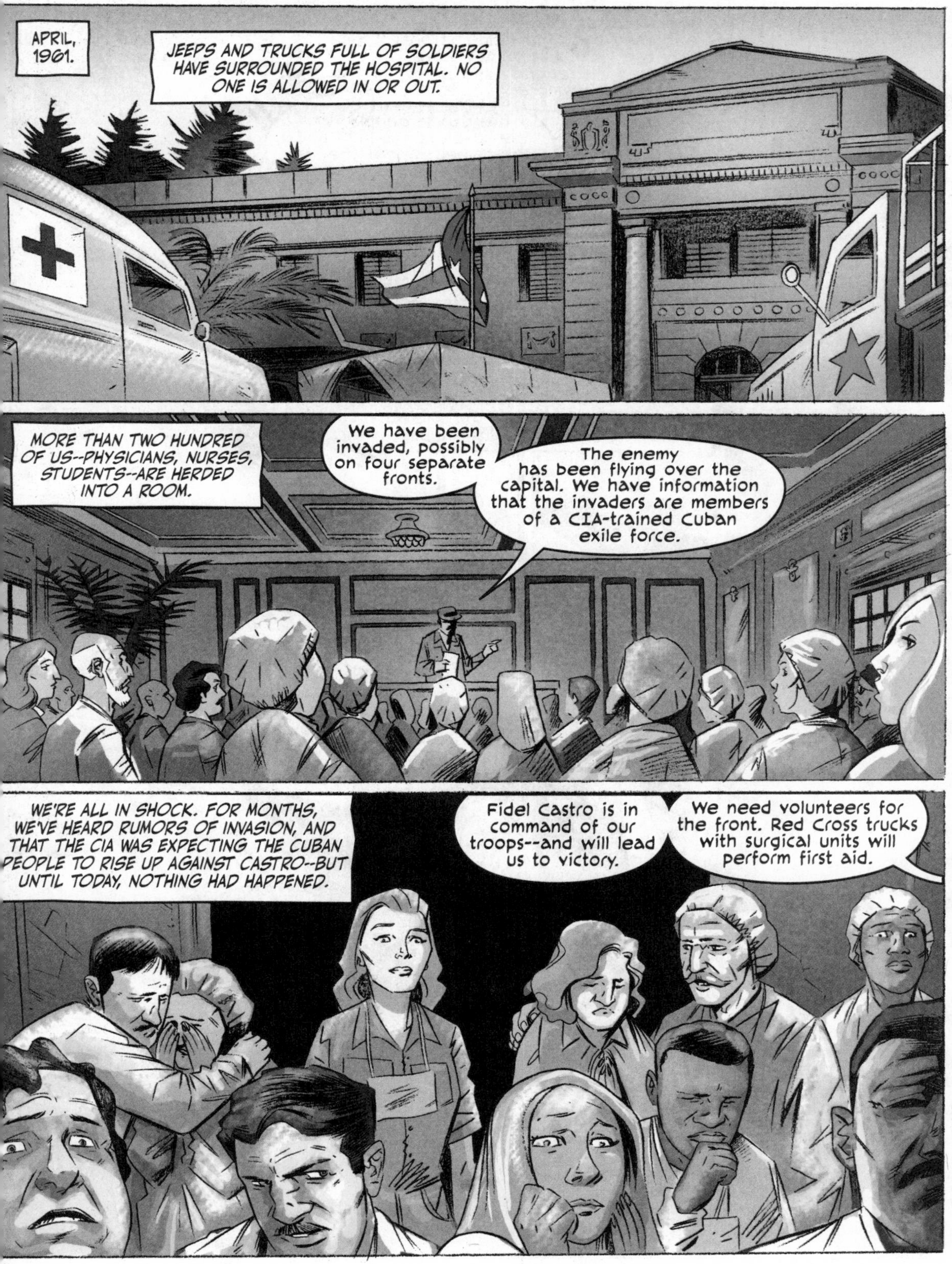
APRIL, 1961.
JEEPS AND TRUCKS FULL OF SOLDIERS HAVE SURROUNDED THE HOSPITAL. NO ONE IS ALLOWED IN OR OUT.
MORE THAN TWO HUNDRED OF US--PHYSICIANS, NURSES, STUDENTS--ARE HERDED INTO A ROOM.
We have been invaded, possibly on four separate fronts.
The enemy has been flying over the capital. We have information that the invaders are members of a CIA-trained Cuban exile force.
WE'RE ALL IN SHOCK. FOR MONTHS, WE'VE HEARD RUMORS OF INVASION, AND THAT THE CIA WAS EXPECTING THE CUBAN PEOPLE TO RISE UP AGAINST CASTRO--BUT UNTIL TODAY, NOTHING HAD HAPPENED.
Fidel Castro is in command of our troops--and will lead us to victory.
We need volunteers for the front. Red Cross trucks with surgical units will perform first aid.

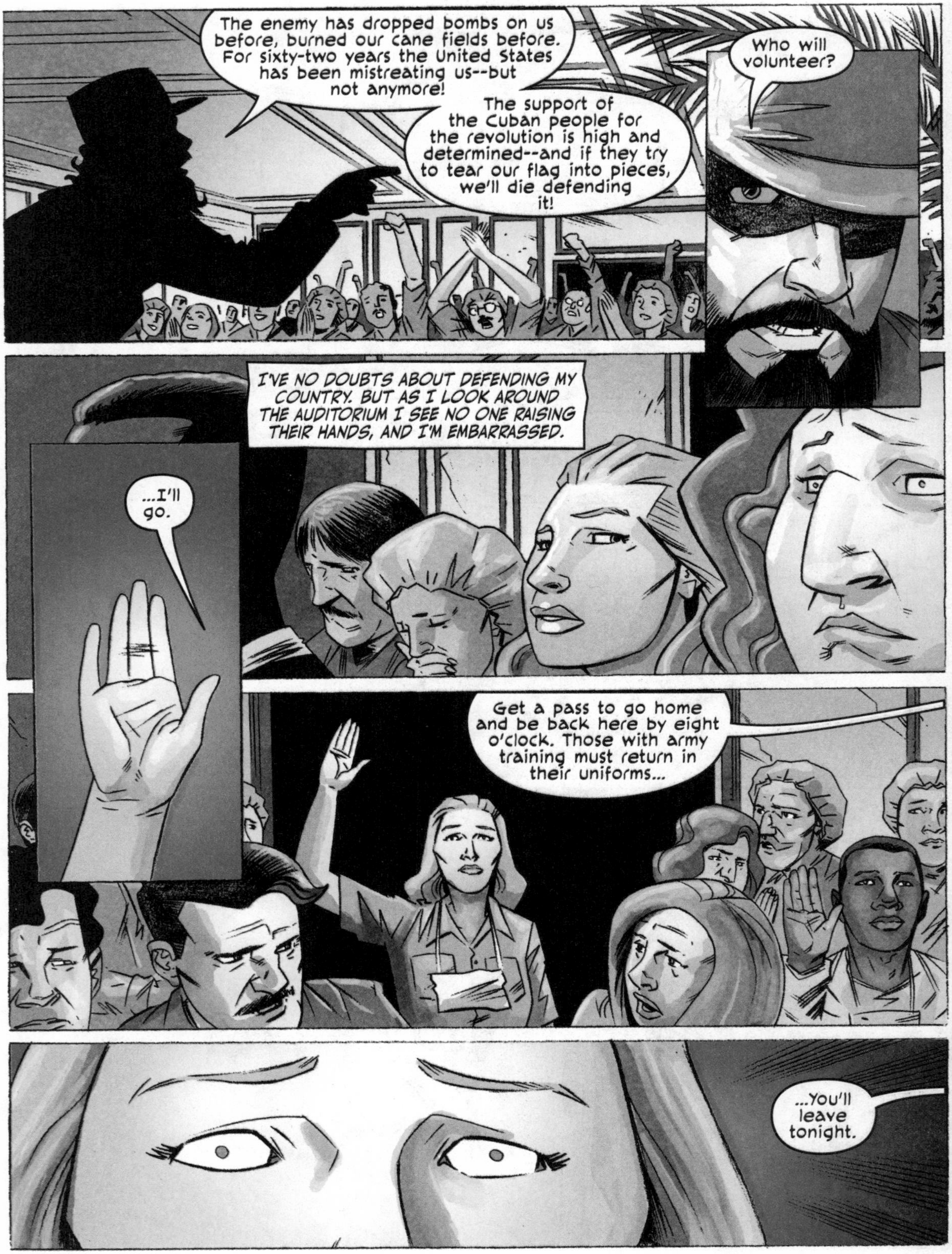
The enemy has dropped bombs on us before, burned our cane fields before. For sixty-two years the United States has been mistreating us--but not anymore!
The support of the Cuban people for the revolution is high and determined--and if they try to tear our flag into pieces, we'll die defending it!
Who will volunteer?
I'VE NO DOUBTS ABOUT DEFENDING MY COUNTRY. BUT AS I LOOK AROUND THE AUDITORIUM I SEE NO ONE RAISING THEIR HANDS, AND I'M EMBARRASSED.
...I'll go.
Get a pass to go home and be back here by eight o'clock. Those with army training must return in their uniforms...
...You'll leave tonight.

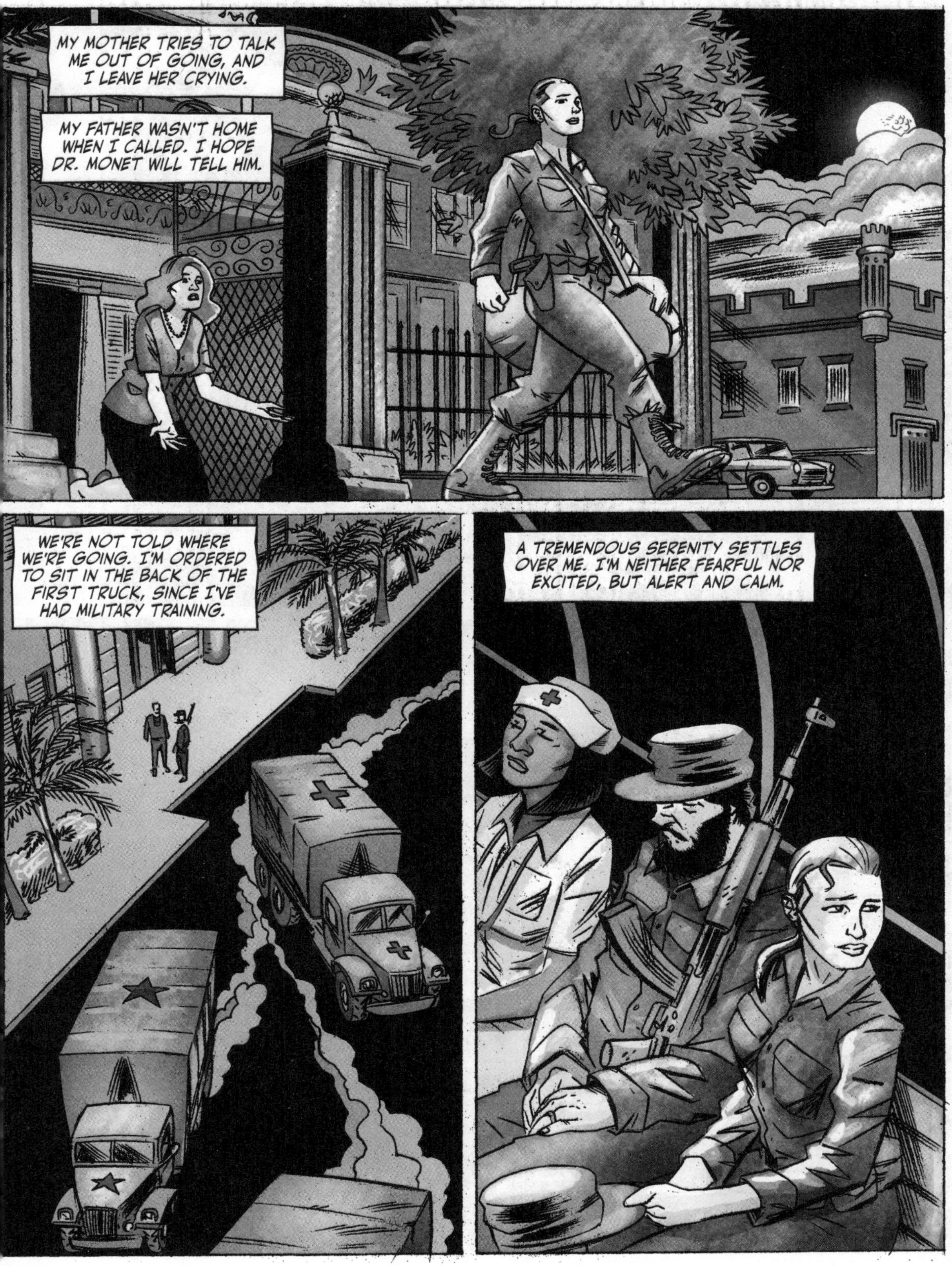
MY MOTHER TRIES TO TALK ME OUT OF GOING, AND I LEAVE HER CRYING.
MY FATHER WASN'T HOME WHEN I CALLED. I HOPE DR. MONET WILL TELL HIM.
WE'RE NOT TOLD WHERE WE'RE GOING. I'M ORDERED TO SIT IN THE BACK OF THE FIRST TRUCK, SINCE I'VE HAD MILITARY TRAINING.
A TREMENDOUS SERENITY SETTLES OVER ME. I'M NEITHER FEARFUL NOR EXCITED, BUT ALERT AND CALM.

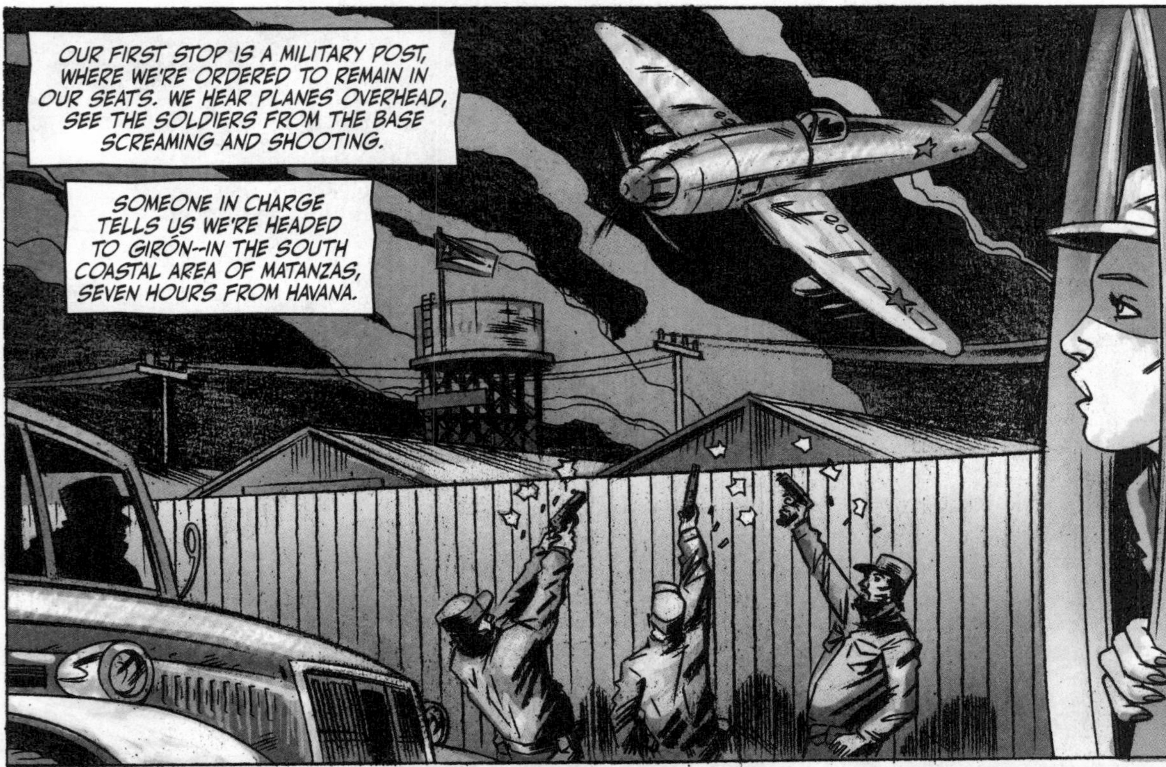
OUR FIRST STOP IS A MILITARY POST, WHERE WE'RE ORDERED TO REMAIN IN OUR SEATS. WE HEAR PLANES OVERHEAD, SEE THE SOLDIERS FROM THE BASE SCREAMING AND SHOOTING.
SOMEONE IN CHARGE TELLS US WE'RE HEADED TO GIRÓN--IN THE SOUTH COASTAL AREA OF MATANZAS, SEVEN HOURS FROM HAVANA.

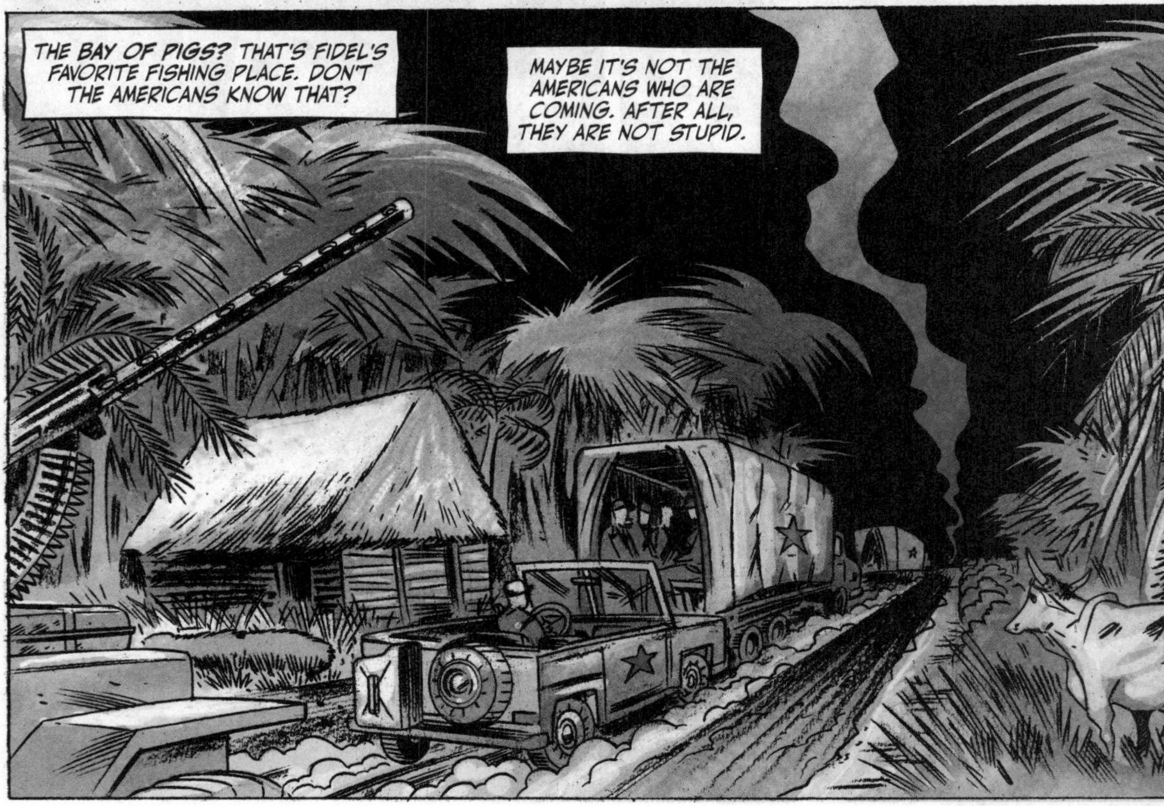
THE BAY OF PIGS? THAT'S FIDEL'S FAVORITE FISHING PLACE. DON'T THE AMERICANS KNOW THAT?
MAYBE IT'S NOT THE AMERICANS WHO ARE COMING. AFTER ALL, THEY ARE NOT STUPID.

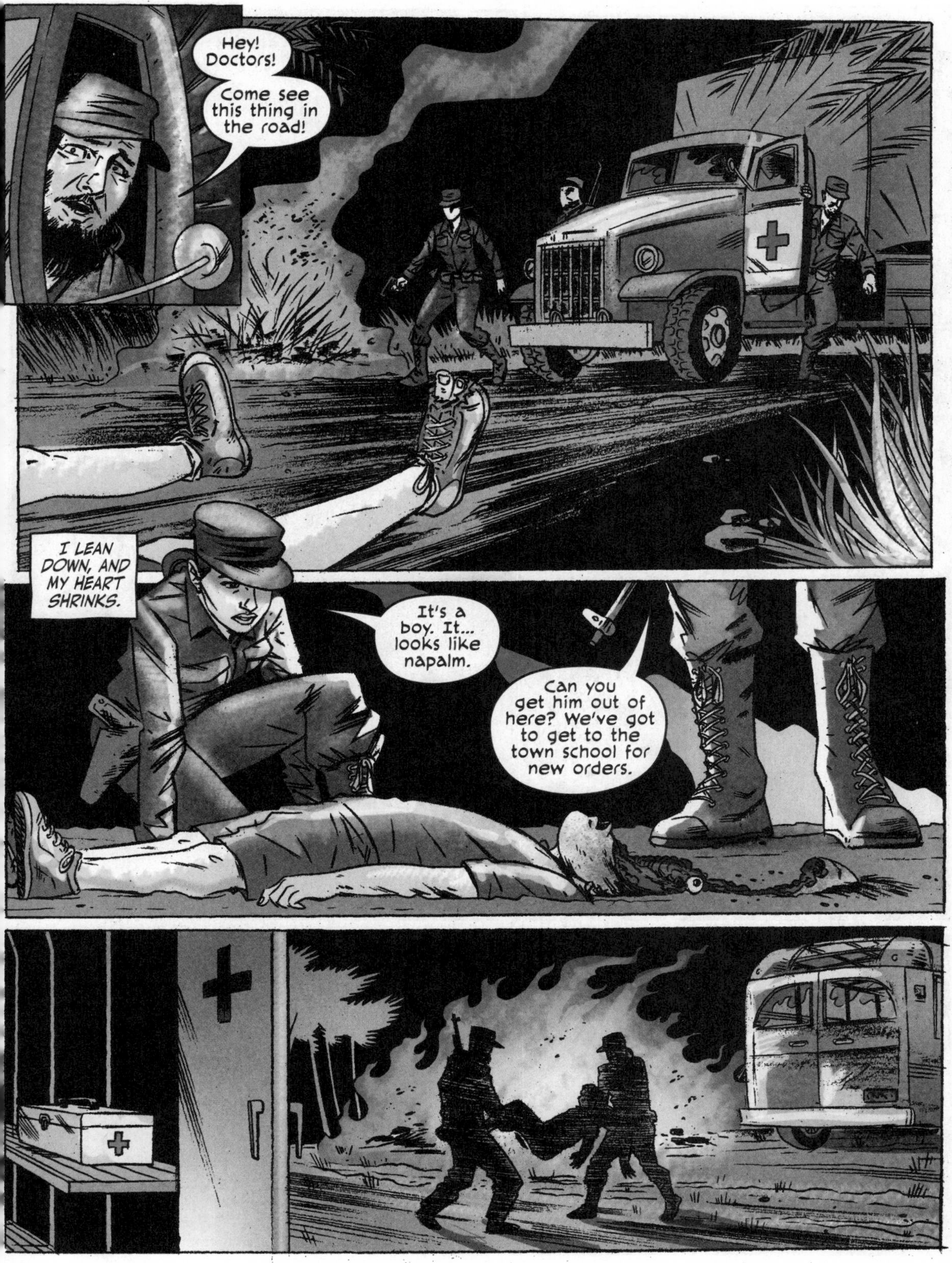
Hey! Doctors!
Come see this thing in the road!
I LEAN DOWN, AND MY HEART SHRINKS.
It's a boy. It... looks like napalm.
Can you get him out of here? We've got to get to the town school for new orders.

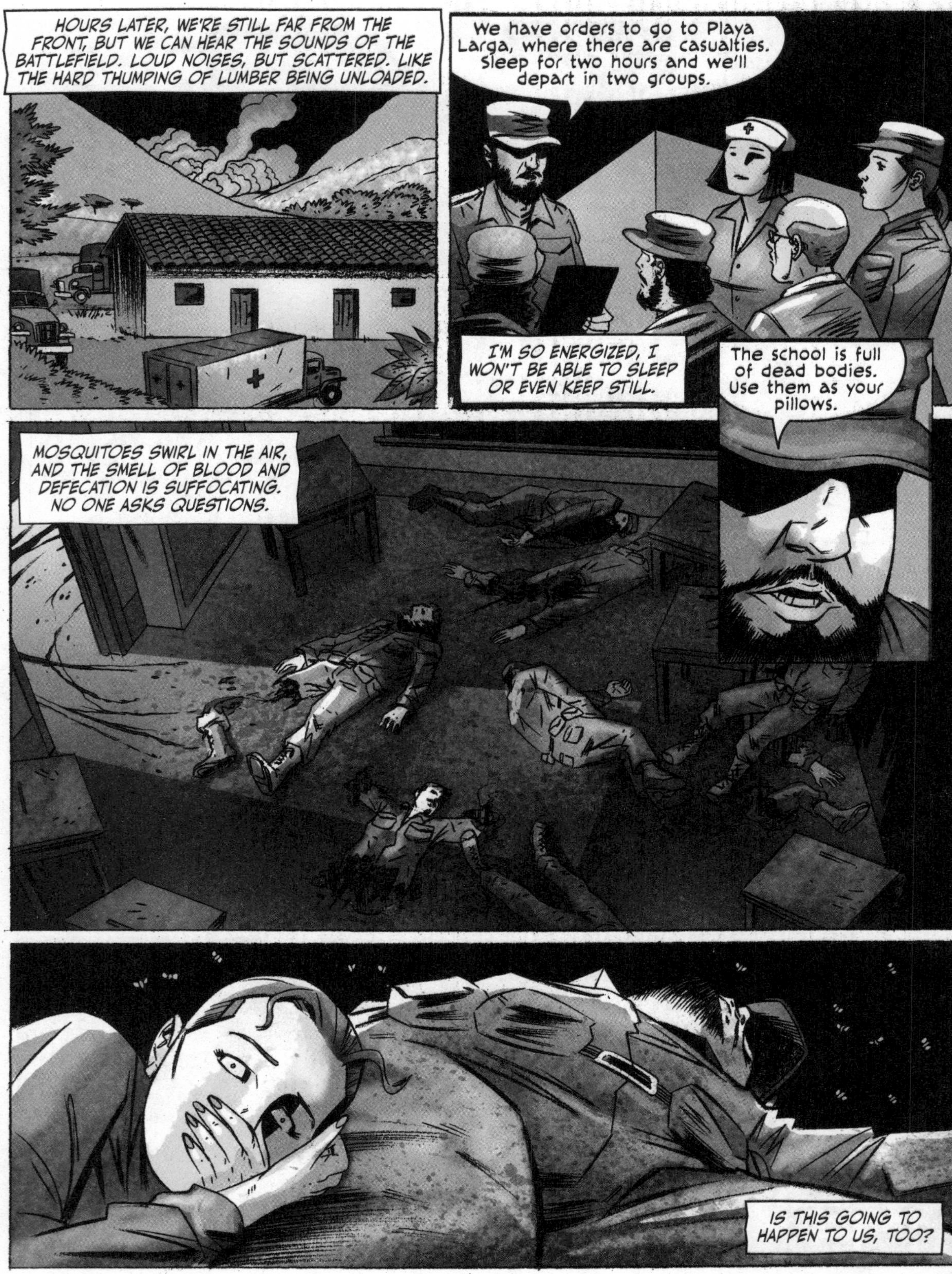
HOURS LATER, WE'RE STILL FAR FROM THE FRONT, BUT WE CAN HEAR THE SOUNDS OF THE BATTLEFIELD. LOUD NOISES, BUT SCATTERED. LIKE THE HARD THUMPING OF LUMBER BEING UNLOADED.
We have orders to go to Playa Larga, where there are casualties. Sleep for two hours and we'll depart in two groups.
I'M SO ENERGIZED, I WON'T BE ABLE TO SLEEP OR EVEN KEEP STILL.
The school is full of dead bodies. Use them as your pillows.
MOSQUITOES SWIRL IN THE AIR, AND THE SMELL OF BLOOD AND DEFECATION IS SUFFOCATING. NO ONE ASKS QUESTIONS.
IS THIS GOING TO HAPPEN TO US, TOO?

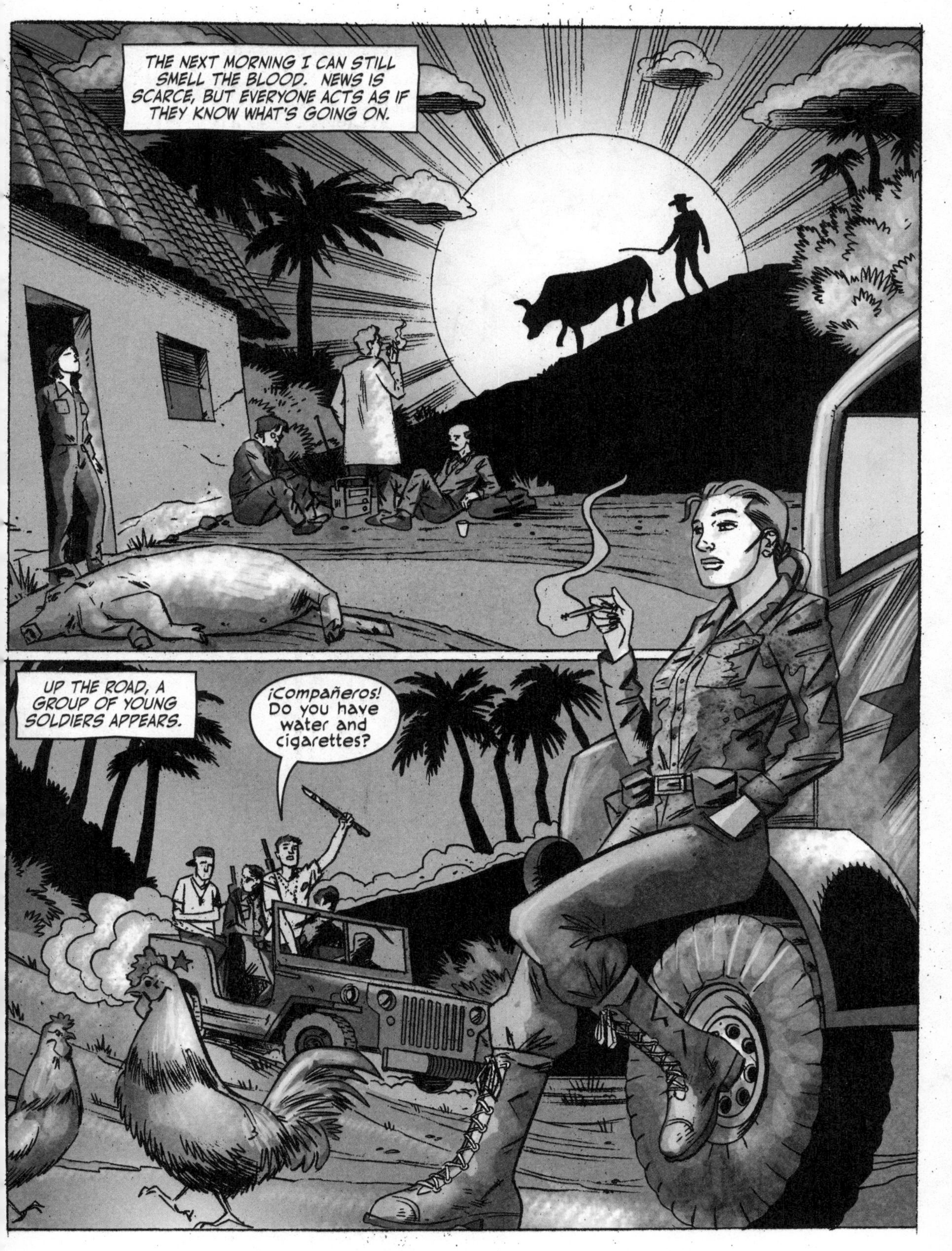
THE NEXT MORNING I CAN STILL SMELL THE BLOOD. NEWS IS SCARCE, BUT EVERYONE ACTS AS IF THEY KNOW WHAT'S GOING ON.
UP THE ROAD, A GROUP OF YOUNG SOLDIERS APPEARS.
¡Compañeros! Do you have water and cigarettes?

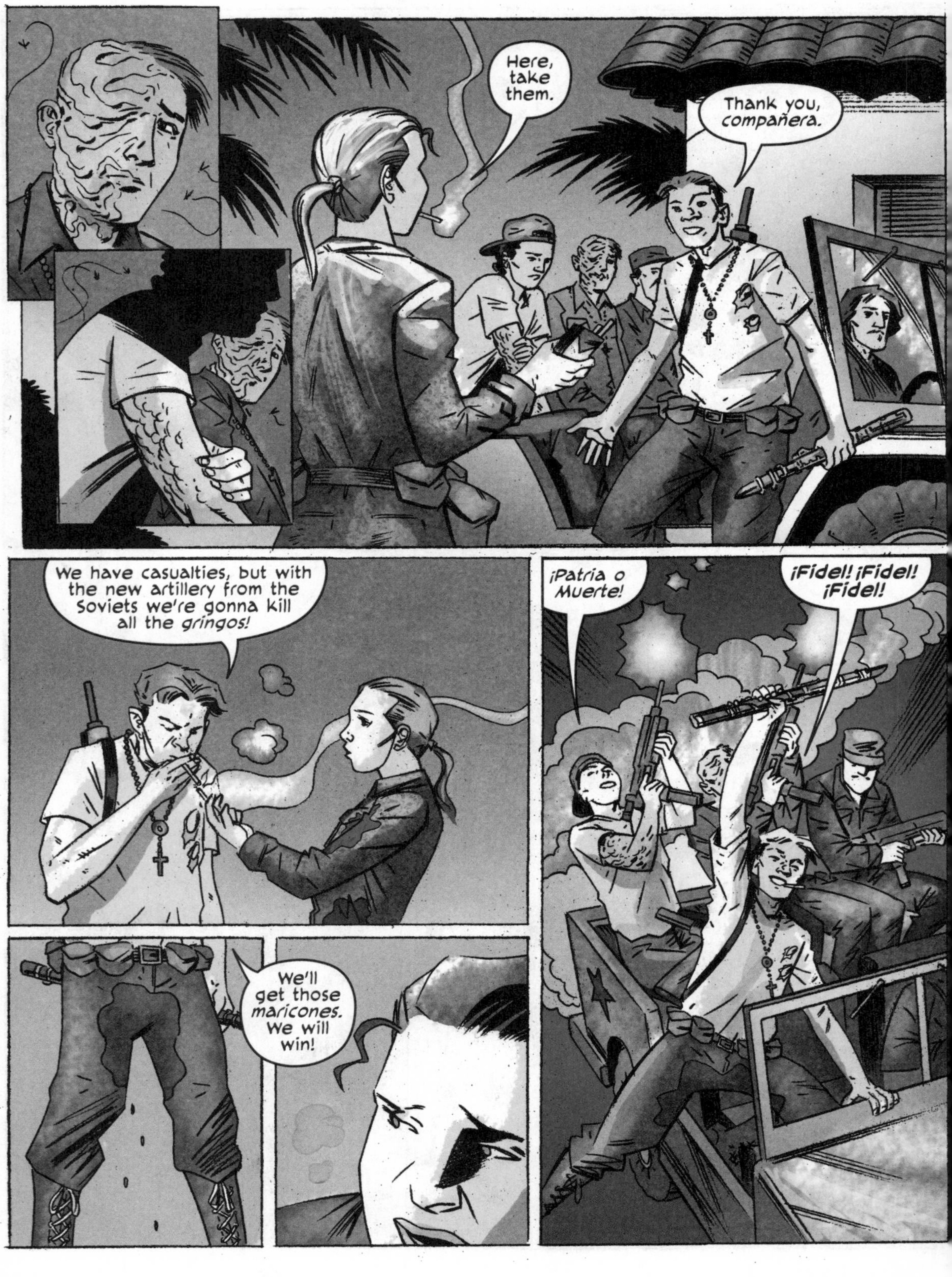
Here, take them.
Thank you, *compañera.*
We have casualties, but with the new artillery from the Soviets we're gonna kill all the *gringos!*
We'll get those *maricones.* We will win!
¡Patria o Muerte!
¡Fidel! ¡Fidel! ¡Fidel!

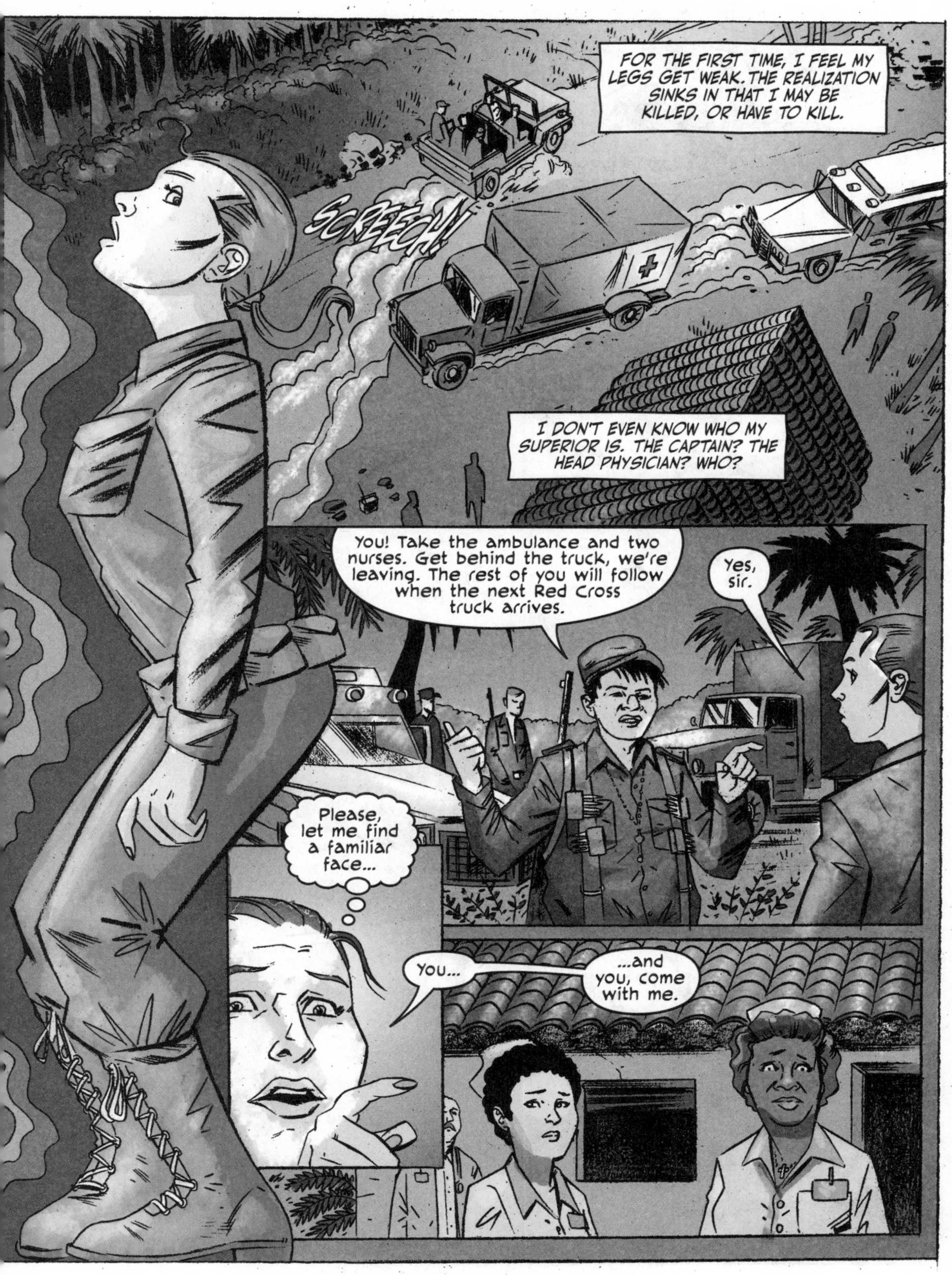
FOR THE FIRST TIME, I FEEL MY LEGS GET WEAK. THE REALIZATION SINKS IN THAT I MAY BE KILLED, OR HAVE TO KILL.
SCREECH!
I DON'T EVEN KNOW WHO MY SUPERIOR IS. THE CAPTAIN? THE HEAD PHYSICIAN? WHO?
You! Take the ambulance and two nurses. Get behind the truck, we're leaving. The rest of you will follow when the next Red Cross truck arrives.
Yes, sir.
Please, let me find a familiar face...
You...
...and you, come with me.

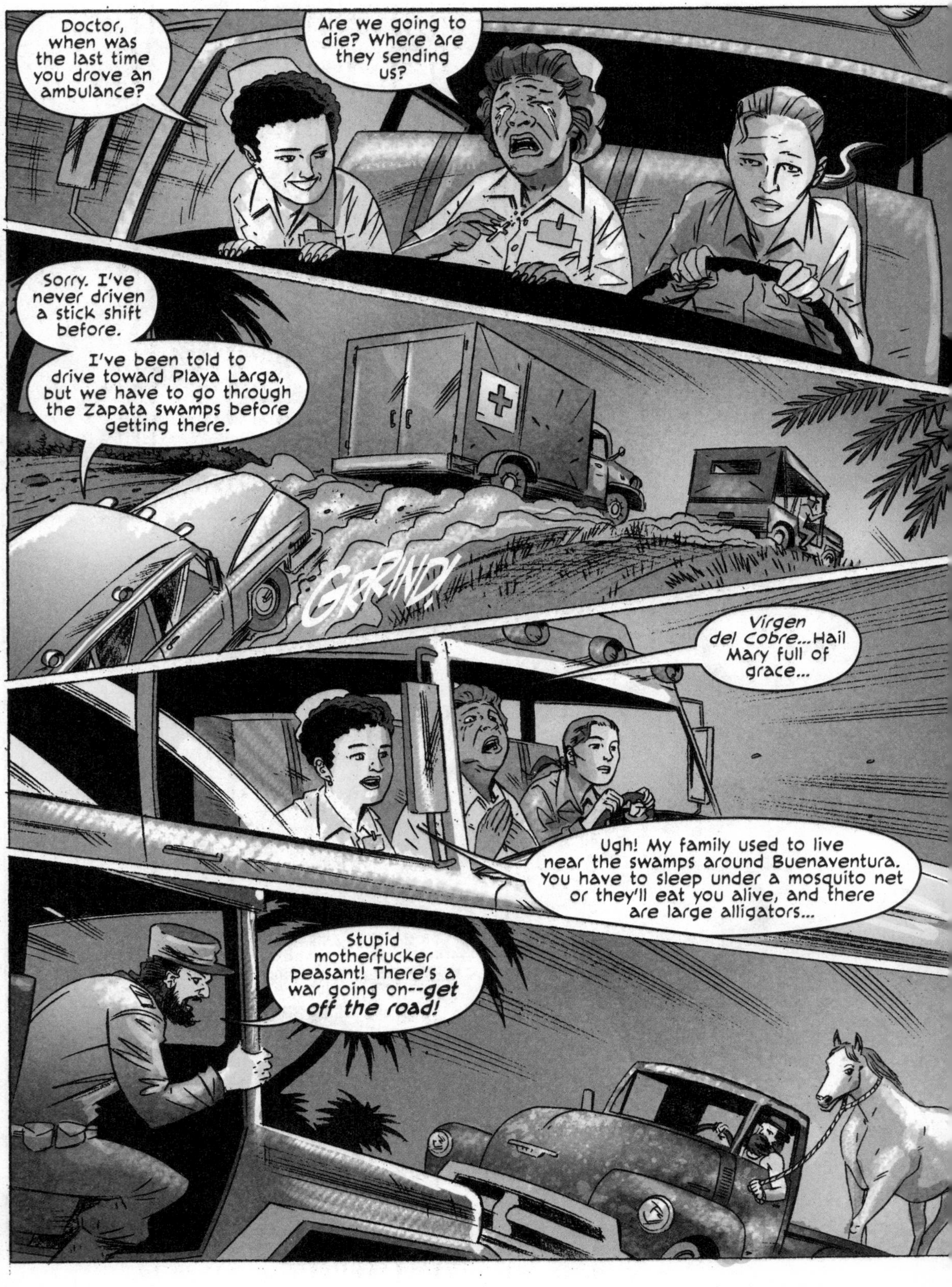

Doctor, when was the last time you drove an ambulance?
Are we going to die? Where are they sending us?
Sorry. I've never driven a stick shift before.
I've been told to drive toward Playa Larga, but we have to go through the Zapata swamps before getting there.
GRRIND!
Virgen del Cobre...Hail Mary full of grace...
Ugh! My family used to live near the swamps around Buenaventura. You have to sleep under a mosquito net or they'll eat you alive, and there are large alligators...
Stupid motherfucker peasant! There's a war going on--***get off the road!***

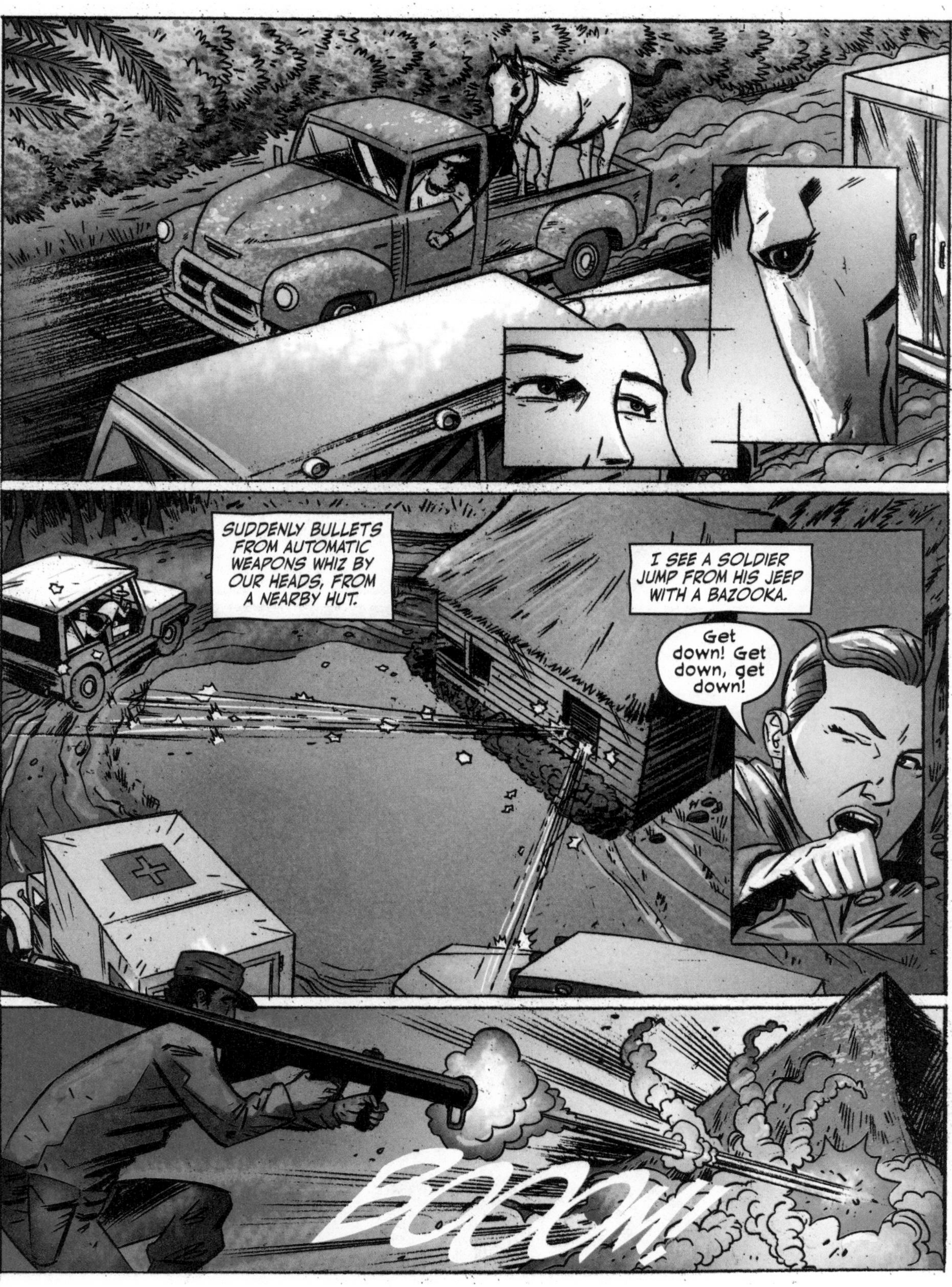
SUDDENLY BULLETS FROM AUTOMATIC WEAPONS WHIZ BY OUR HEADS, FROM A NEARBY HUT.
I SEE A SOLDIER JUMP FROM HIS JEEP WITH A BAZOOKA.
Get down! Get down, get down!
BOOOM!

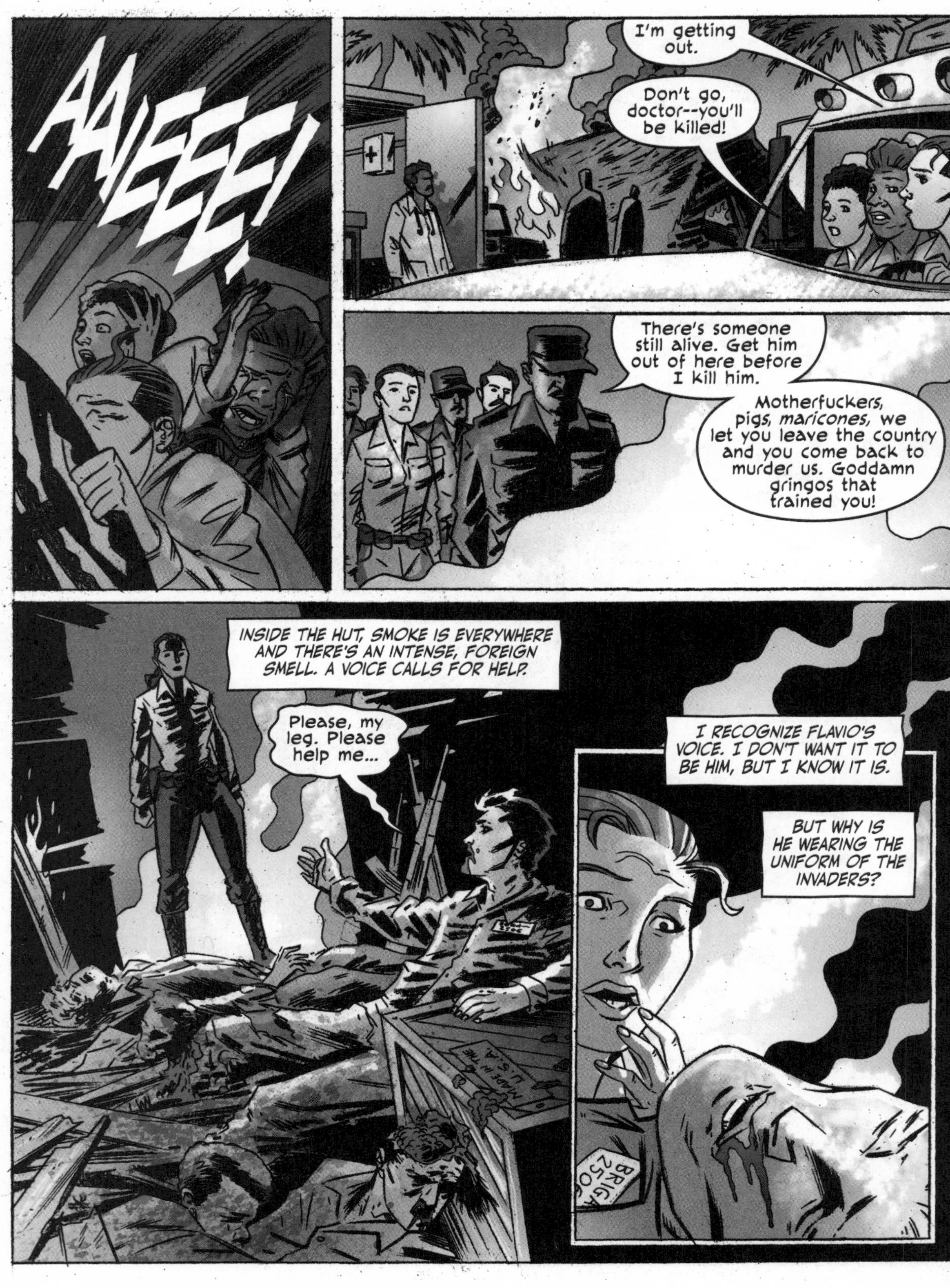
AAIEEE!
I'm getting out.
Don't go, doctor--you'll be killed!
There's someone still alive. Get him out of here before I kill him.
Motherfuckers, pigs, *maricones,* we let you leave the country and you come back to murder us. Goddamn gringos that trained you!
INSIDE THE HUT, SMOKE IS EVERYWHERE AND THERE'S AN INTENSE, FOREIGN SMELL. A VOICE CALLS FOR HELP.
Please, my leg. Please help me...
I RECOGNIZE FLAVIO'S VOICE. I DON'T WANT IT TO BE HIM, BUT I KNOW IT IS.
BUT WHY IS HE WEARING THE UNIFORM OF THE INVADERS?

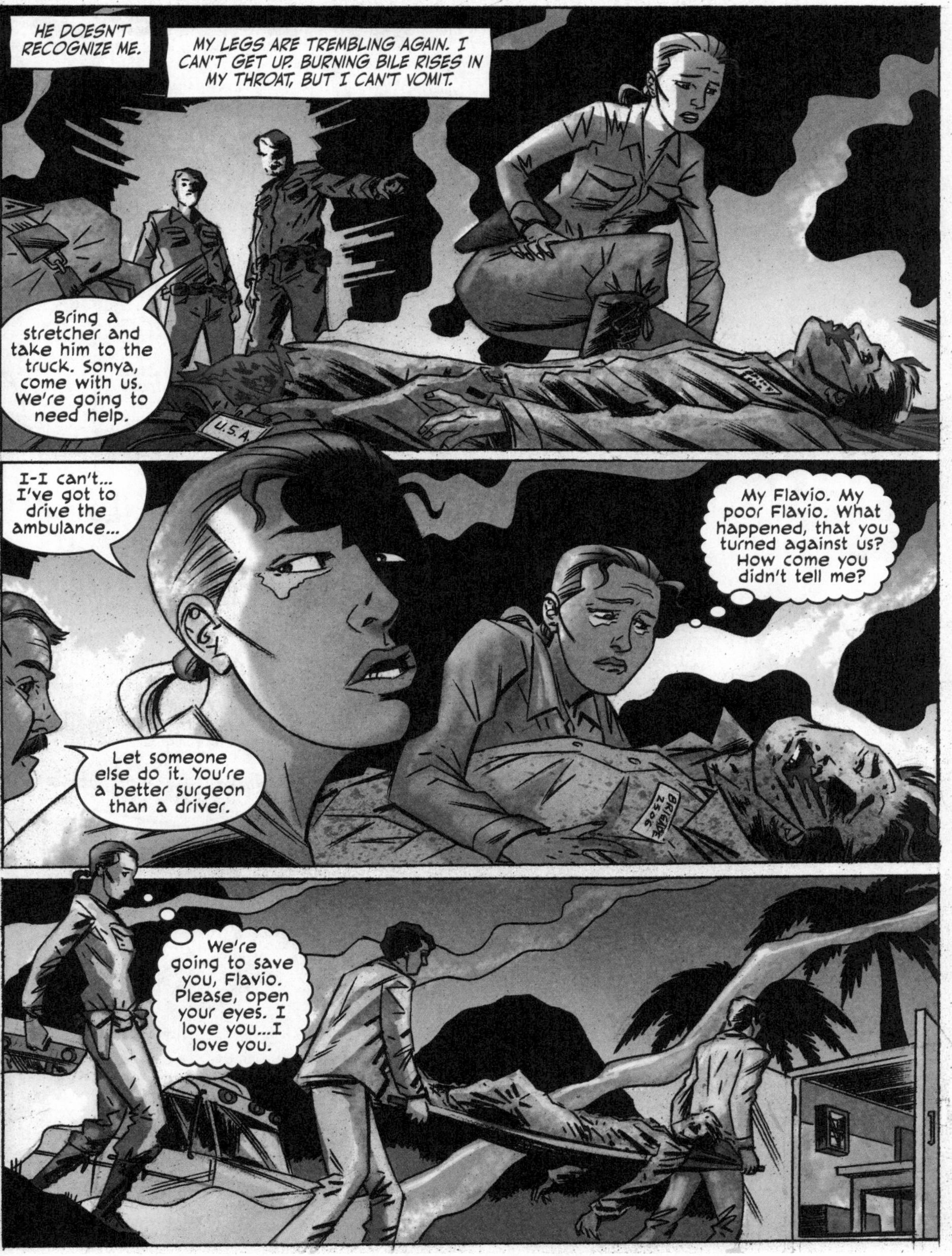
HE DOESN'T RECOGNIZE ME.
MY LEGS ARE TREMBLING AGAIN. I CAN'T GET UP. BURNING BILE RISES IN MY THROAT, BUT I CAN'T VOMIT.
Bring a stretcher and take him to the truck. Sonya, come with us. We're going to need help.
U.S.A.
I-I can't... I've got to drive the ambulance...
My Flavio. My poor Flavio. What happened, that you turned against us? How come you didn't tell me?
Let someone else do it. You're a better surgeon than a driver.
BRIGADE 2506
We're going to save you, Flavio. Please, open your eyes. I love you...I love you.

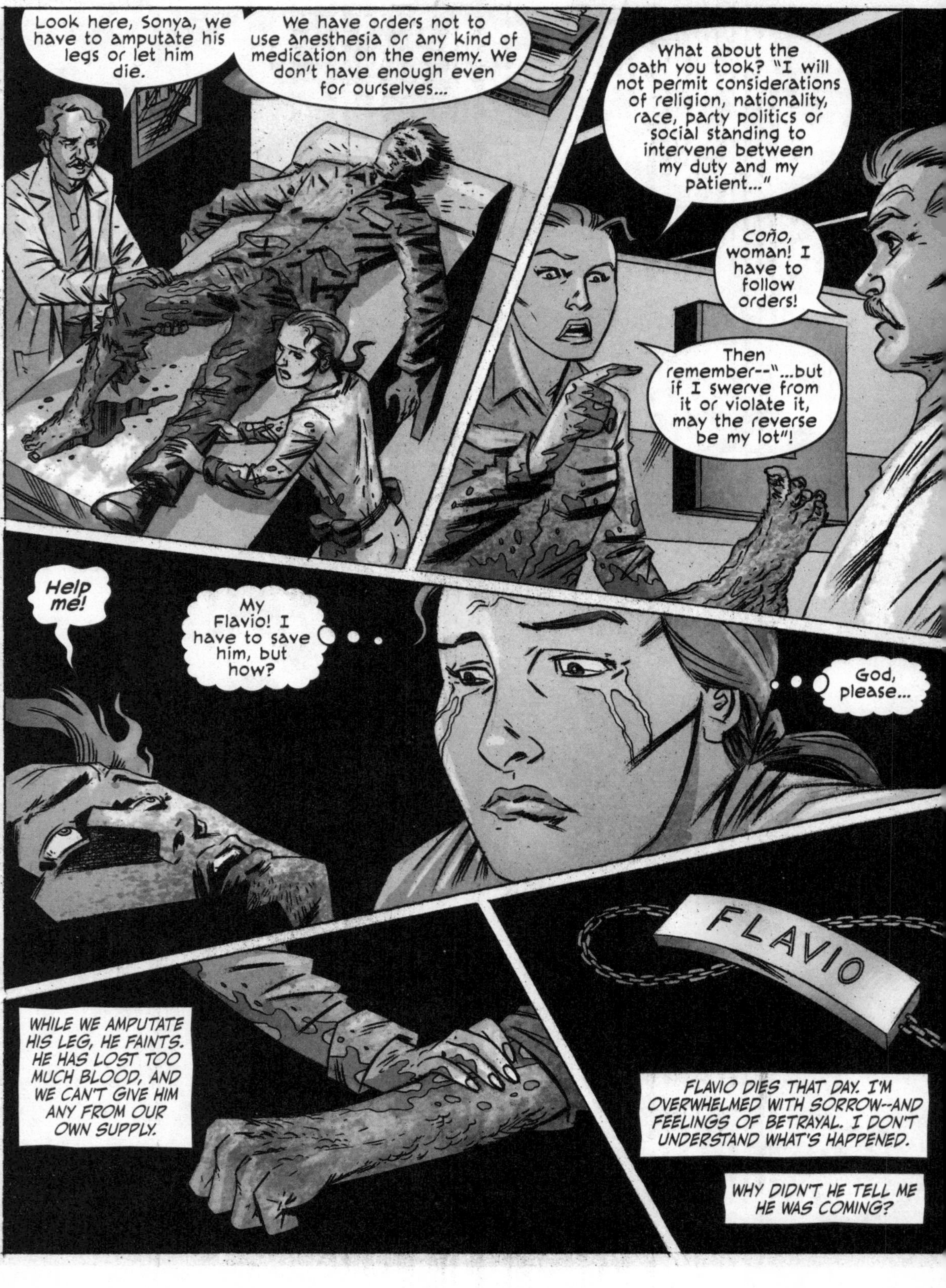

Look here, Sonya, we have to amputate his legs or let him die.
We have orders not to use anesthesia or any kind of medication on the enemy. We don't have enough even for ourselves...
What about the oath you took? "I will not permit considerations of religion, nationality, race, party politics or social standing to intervene between my duty and my patient..."
Coño, woman! I have to follow orders!
Then remember--"...but if I swerve from it or violate it, may the reverse be my lot"!
Help me!
My Flavio! I have to save him, but how?
God, please...
WHILE WE AMPUTATE HIS LEG, HE FAINTS. HE HAS LOST TOO MUCH BLOOD, AND WE CAN'T GIVE HIM ANY FROM OUR OWN SUPPLY.
FLAVIO
FLAVIO DIES THAT DAY. I'M OVERWHELMED WITH SORROW--AND FEELINGS OF BETRAYAL. I DON'T UNDERSTAND WHAT'S HAPPENED.
WHY DIDN'T HE TELL ME HE WAS COMING?

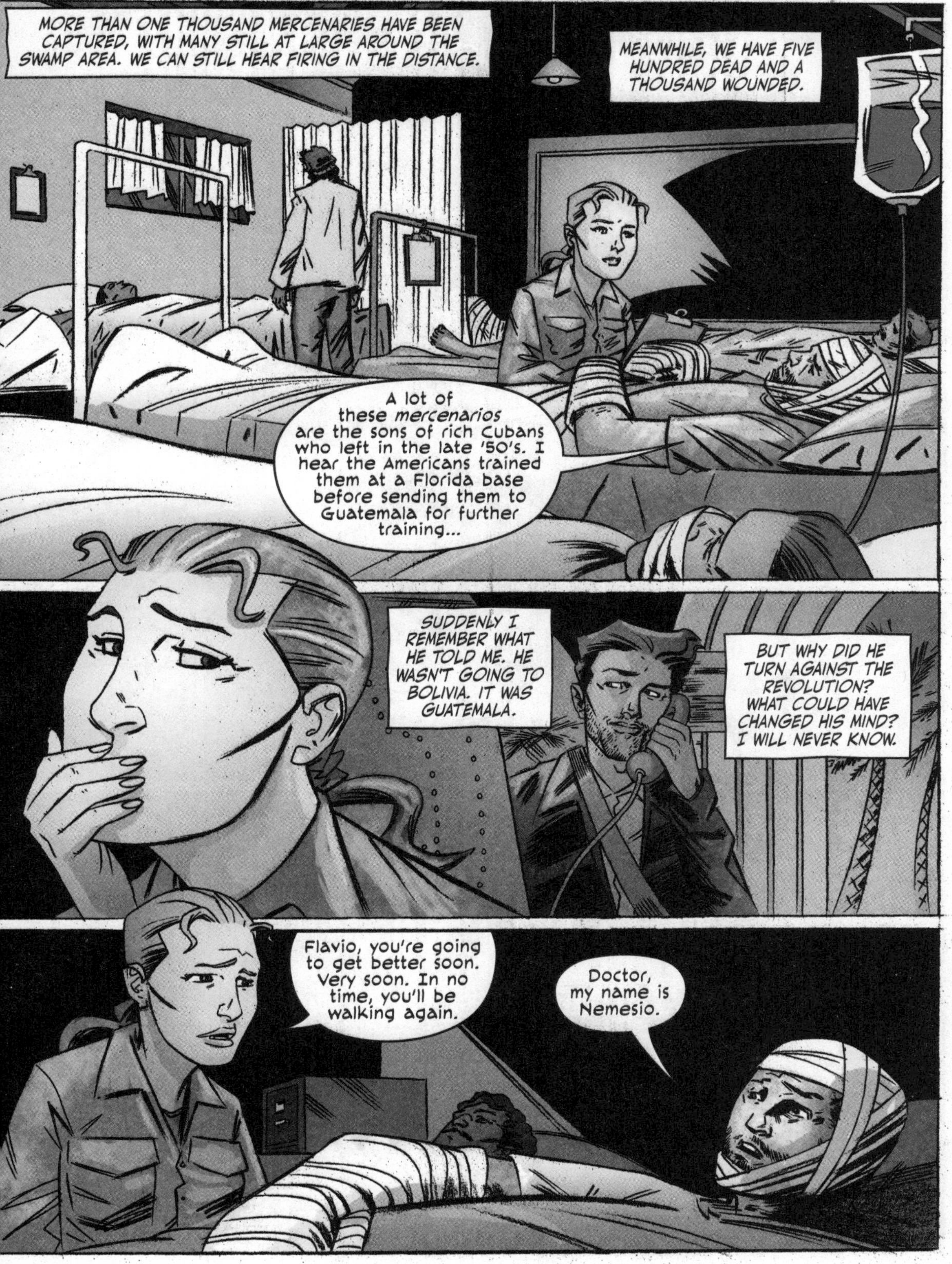
MORE THAN ONE THOUSAND MERCENARIES HAVE BEEN CAPTURED, WITH MANY STILL AT LARGE AROUND THE SWAMP AREA. WE CAN STILL HEAR FIRING IN THE DISTANCE.
MEANWHILE, WE HAVE FIVE HUNDRED DEAD AND A THOUSAND WOUNDED.
A lot of these *mercenarios* are the sons of rich Cubans who left in the late '50's. I hear the Americans trained them at a Florida base before sending them to Guatemala for further training...
SUDDENLY I REMEMBER WHAT HE TOLD ME. HE WASN'T GOING TO BOLIVIA. IT WAS GUATEMALA.
BUT WHY DID HE TURN AGAINST THE REVOLUTION? WHAT COULD HAVE CHANGED HIS MIND? I WILL NEVER KNOW.
Flavio, you're going to get better soon. Very soon. In no time, you'll be walking again.
Doctor, my name is Nemesio.

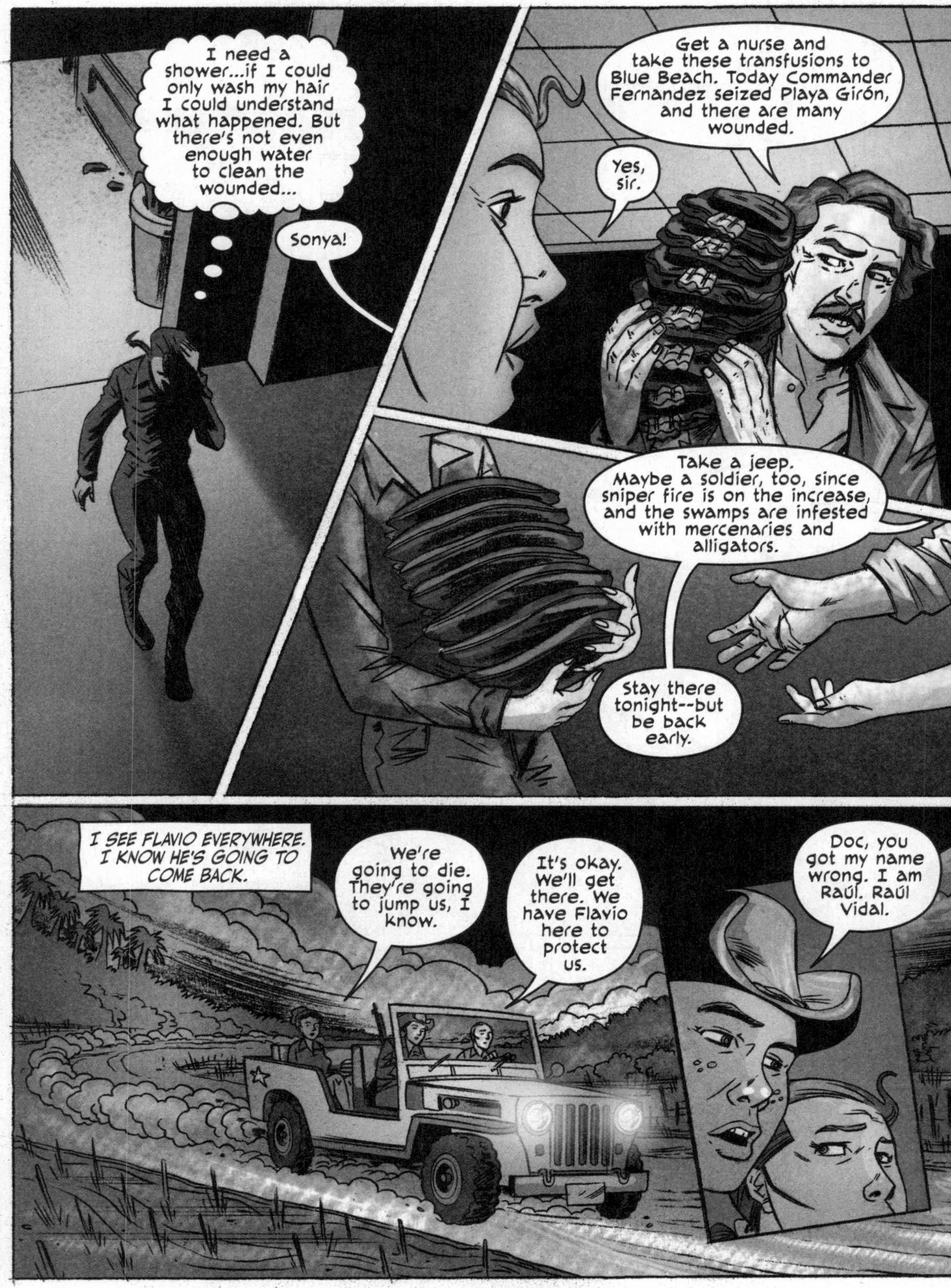

I need a shower...if I could only wash my hair I could understand what happened. But there's not even enough water to clean the wounded...
Sonya!
Get a nurse and take these transfusions to Blue Beach. Today Commander Fernandez seized Playa Girón, and there are many wounded.
Yes, sir.
Take a jeep. Maybe a soldier, too, since sniper fire is on the increase, and the swamps are infested with mercenaries and alligators.
Stay there tonight--but be back early.
I SEE FLAVIO EVERYWHERE. I KNOW HE'S GOING TO COME BACK.
We're going to die. They're going to jump us, I know.
It's okay. We'll get there. We have Flavio here to protect us.
Doc, you got my name wrong. I am Raúl. Raúl Vidal.

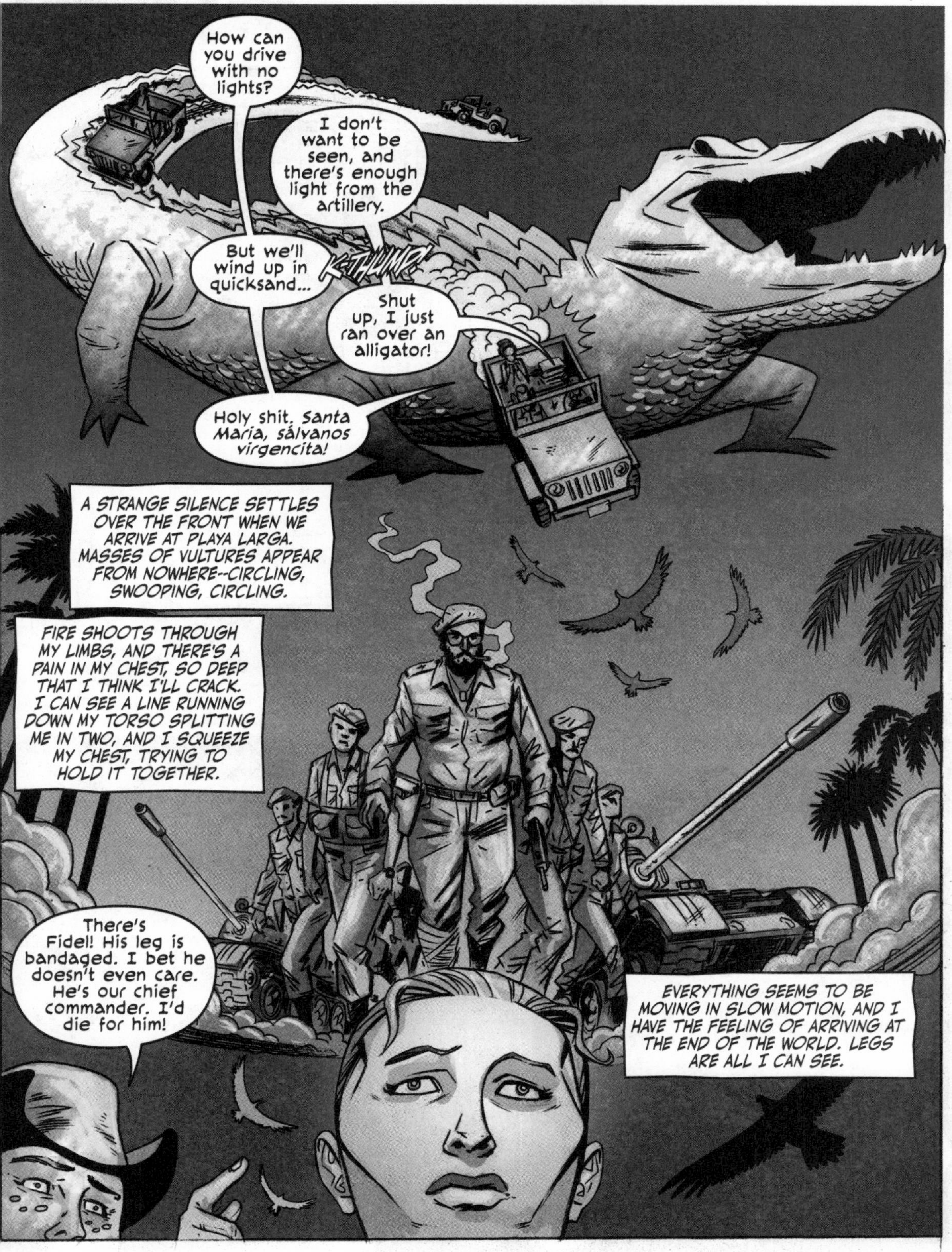
How can you drive with no lights?
I don't want to be seen, and there's enough light from the artillery.
But we'll wind up in quicksand...
K-THUMP!
Shut up, I just ran over an alligator!
Holy shit. Santa Maria, sálvanos virgencita!
A STRANGE SILENCE SETTLES OVER THE FRONT WHEN WE ARRIVE AT PLAYA LARGA. MASSES OF VULTURES APPEAR FROM NOWHERE--CIRCLING, SWOOPING, CIRCLING.
FIRE SHOOTS THROUGH MY LIMBS, AND THERE'S A PAIN IN MY CHEST, SO DEEP THAT I THINK I'LL CRACK. I CAN SEE A LINE RUNNING DOWN MY TORSO SPLITTING ME IN TWO, AND I SQUEEZE MY CHEST, TRYING TO HOLD IT TOGETHER.
There's Fidel! His leg is bandaged. I bet he doesn't even care. He's our chief commander. I'd die for him!
EVERYTHING SEEMS TO BE MOVING IN SLOW MOTION, AND I HAVE THE FEELING OF ARRIVING AT THE END OF THE WORLD. LEGS ARE ALL I CAN SEE.

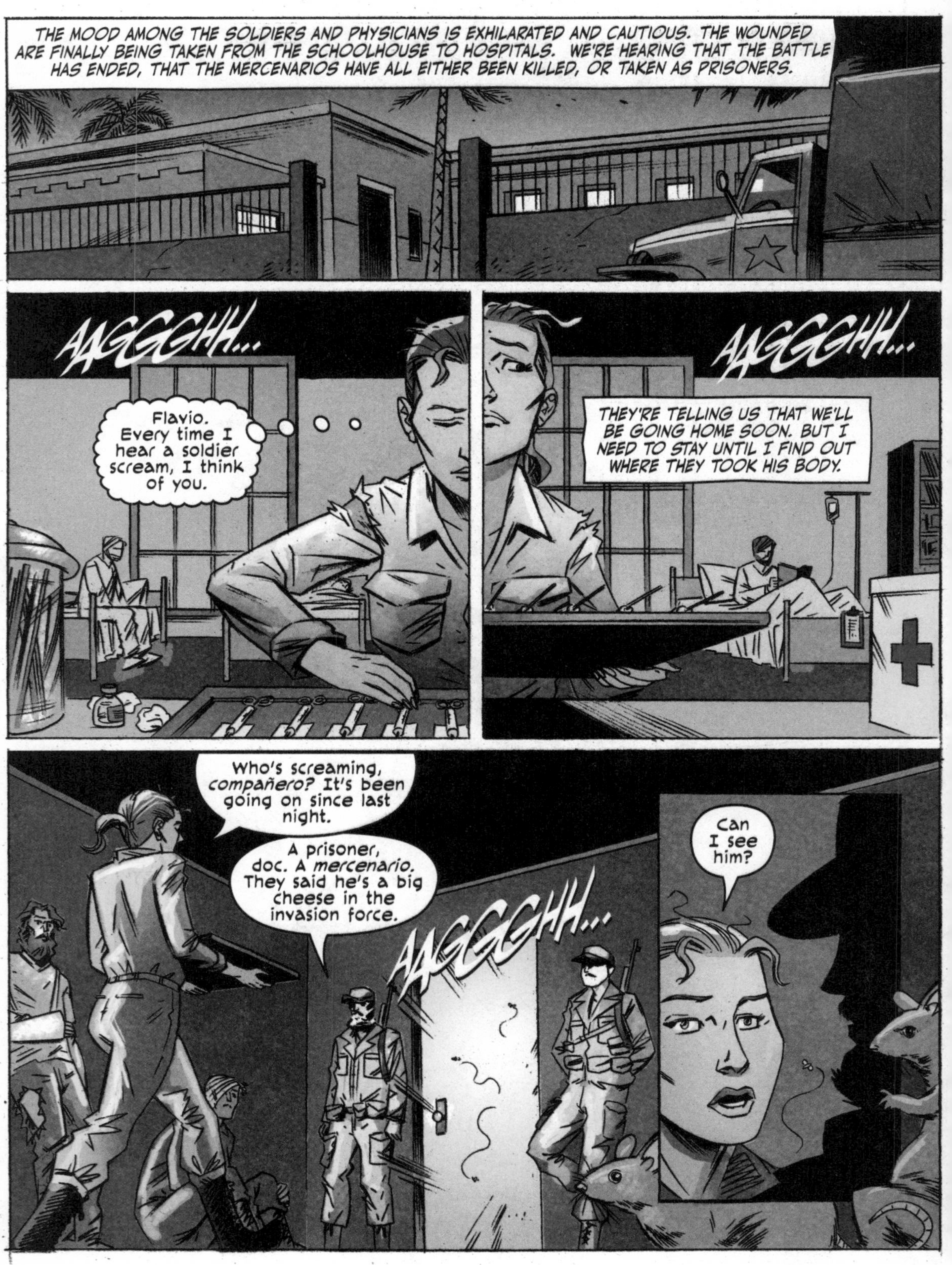
THE MOOD AMONG THE SOLDIERS AND PHYSICIANS IS EXHILARATED AND CAUTIOUS. THE WOUNDED ARE FINALLY BEING TAKEN FROM THE SCHOOLHOUSE TO HOSPITALS. WE'RE HEARING THAT THE BATTLE HAS ENDED, THAT THE MERCENARIOS HAVE ALL EITHER BEEN KILLED, OR TAKEN AS PRISONERS.
AAGGGHH...
Flavio. Every time I hear a soldier scream, I think of you.
AAGGGHH...
THEY'RE TELLING US THAT WE'LL BE GOING HOME SOON. BUT I NEED TO STAY UNTIL I FIND OUT WHERE THEY TOOK HIS BODY.
Who's screaming, *compañero?* It's been going on since last night.
A prisoner, doc. A *mercenario.* They said he's a big cheese in the invasion force.
AAGGGHH...
Can I see him?

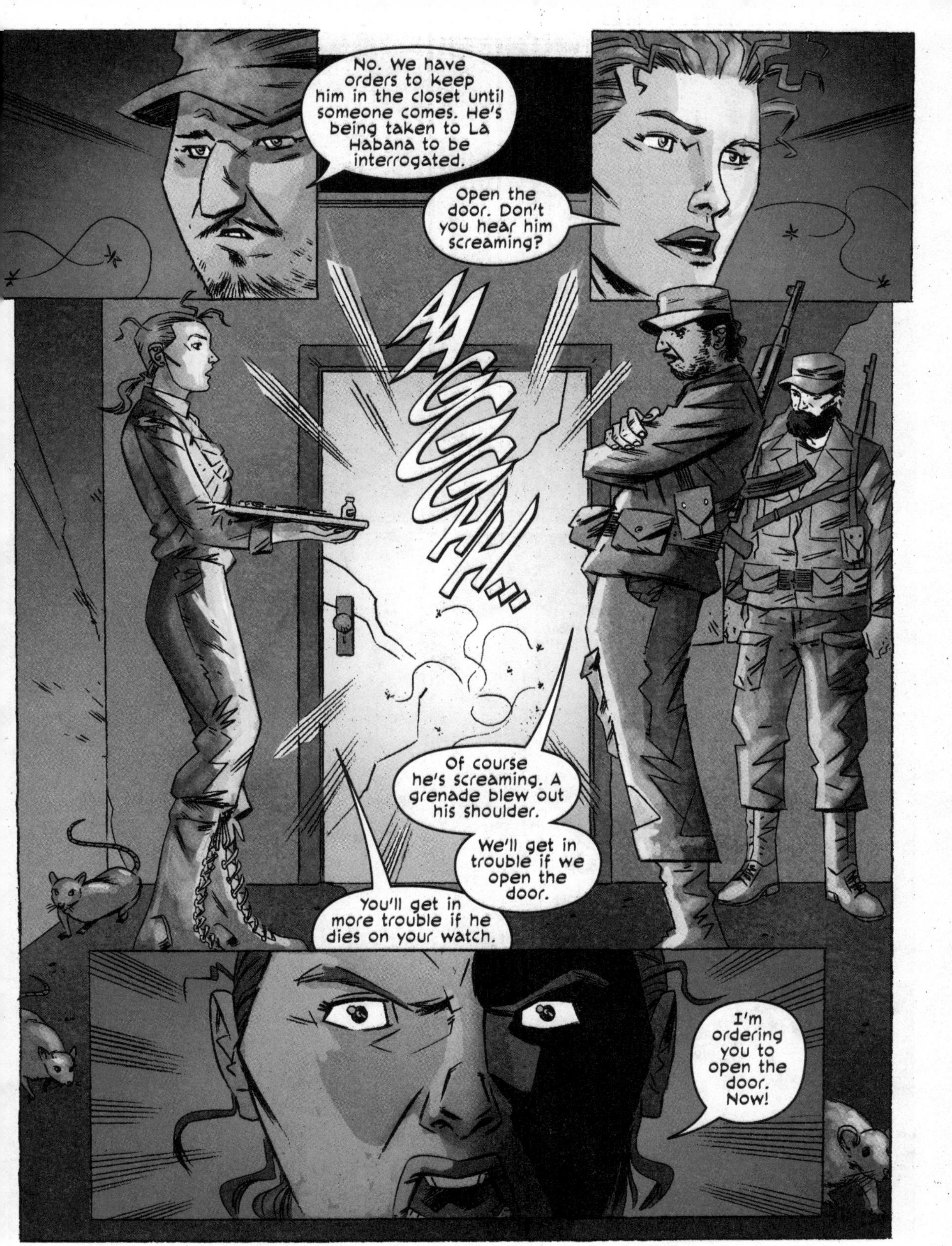
No. We have orders to keep him in the closet until someone comes. He's being taken to La Habana to be interrogated.
Open the door. Don't you hear him screaming?
AAGGGGHH...
Of course he's screaming. A grenade blew out his shoulder.
We'll get in trouble if we open the door.
You'll get in more trouble if he dies on your watch.
I'm ordering you to open the door. Now!

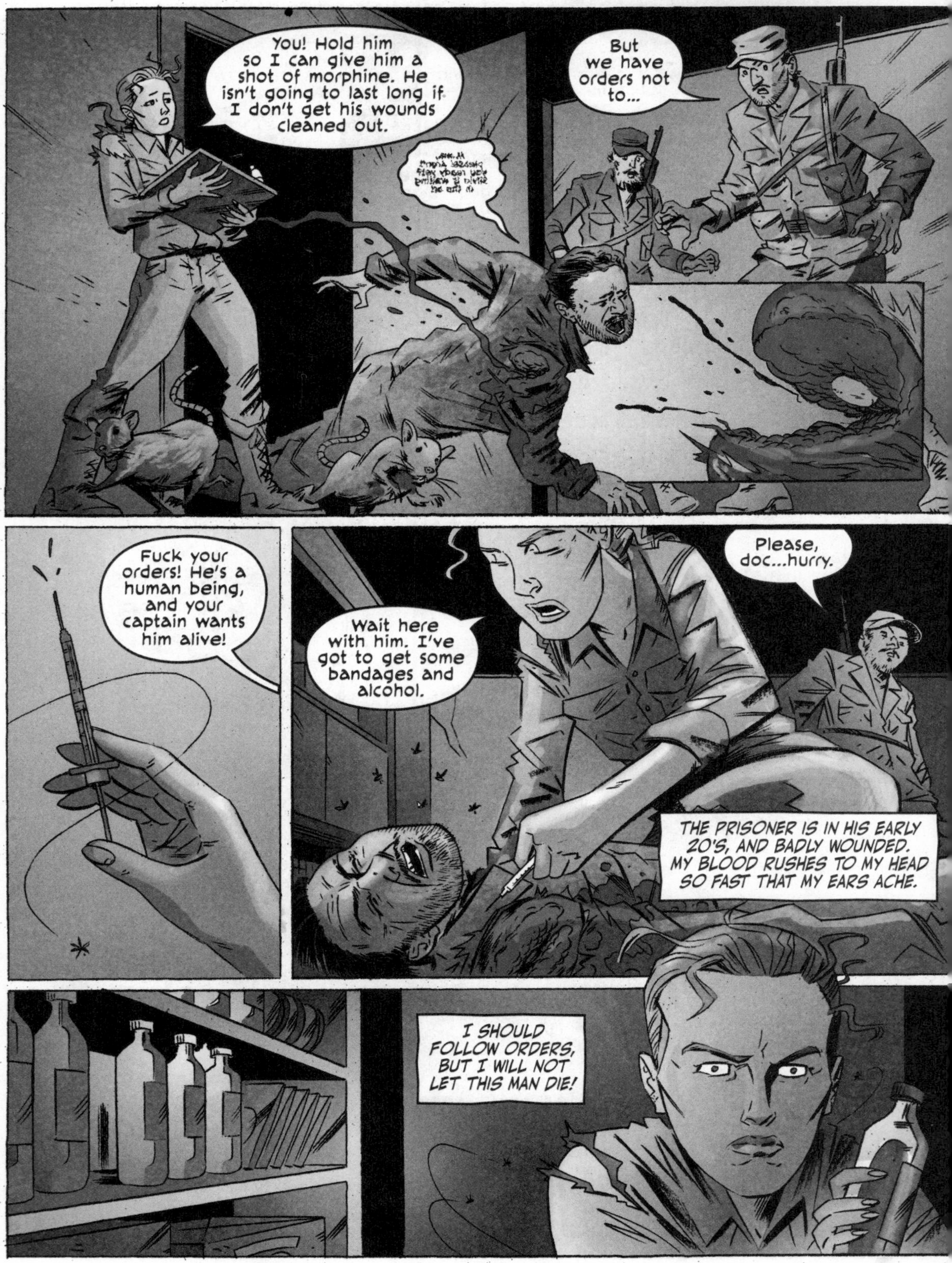
You! Hold him so I can give him a shot of morphine. He isn't going to last long if I don't get his wounds cleaned out.
But we have orders not to...
Fuck your orders! He's a human being, and your captain wants him alive!
Wait here with him. I've got to get some bandages and alcohol.
Please, doc...hurry.
THE PRISONER IS IN HIS EARLY 20'S, AND BADLY WOUNDED. MY BLOOD RUSHES TO MY HEAD SO FAST THAT MY EARS ACHE.
I SHOULD FOLLOW ORDERS, BUT I WILL NOT LET THIS MAN DIE!

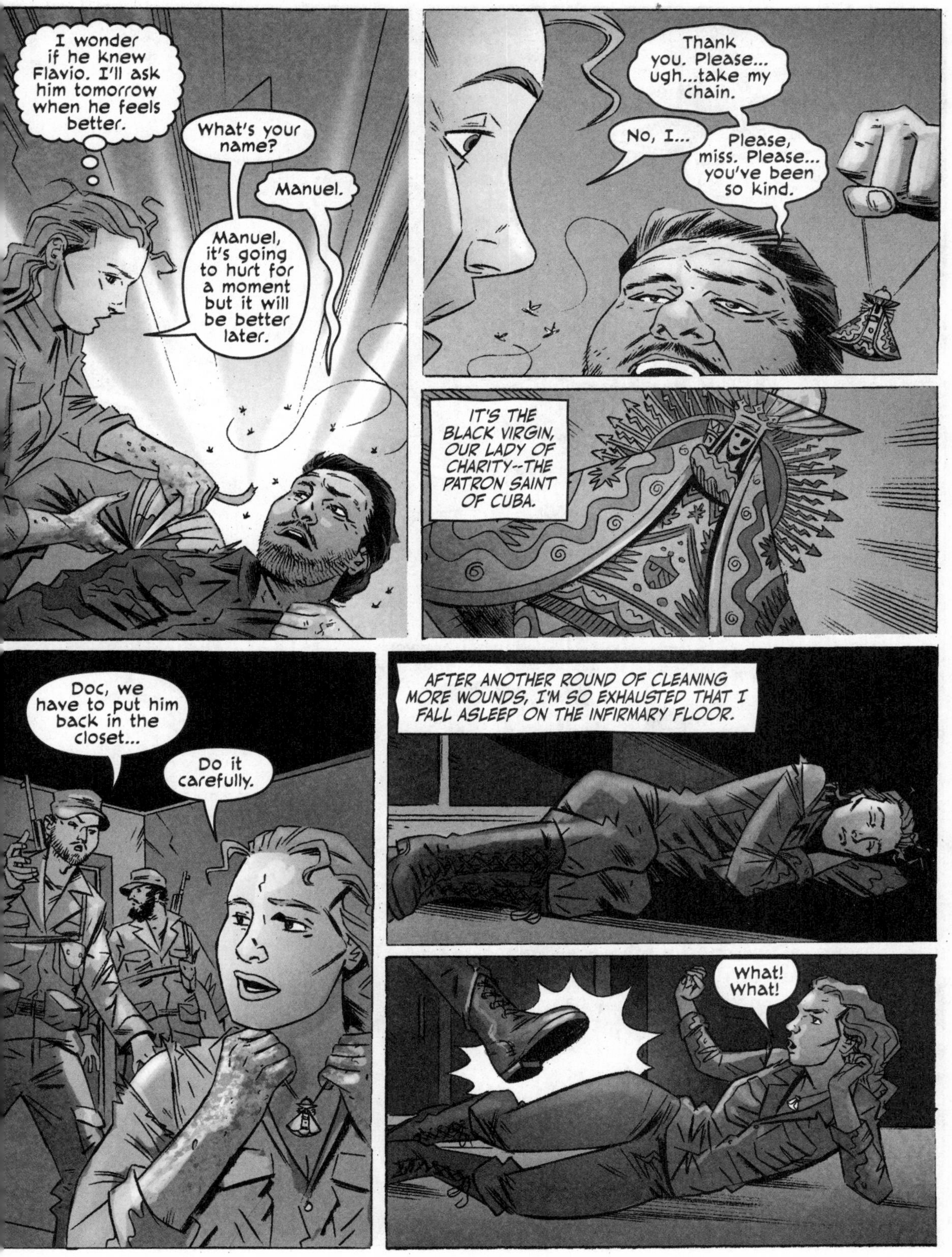
I wonder if he knew Flavio. I'll ask him tomorrow when he feels better.
What's your name?
Manuel.
Manuel, it's going to hurt for a moment but it will be better later.
Thank you. Please... ugh...take my chain.
No, I...
Please, miss. Please... you've been so kind.
IT'S THE BLACK VIRGIN, OUR LADY OF CHARITY--THE PATRON SAINT OF CUBA.
Doc, we have to put him back in the closet...
Do it carefully.
AFTER ANOTHER ROUND OF CLEANING MORE WOUNDS, I'M SO EXHAUSTED THAT I FALL ASLEEP ON THE INFIRMARY FLOOR.
What! What!

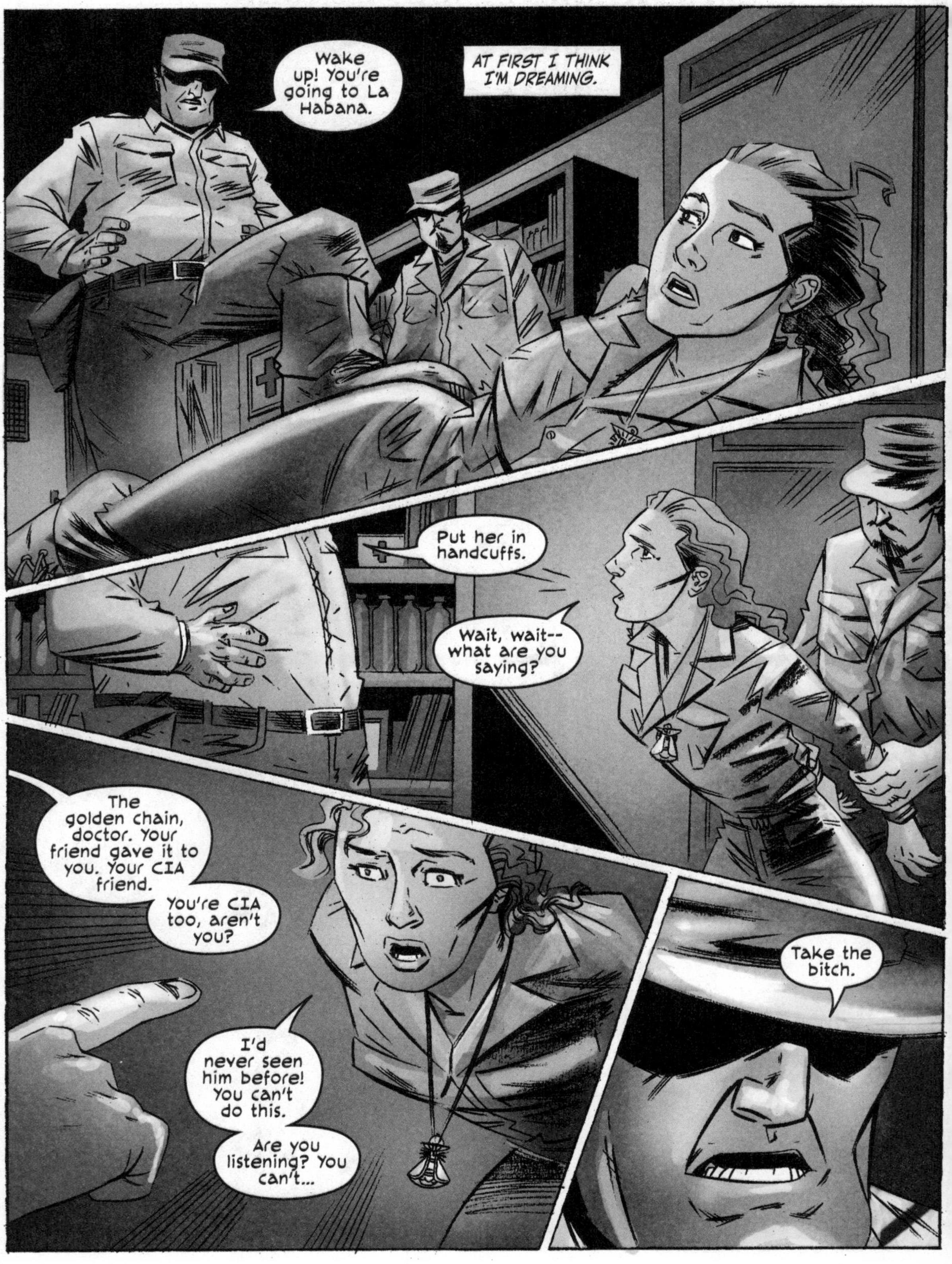
Wake up! You're going to La Habana.
AT FIRST I THINK I'M DREAMING.
Put her in handcuffs.
Wait, wait-- what are you saying?
The golden chain, doctor. Your friend gave it to you. Your CIA friend.
You're CIA too, aren't you?
I'd never seen him before! You can't do this.
Are you listening? You can't...
Take the bitch.

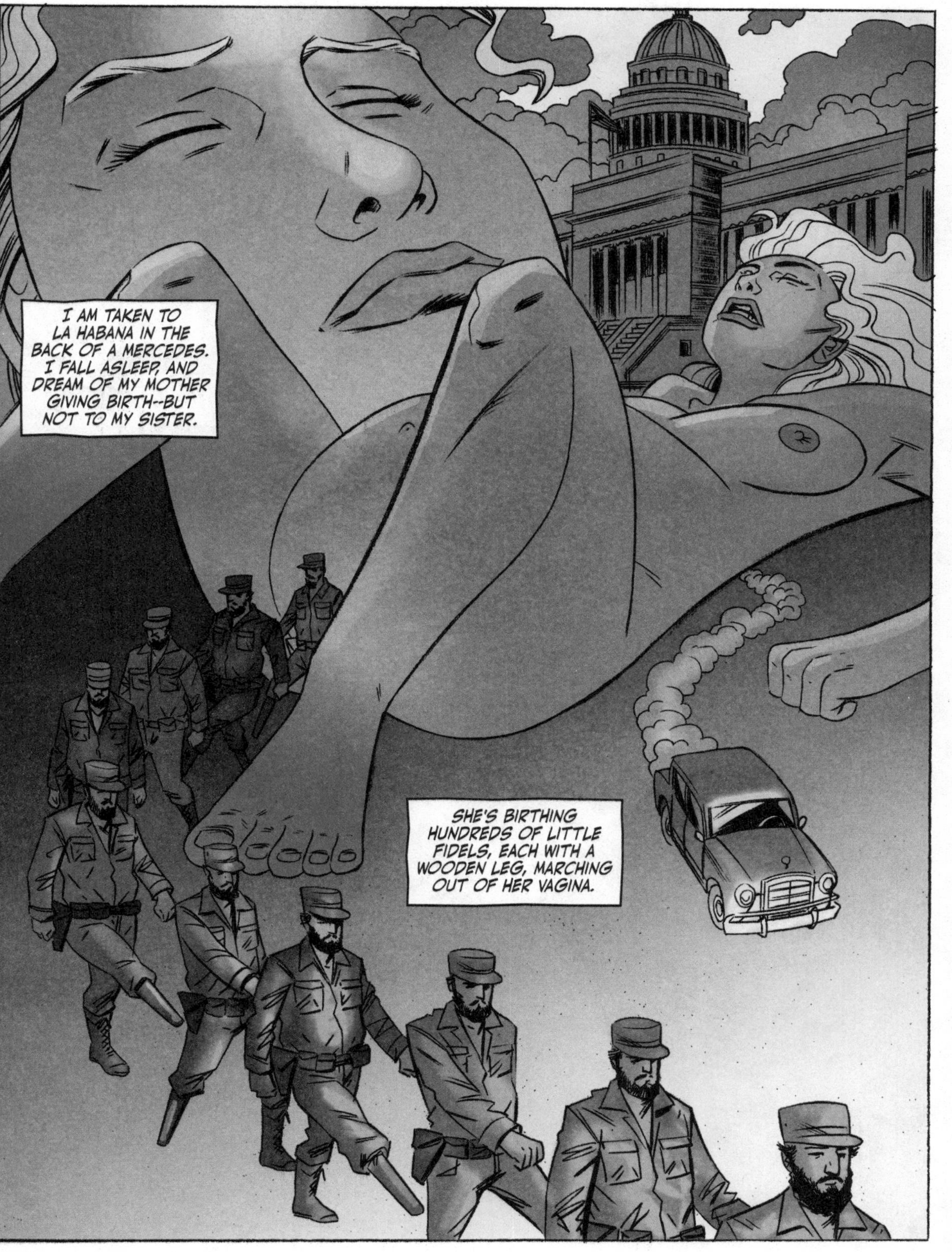
I AM TAKEN TO LA HABANA IN THE BACK OF A MERCEDES. I FALL ASLEEP, AND DREAM OF MY MOTHER GIVING BIRTH--BUT NOT TO MY SISTER.
SHE'S BIRTHING HUNDREDS OF LITTLE FIDELS, EACH WITH A WOODEN LEG, MARCHING OUT OF HER VAGINA.

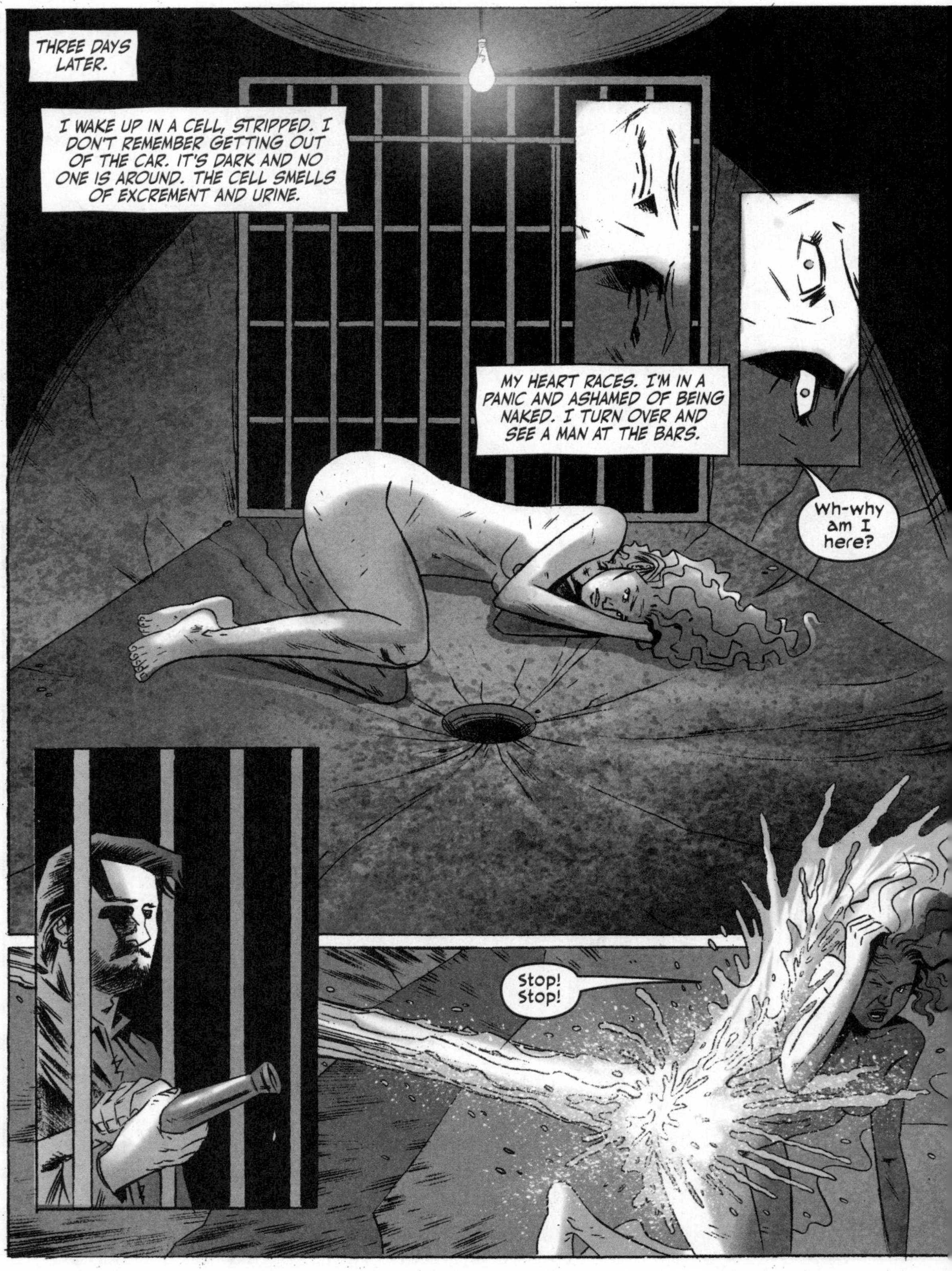
THREE DAYS LATER.
I WAKE UP IN A CELL, STRIPPED. I DON'T REMEMBER GETTING OUT OF THE CAR. IT'S DARK AND NO ONE IS AROUND. THE CELL SMELLS OF EXCREMENT AND URINE.
MY HEART RACES. I'M IN A PANIC AND ASHAMED OF BEING NAKED. I TURN OVER AND SEE A MAN AT THE BARS.
Wh-why am I here?
Stop! Stop!

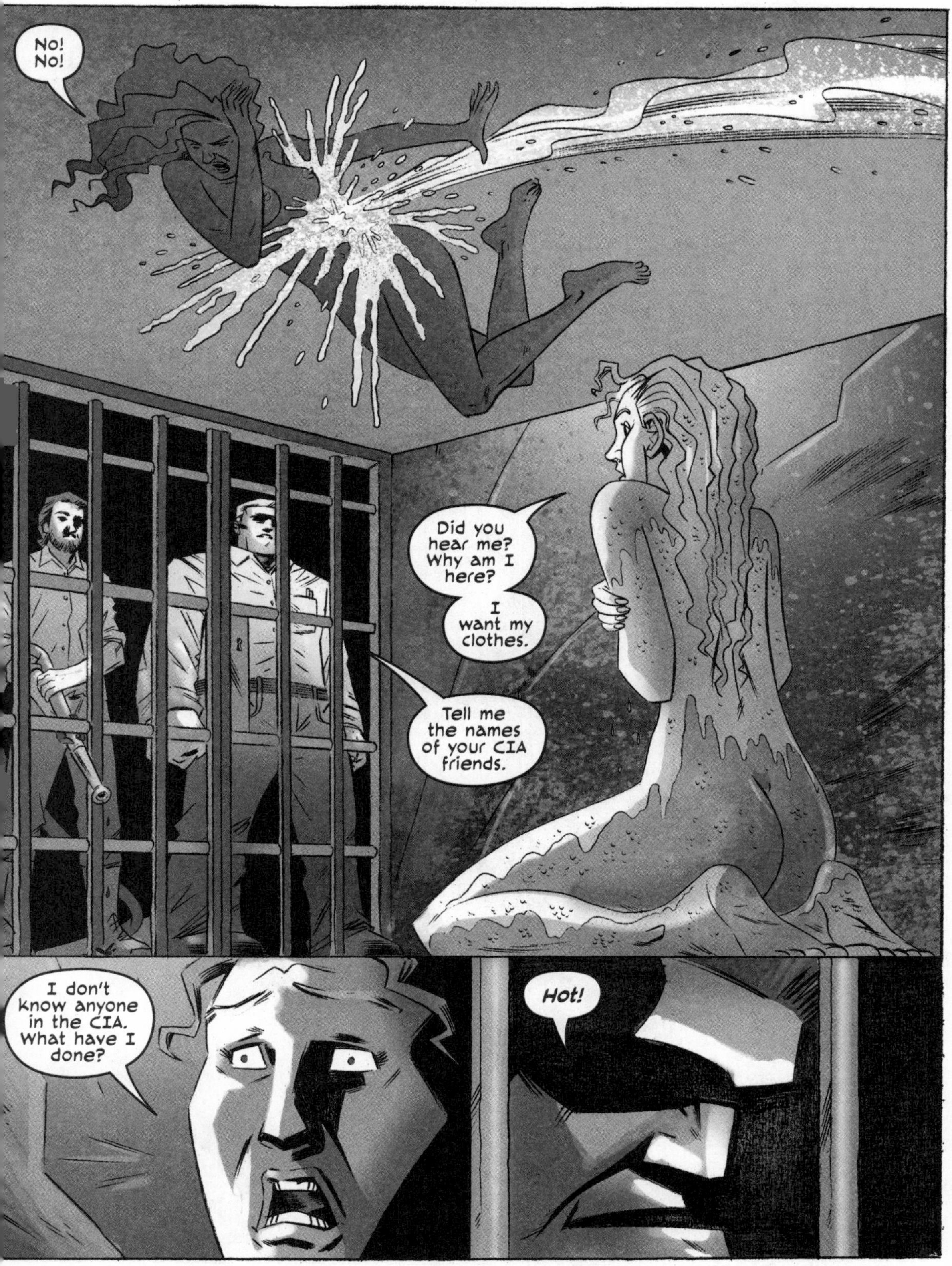
No! No!
Did you hear me? Why am I here?
I want my clothes.
Tell me the names of your CIA friends.
I don't know anyone in the CIA. What have I done?
Hot!

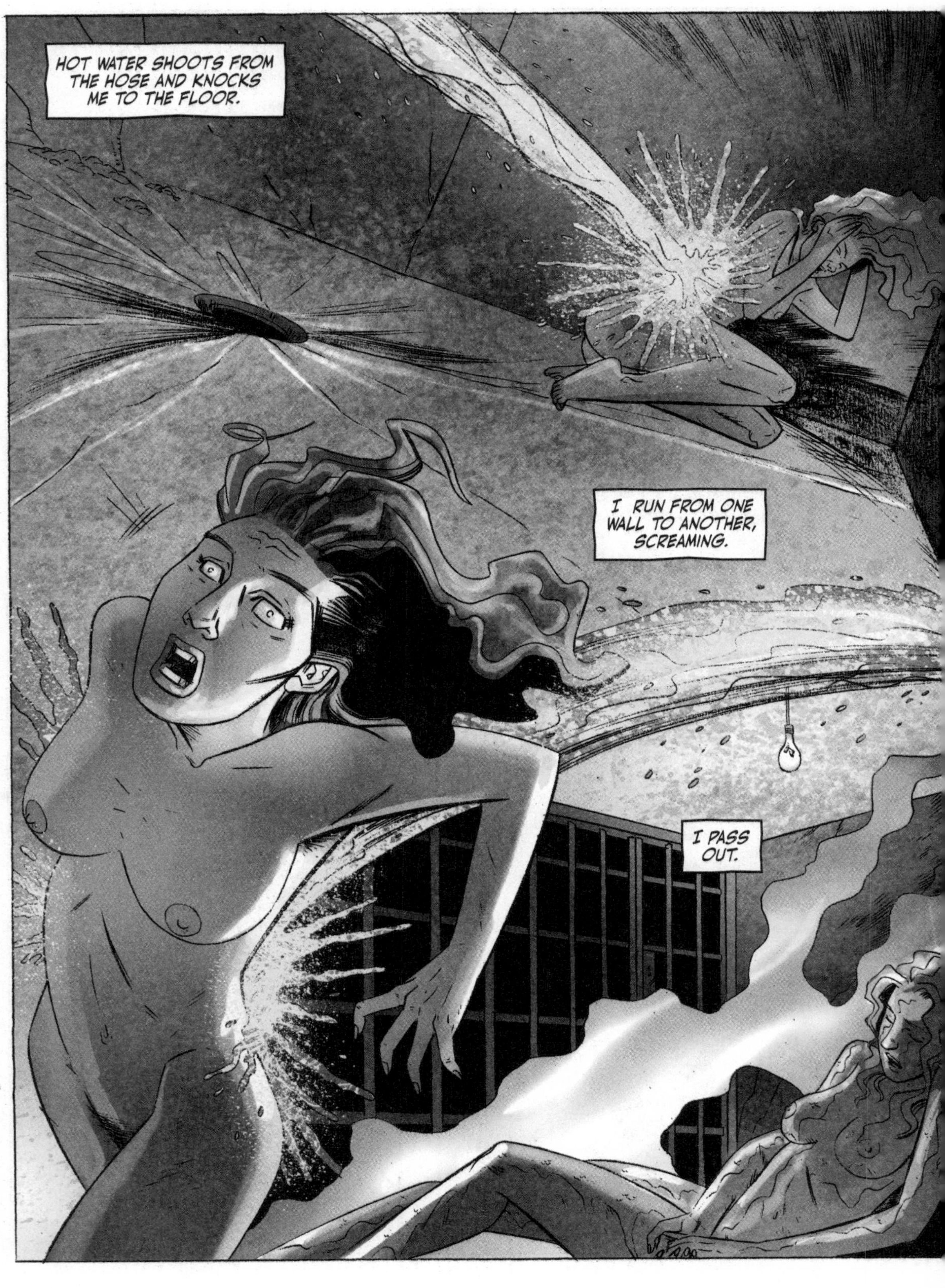
HOT WATER SHOOTS FROM THE HOSE AND KNOCKS ME TO THE FLOOR.
I RUN FROM ONE WALL TO ANOTHER, SCREAMING.
I PASS OUT.

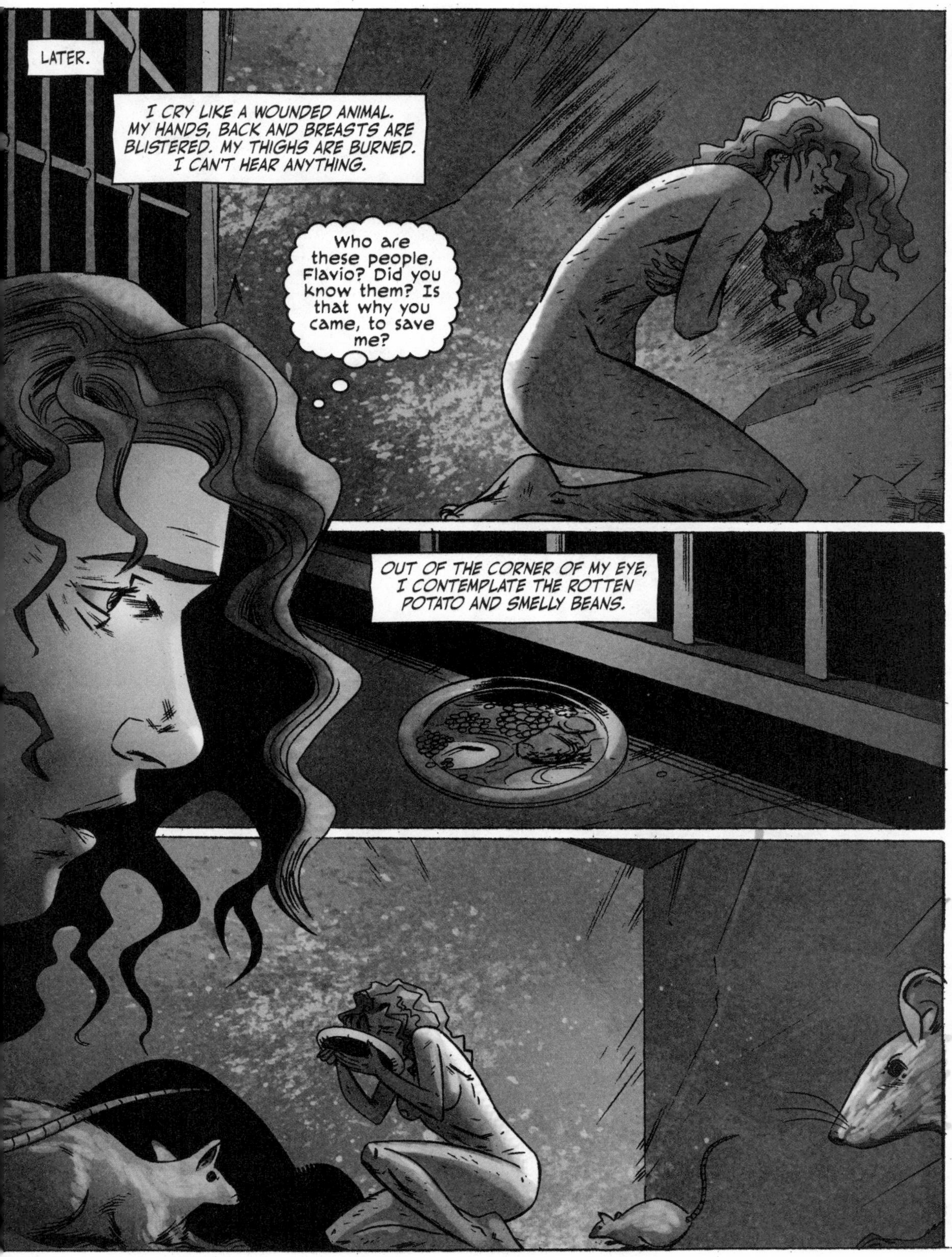
LATER.
I CRY LIKE A WOUNDED ANIMAL. MY HANDS, BACK AND BREASTS ARE BLISTERED. MY THIGHS ARE BURNED. I CAN'T HEAR ANYTHING.
Who are these people, Flavio? Did you know them? Is that why you came, to save me?
OUT OF THE CORNER OF MY EYE, I CONTEMPLATE THE ROTTEN POTATO AND SMELLY BEANS.

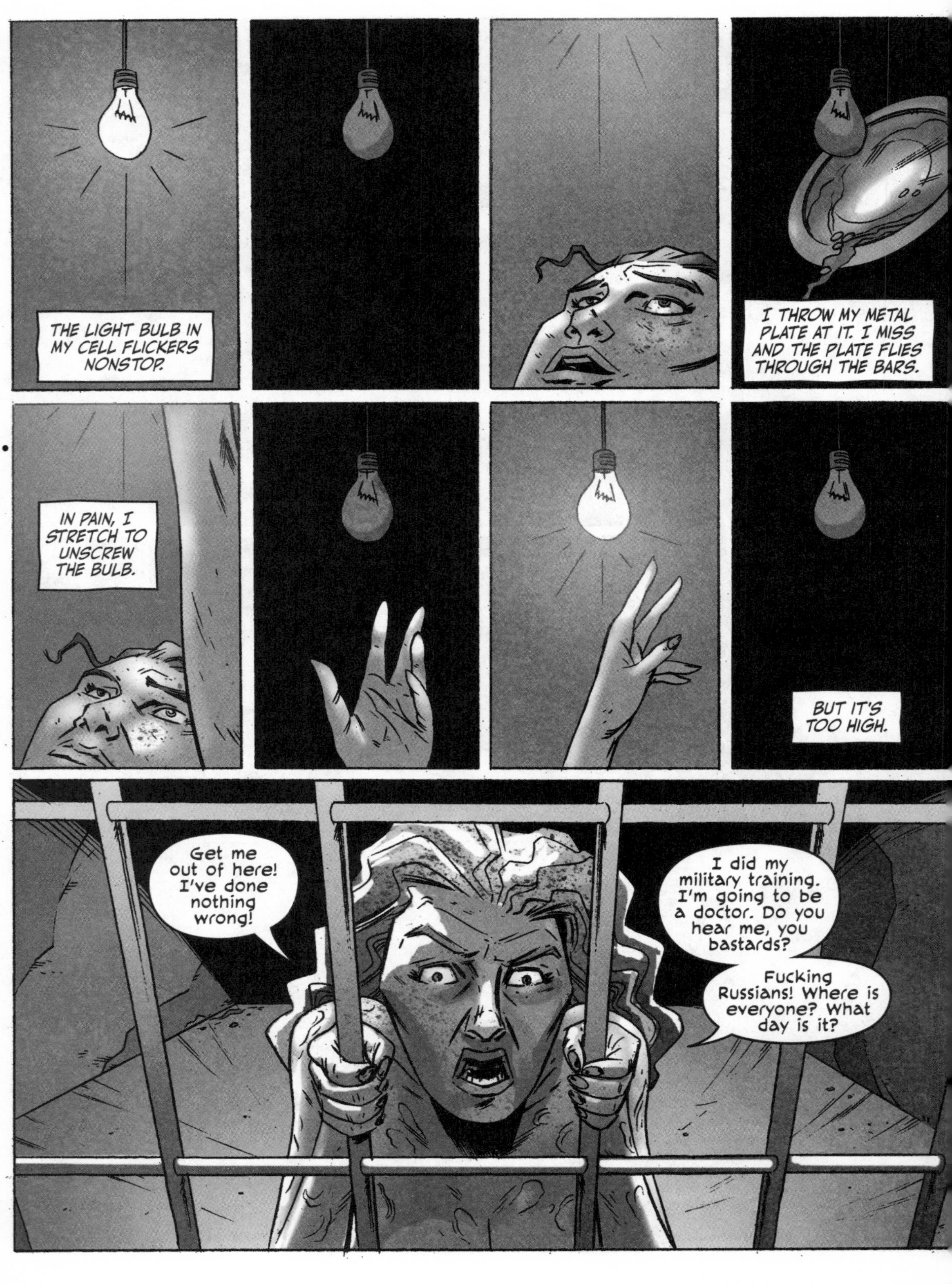
THE LIGHT BULB IN MY CELL FLICKERS NONSTOP.
I THROW MY METAL PLATE AT IT. I MISS AND THE PLATE FLIES THROUGH THE BARS.
IN PAIN, I STRETCH TO UNSCREW THE BULB.
BUT IT'S TOO HIGH.
Get me out of here! I've done nothing wrong!
I did my military training. I'm going to be a doctor. Do you hear me, you bastards?
Fucking Russians! Where is everyone? What day is it?

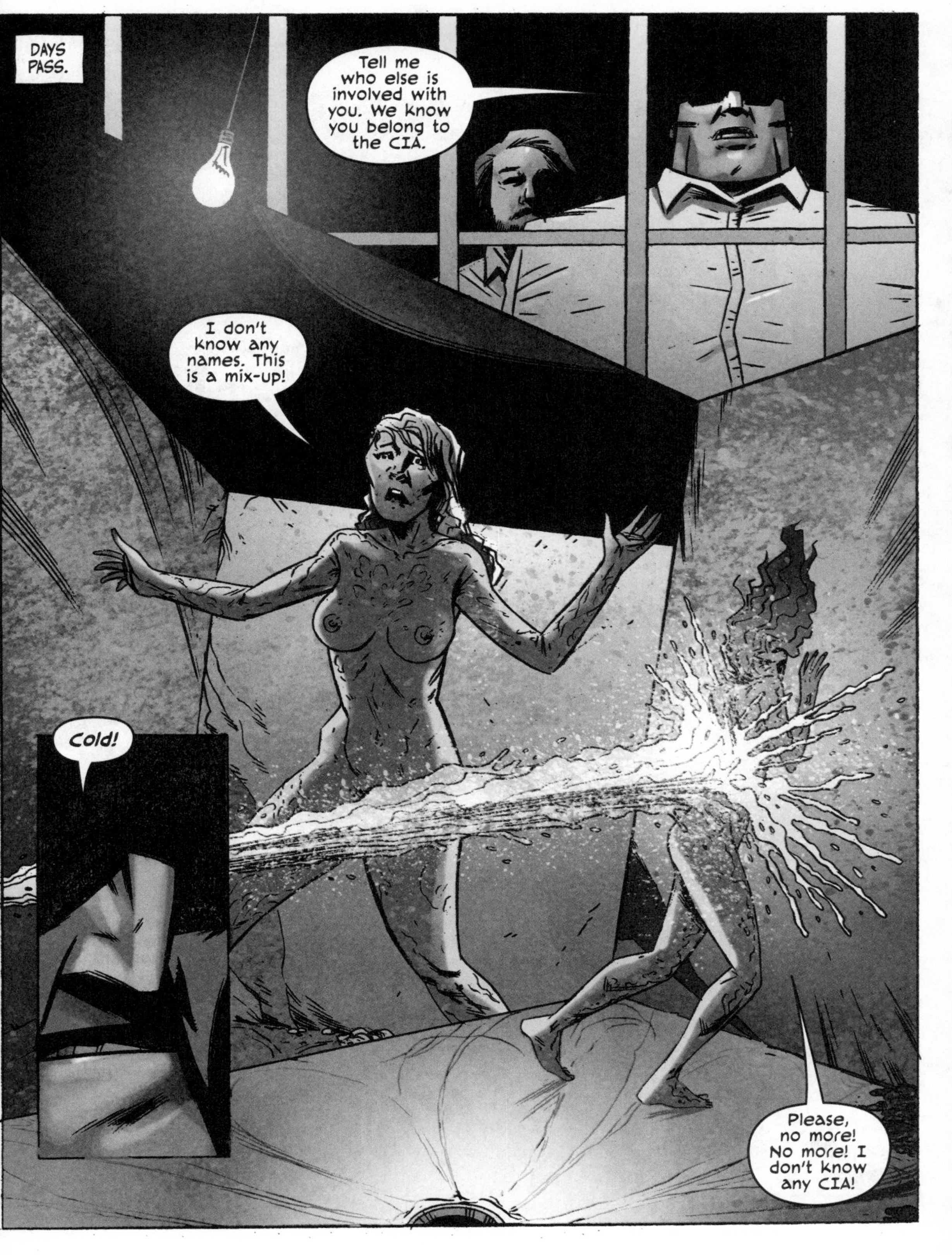
DAYS PASS.
Tell me who else is involved with you. We know you belong to the CIA.
I don't know any names. This is a mix-up!
Cold!
Please, no more! No more! I don't know any CIA!

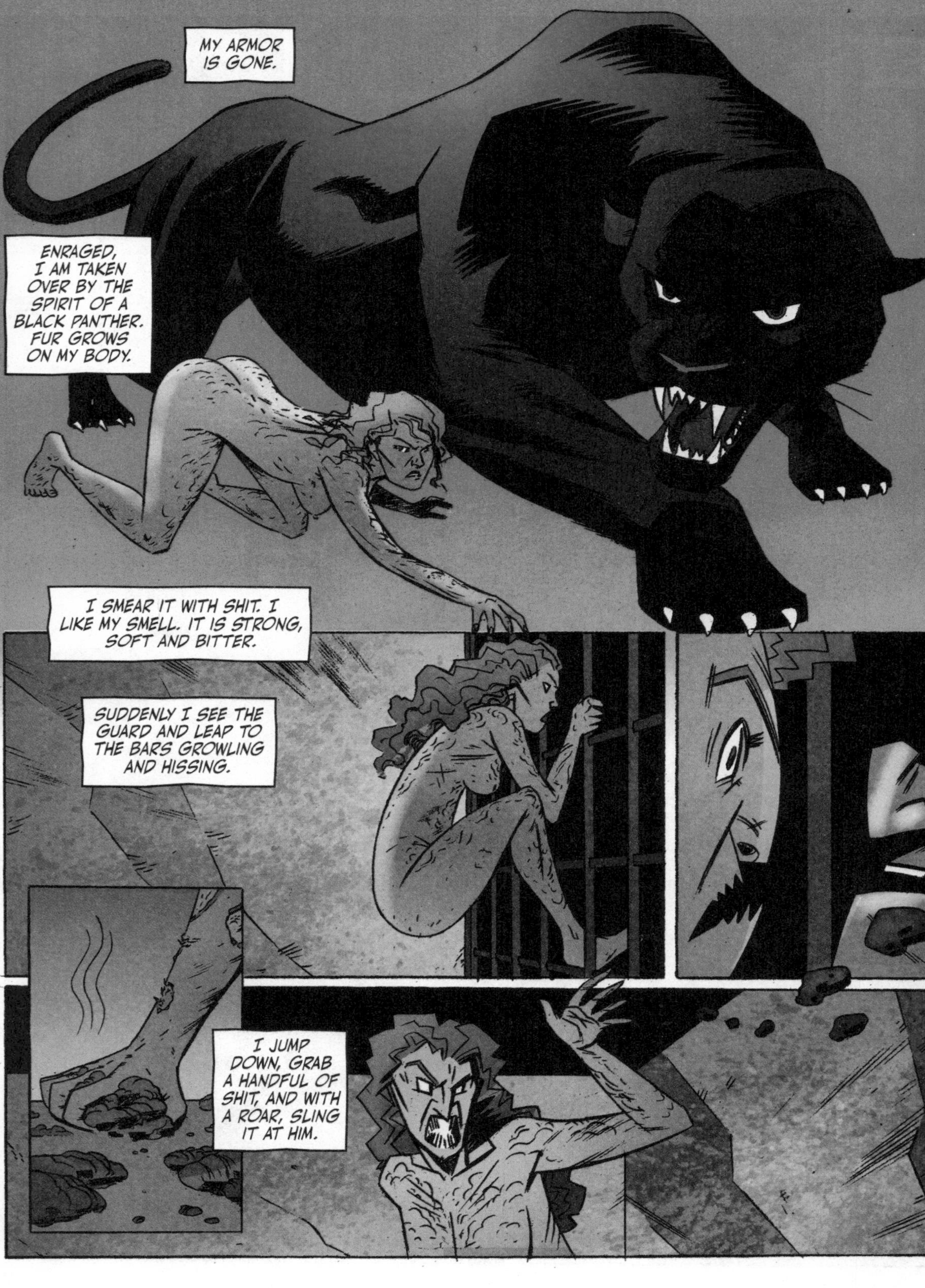
MY ARMOR IS GONE.
ENRAGED, I AM TAKEN OVER BY THE SPIRIT OF A BLACK PANTHER. FUR GROWS ON MY BODY.
I SMEAR IT WITH SHIT. I LIKE MY SMELL. IT IS STRONG, SOFT AND BITTER.
SUDDENLY I SEE THE GUARD AND LEAP TO THE BARS GROWLING AND HISSING.
I JUMP DOWN, GRAB A HANDFUL OF SHIT, AND WITH A ROAR, SLING IT AT HIM.

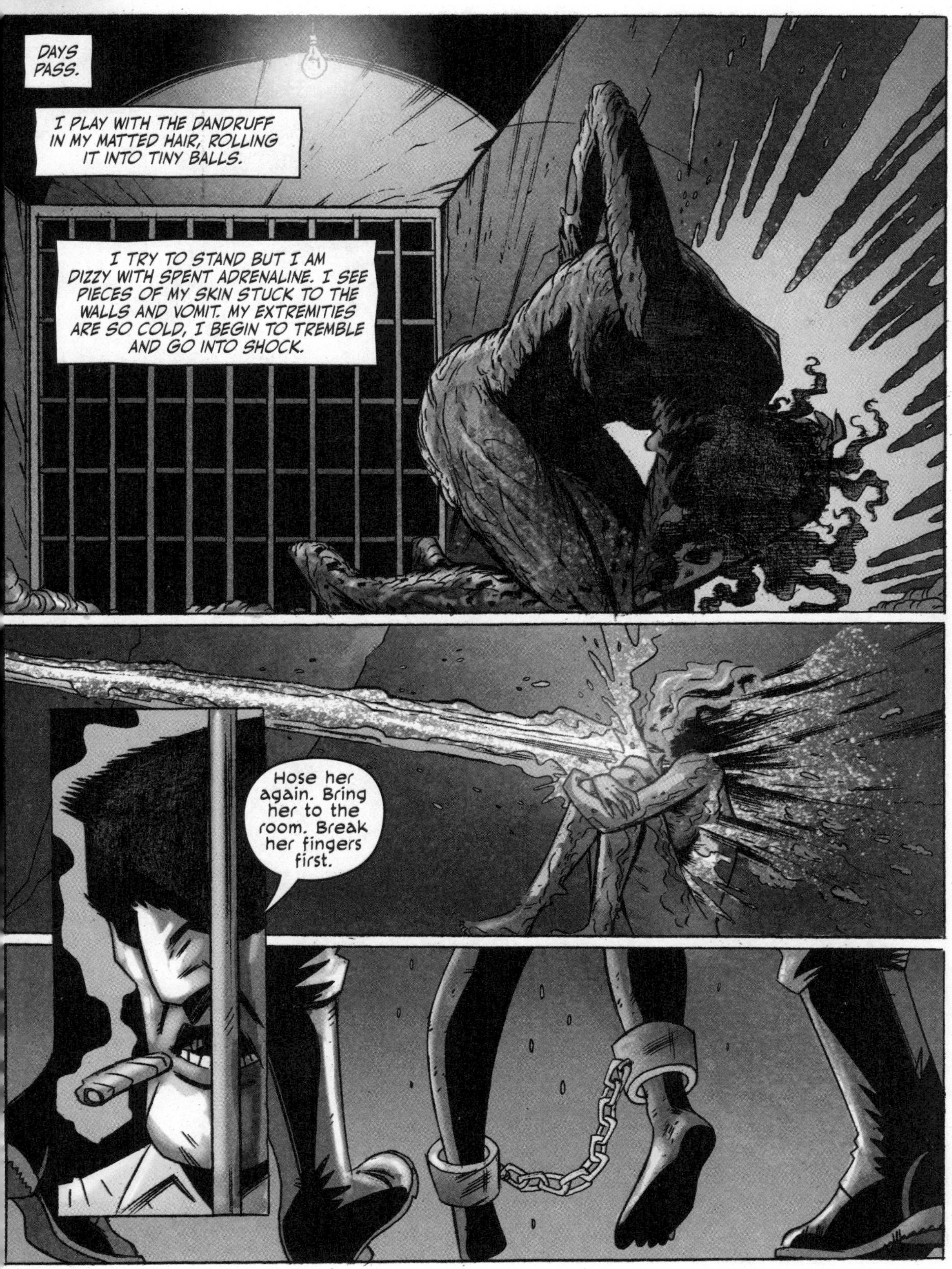
DAYS PASS.
I PLAY WITH THE DANDRUFF IN MY MATTED HAIR, ROLLING IT INTO TINY BALLS.
I TRY TO STAND BUT I AM DIZZY WITH SPENT ADRENALINE. I SEE PIECES OF MY SKIN STUCK TO THE WALLS AND VOMIT. MY EXTREMITIES ARE SO COLD, I BEGIN TO TREMBLE AND GO INTO SHOCK.
Hose her again. Bring her to the room. Break her fingers first.

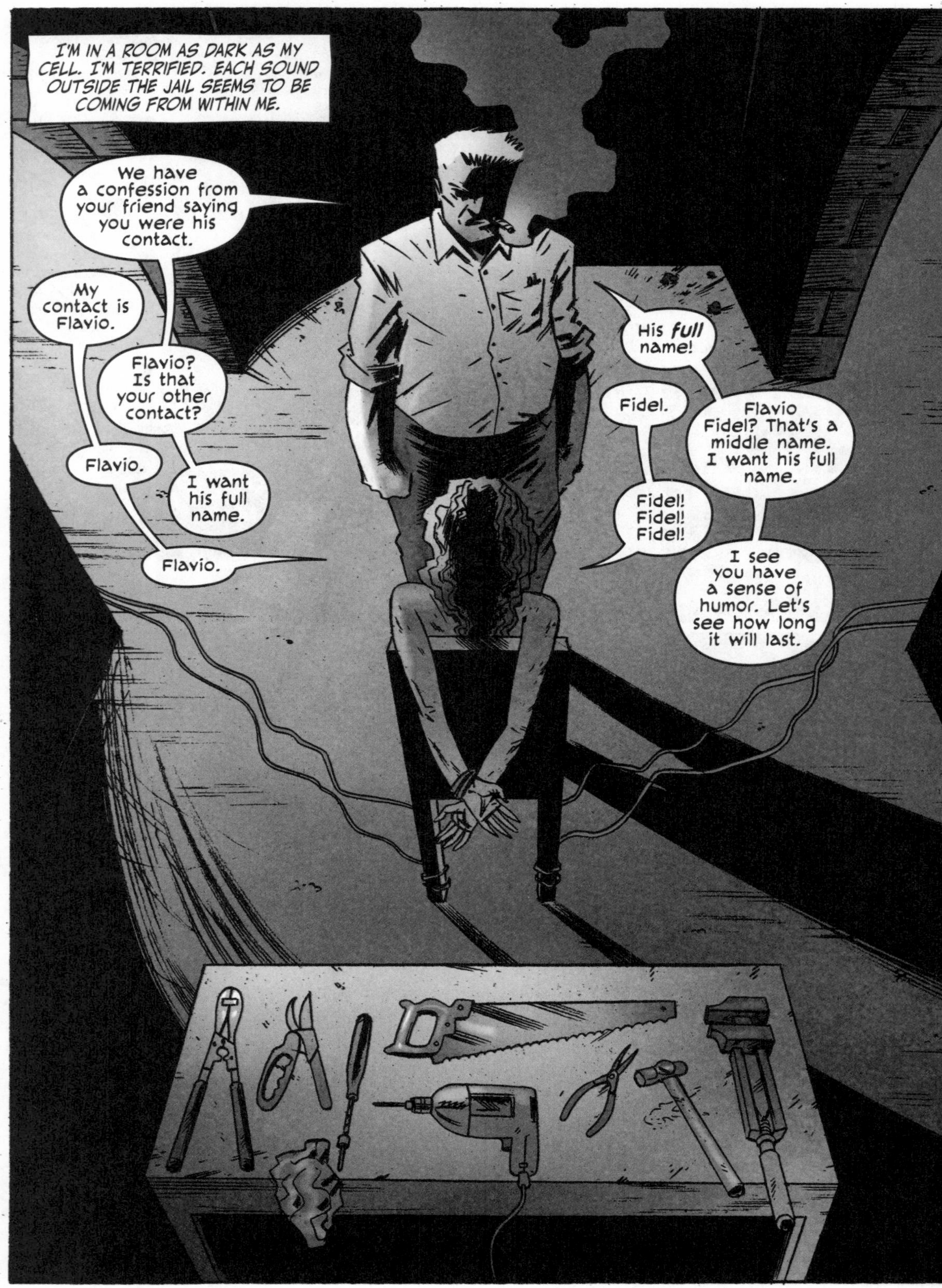
I'M IN A ROOM AS DARK AS MY CELL. I'M TERRIFIED. EACH SOUND OUTSIDE THE JAIL SEEMS TO BE COMING FROM WITHIN ME.
We have a confession from your friend saying you were his contact.
My contact is Flavio.
Flavio? Is that your other contact?
Flavio.
I want his full name.
Flavio.
His *full* name!
Fidel.
Flavio Fidel? That's a middle name. I want his full name.
Fidel! Fidel! Fidel!
I see you have a sense of humor. Let's see how long it will last.

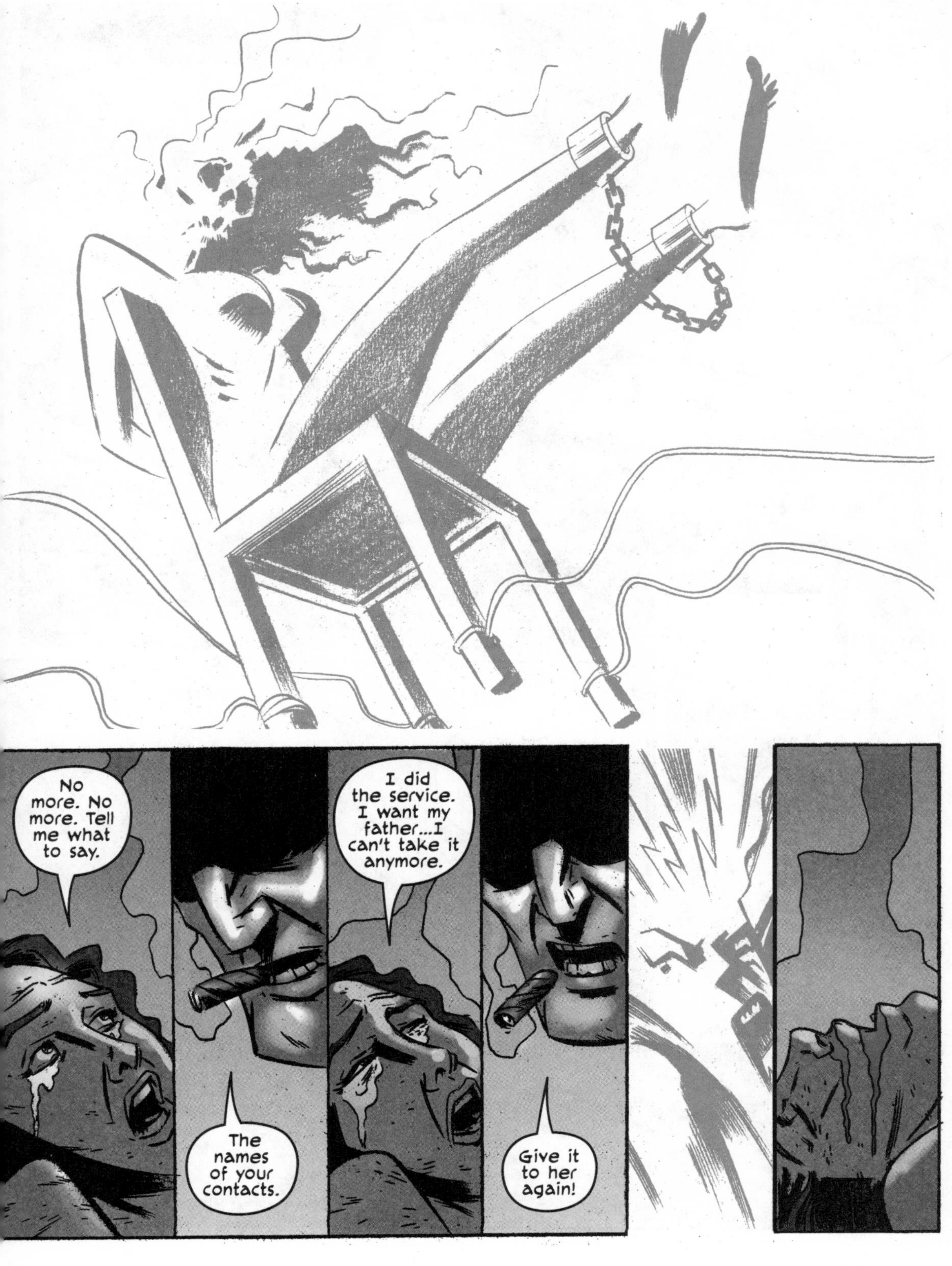

No more. No more. Tell me what to say.
The names of your contacts.
I did the service. I want my father...I can't take it anymore.
Give it to her again!

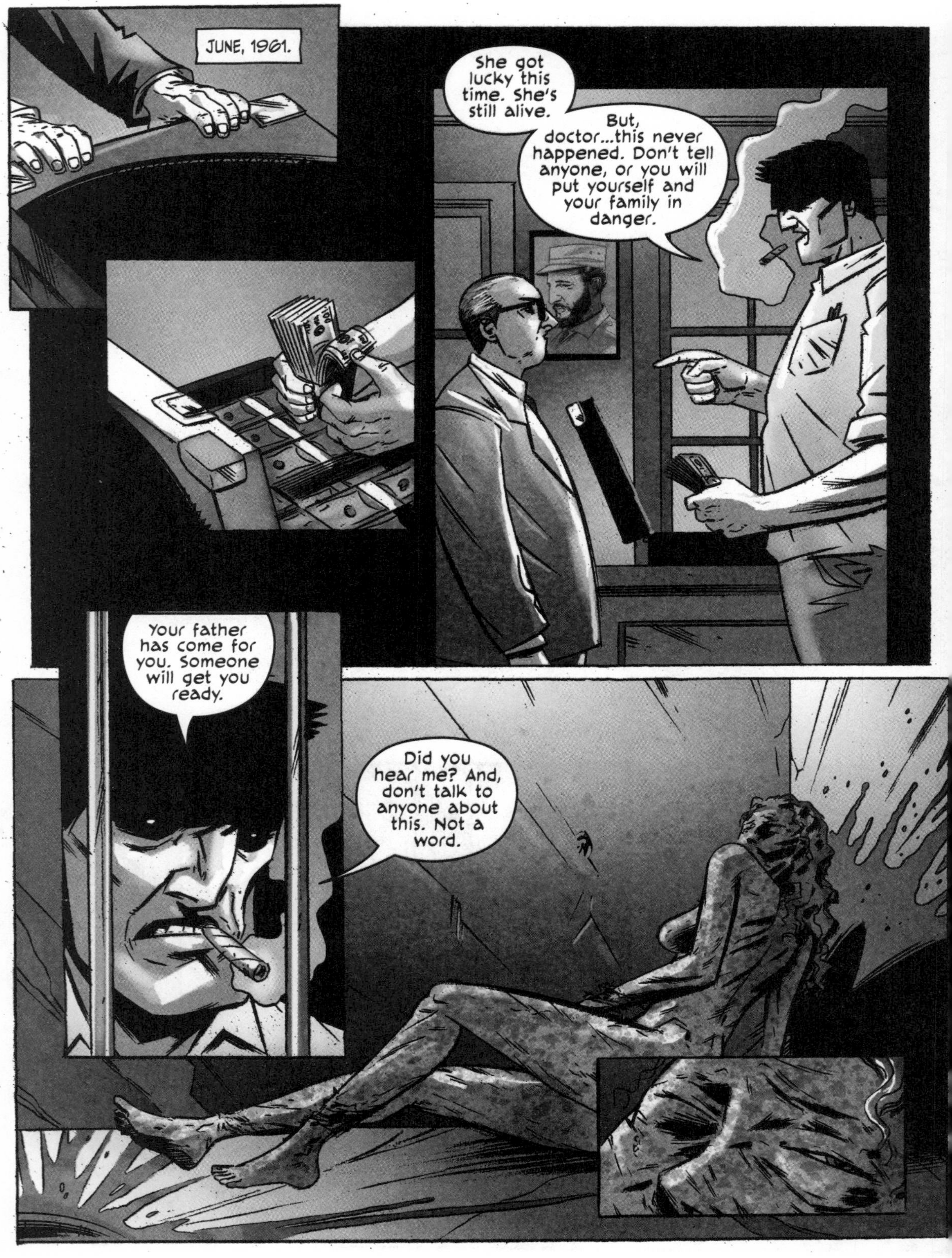
JUNE, 1961.
She got lucky this time. She's still alive.
But, doctor...this never happened. Don't tell anyone, or you will put yourself and your family in danger.
Your father has come for you. Someone will get you ready.
Did you hear me? And, don't talk to anyone about this. Not a word.

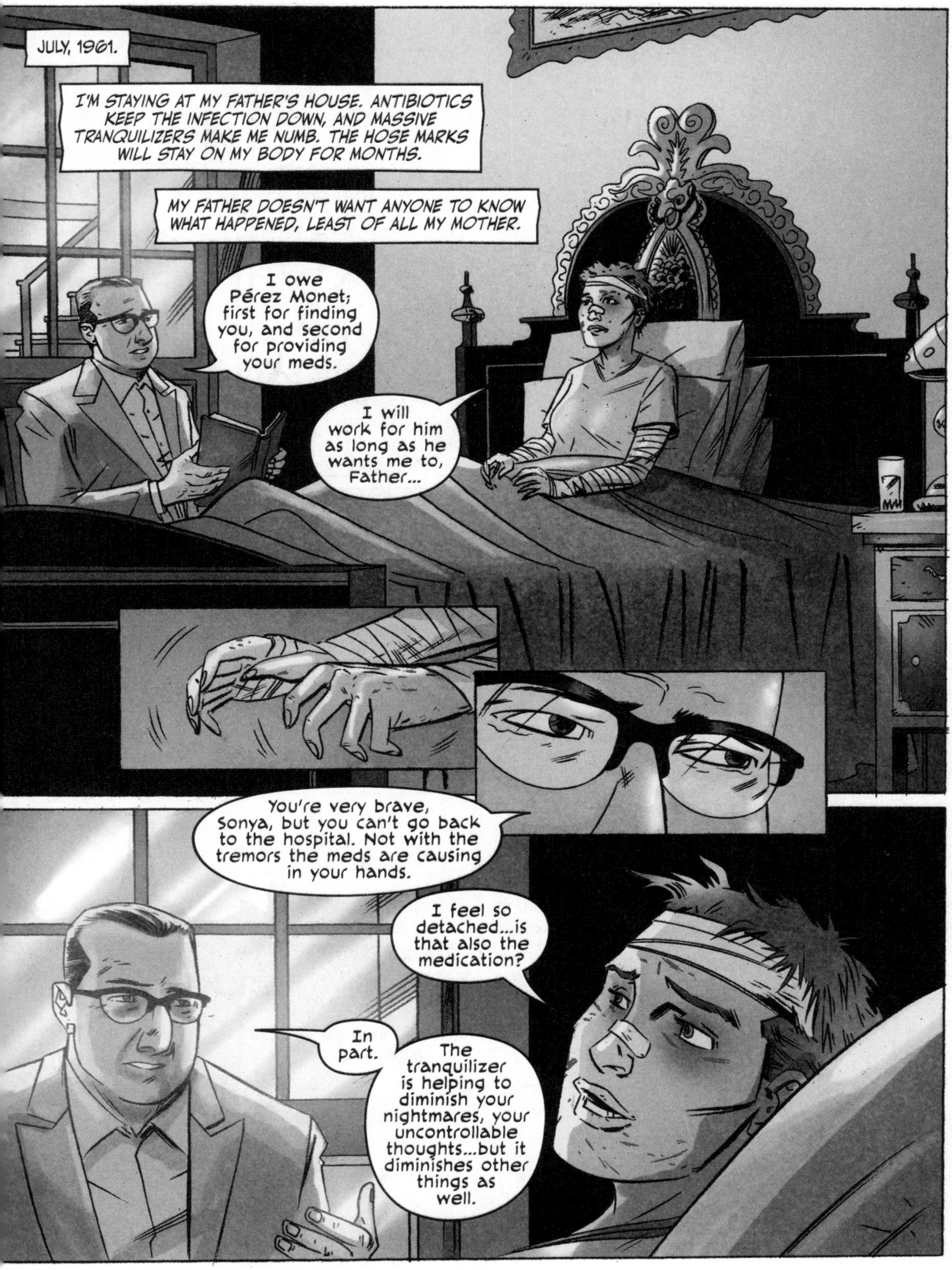
JULY, 1961.
I'M STAYING AT MY FATHER'S HOUSE. ANTIBIOTICS KEEP THE INFECTION DOWN, AND MASSIVE TRANQUILIZERS MAKE ME NUMB. THE HOSE MARKS WILL STAY ON MY BODY FOR MONTHS.
MY FATHER DOESN'T WANT ANYONE TO KNOW WHAT HAPPENED, LEAST OF ALL MY MOTHER.
I owe Pérez Monet; first for finding you, and second for providing your meds.
I will work for him as long as he wants me to, Father...
You're very brave, Sonya, but you can't go back to the hospital. Not with the tremors the meds are causing in your hands.
I feel so detached...is that also the medication?
In part.
The tranquilizer is helping to diminish your nightmares, your uncontrollable thoughts...but it diminishes other things as well.

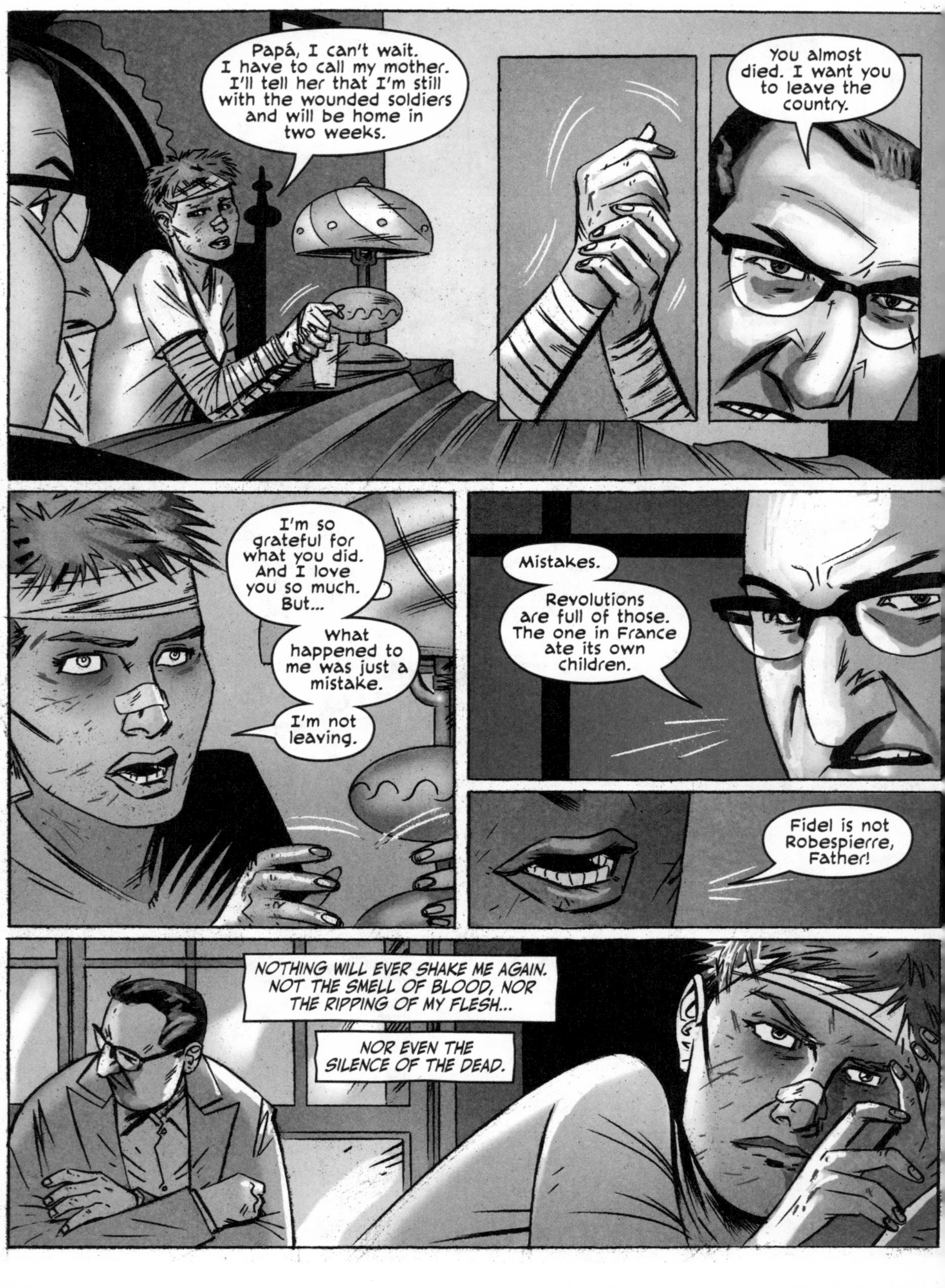
Papá, I can't wait. I have to call my mother. I'll tell her that I'm still with the wounded soldiers and will be home in two weeks.
You almost died. I want you to leave the country.
I'm so grateful for what you did. And I love you so much. But...
What happened to me was just a mistake.
I'm not leaving.
Mistakes.
Revolutions are full of those. The one in France ate its own children.
Fidel is not Robespierre, Father!
NOTHING WILL EVER SHAKE ME AGAIN. NOT THE SMELL OF BLOOD, NOR THE RIPPING OF MY FLESH...
NOR EVEN THE SILENCE OF THE DEAD.

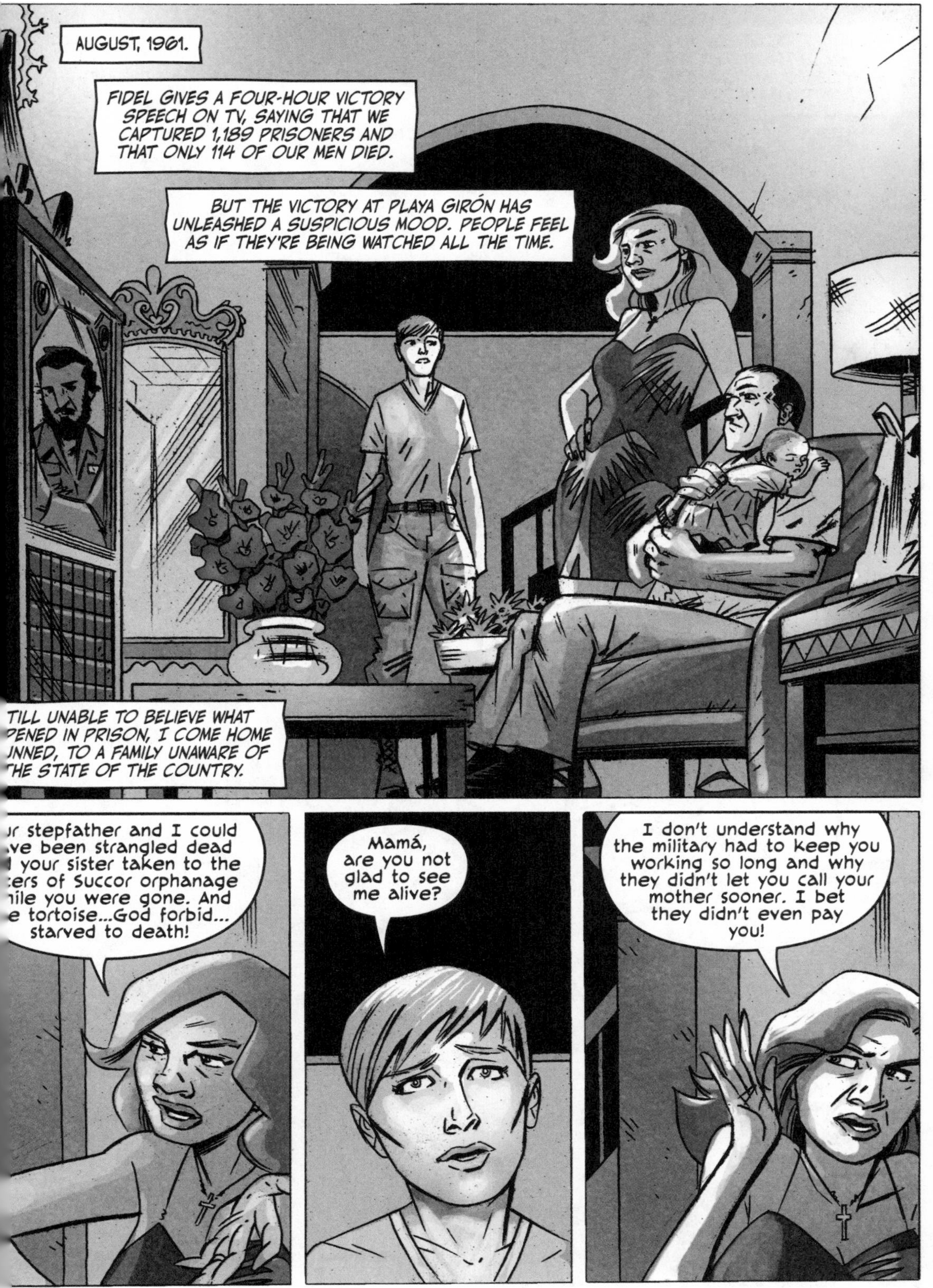
AUGUST, 1961.
FIDEL GIVES A FOUR-HOUR VICTORY SPEECH ON TV, SAYING THAT WE CAPTURED 1,189 PRISONERS AND THAT ONLY 114 OF OUR MEN DIED.
BUT THE VICTORY AT PLAYA GIRÓN HAS UNLEASHED A SUSPICIOUS MOOD. PEOPLE FEEL AS IF THEY'RE BEING WATCHED ALL THE TIME.
TILL UNABLE TO BELIEVE WHAT PENED IN PRISON, I COME HOME UNNED, TO A FAMILY UNAWARE OF THE STATE OF THE COUNTRY.
r stepfather and I could ve been strangled dead your sister taken to the ters of Succor orphanage hile you were gone. And e tortoise...God forbid... starved to death!
Mamá, are you not glad to see me alive?
I don't understand why the military had to keep you working so long and why they didn't let you call your mother sooner. I bet they didn't even pay you!

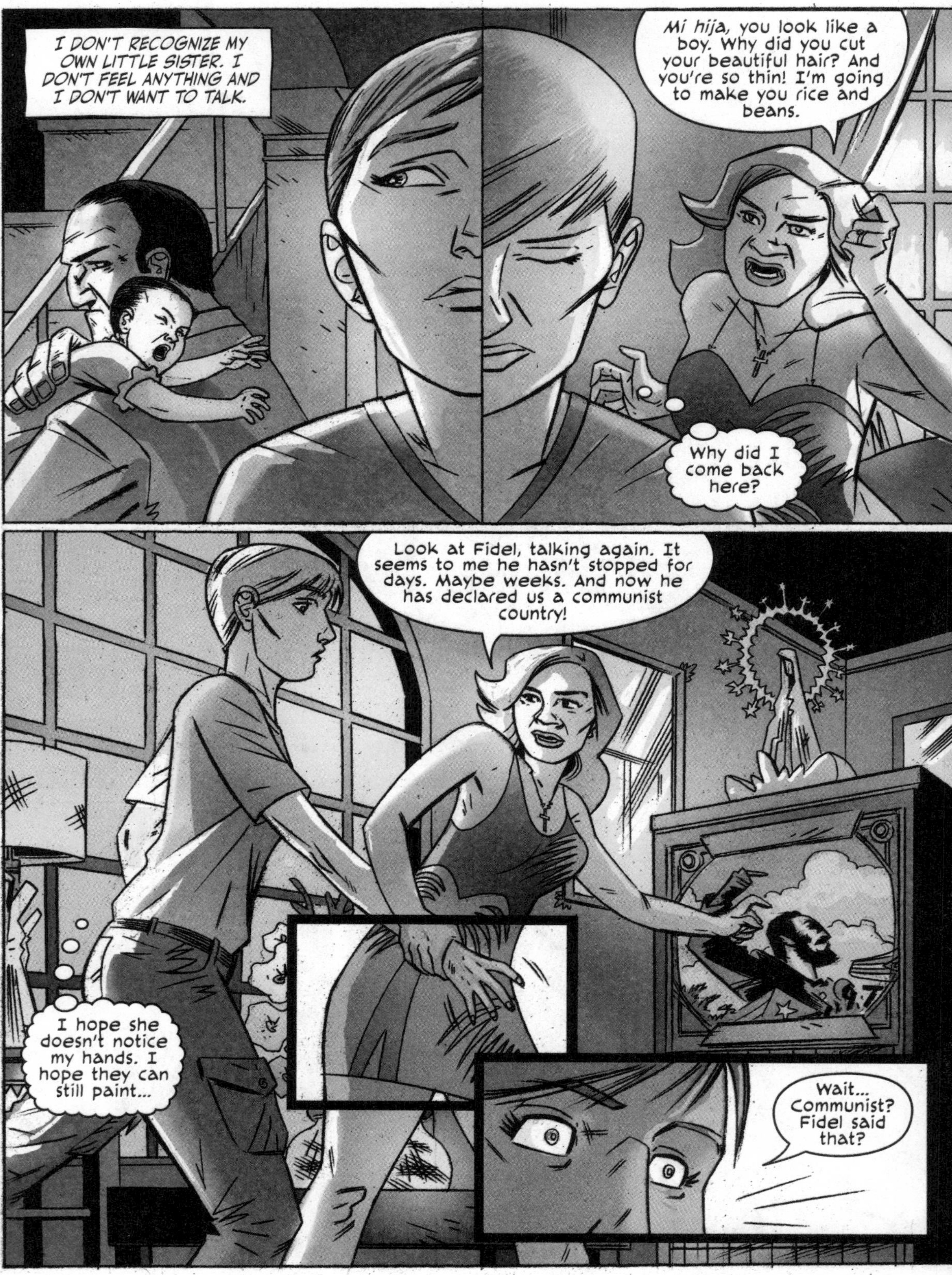
I DON'T RECOGNIZE MY OWN LITTLE SISTER. I DON'T FEEL ANYTHING AND I DON'T WANT TO TALK.
Mi hija, you look like a boy. Why did you cut your beautiful hair? And you're so thin! I'm going to make you rice and beans.
Why did I come back here?
Look at Fidel, talking again. It seems to me he hasn't stopped for days. Maybe weeks. And now he has declared us a communist country!
I hope she doesn't notice my hands. I hope they can still paint...
Wait... Communist? Fidel said that?

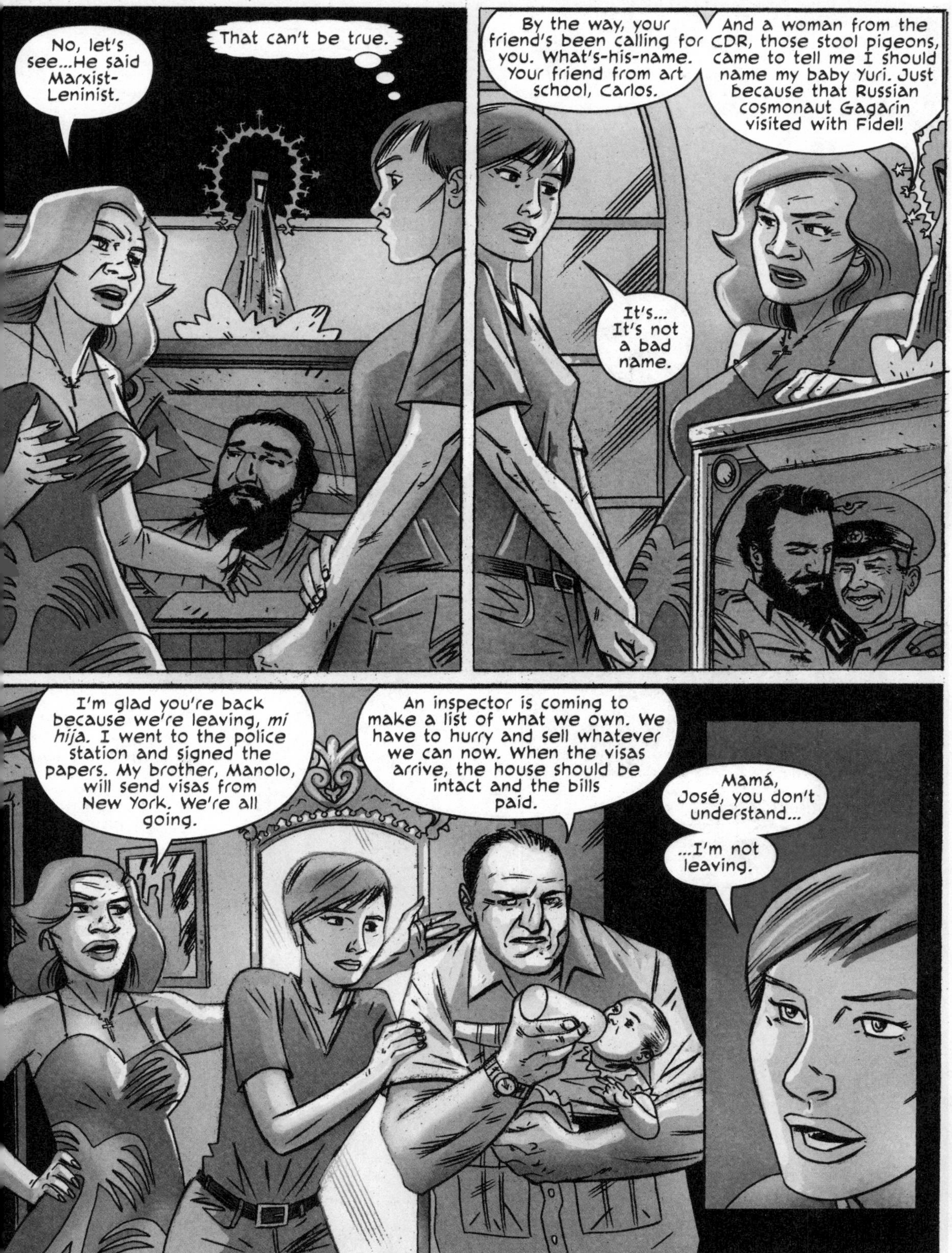
No, let's see...He said Marxist-Leninist.
That can't be true.
By the way, your friend's been calling for you. What's-his-name. Your friend from art school, Carlos.
And a woman from the CDR, those stool pigeons, came to tell me I should name my baby Yuri. Just because that Russian cosmonaut Gagarin visited with Fidel!
It's... It's not a bad name.
I'm glad you're back because we're leaving, *mi hija.* I went to the police station and signed the papers. My brother, Manolo, will send visas from New York. We're all going.
An inspector is coming to make a list of what we own. We have to hurry and sell whatever we can now. When the visas arrive, the house should be intact and the bills paid.
Mamá, José, you don't understand...
...I'm not leaving.

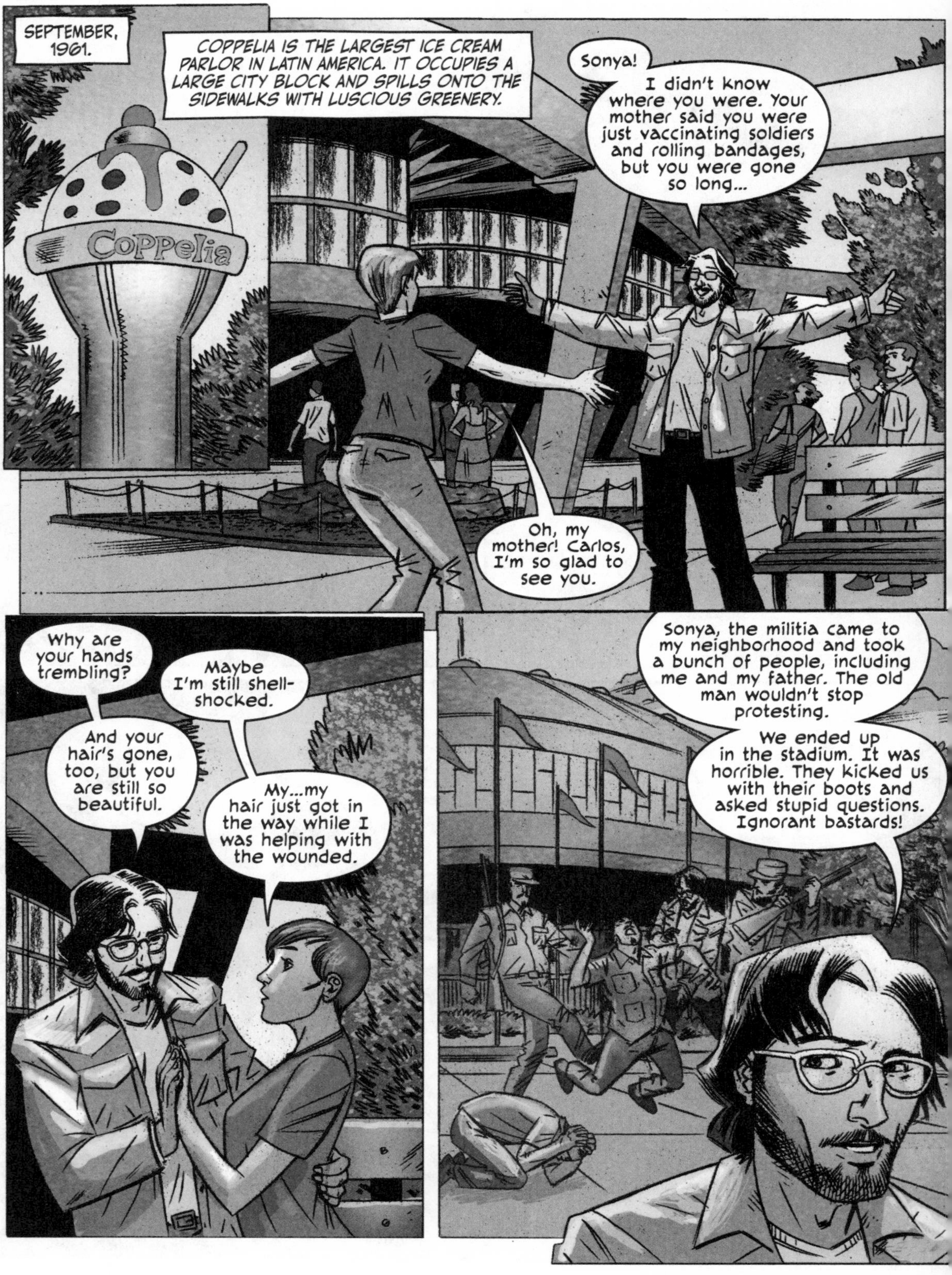
SEPTEMBER, 1961.
COPPELIA IS THE LARGEST ICE CREAM PARLOR IN LATIN AMERICA. IT OCCUPIES A LARGE CITY BLOCK AND SPILLS ONTO THE SIDEWALKS WITH LUSCIOUS GREENERY.
Coppelia
Sonya!
I didn't know where you were. Your mother said you were just vaccinating soldiers and rolling bandages, but you were gone so long...
Oh, my mother! Carlos, I'm so glad to see you.
Why are your hands trembling?
Maybe I'm still shell-shocked.
And your hair's gone, too, but you are still so beautiful.
My...my hair just got in the way while I was helping with the wounded.
Sonya, the militia came to my neighborhood and took a bunch of people, including me and my father. The old man wouldn't stop protesting.
We ended up in the stadium. It was horrible. They kicked us with their boots and asked stupid questions. Ignorant bastards!

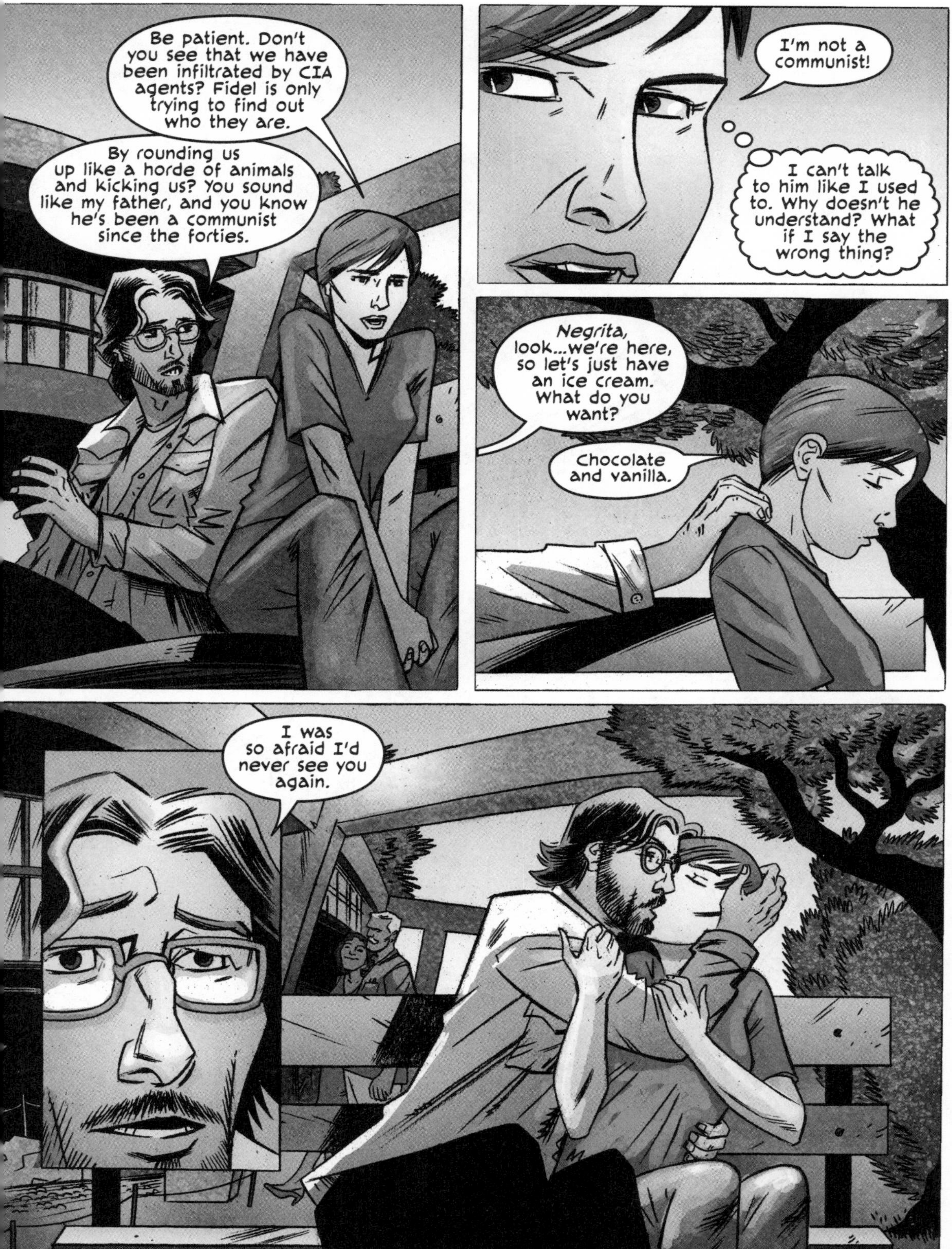
Be patient. Don't you see that we have been infiltrated by CIA agents? Fidel is only trying to find out who they are.
By rounding us up like a horde of animals and kicking us? You sound like my father, and you know he's been a communist since the forties.
I'm not a communist!
I can't talk to him like I used to. Why doesn't he understand? What if I say the wrong thing?
Negrita, look...we're here, so let's just have an ice cream. What do you want?
Chocolate and vanilla.
I was so afraid I'd never see you again.

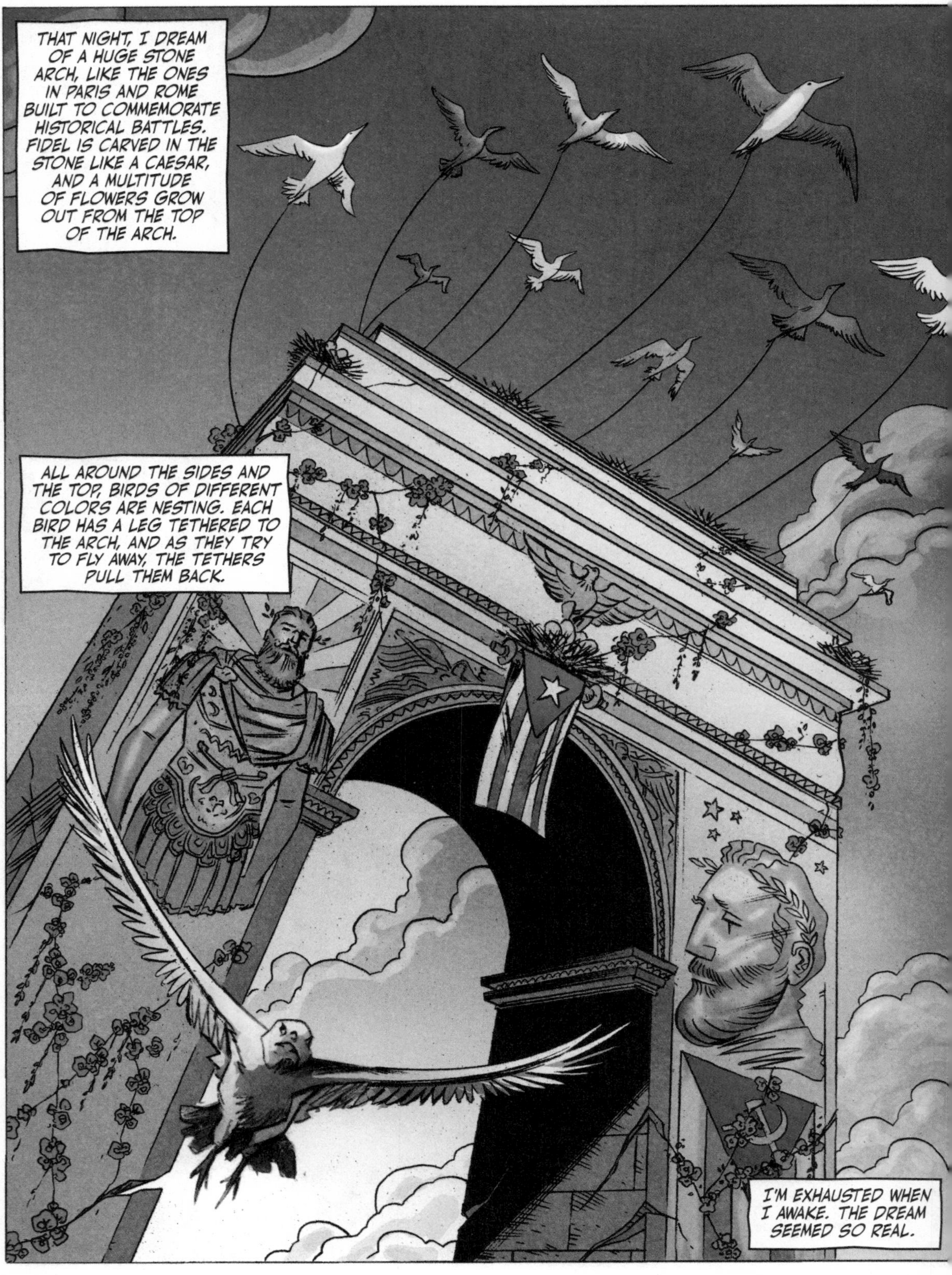
THAT NIGHT, I DREAM OF A HUGE STONE ARCH, LIKE THE ONES IN PARIS AND ROME BUILT TO COMMEMORATE HISTORICAL BATTLES. FIDEL IS CARVED IN THE STONE LIKE A CAESAR, AND A MULTITUDE OF FLOWERS GROW OUT FROM THE TOP OF THE ARCH.
ALL AROUND THE SIDES AND THE TOP, BIRDS OF DIFFERENT COLORS ARE NESTING. EACH BIRD HAS A LEG TETHERED TO THE ARCH, AND AS THEY TRY TO FLY AWAY, THE TETHERS PULL THEM BACK.
I'M EXHAUSTED WHEN I AWAKE. THE DREAM SEEMED SO REAL.

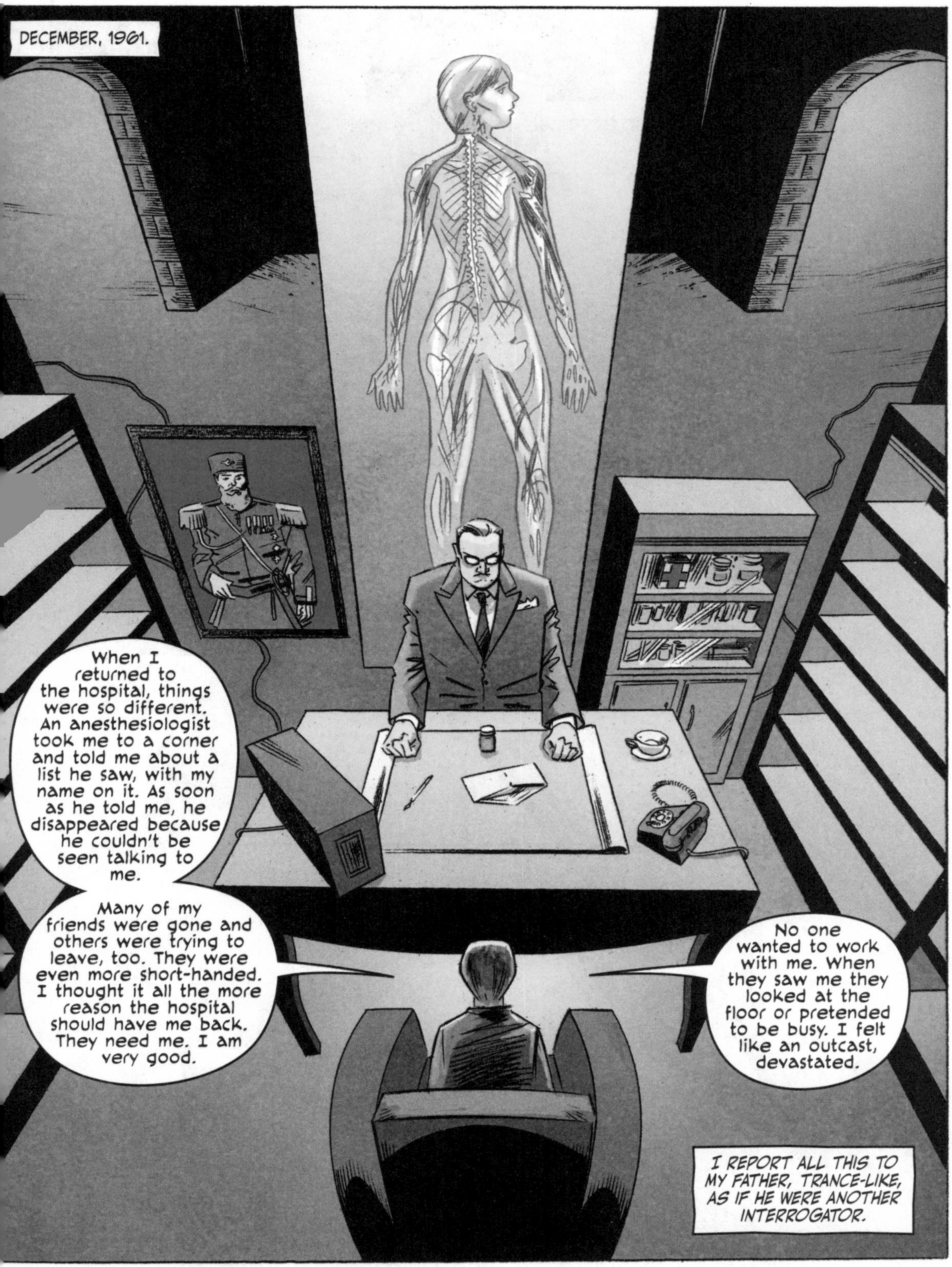
DECEMBER, 1961.
When I returned to the hospital, things were so different. An anesthesiologist took me to a corner and told me about a list he saw, with my name on it. As soon as he told me, he disappeared because he couldn't be seen talking to me.
Many of my friends were gone and others were trying to leave, too. They were even more short-handed. I thought it all the more reason the hospital should have me back. They need me. I am very good.
No one wanted to work with me. When they saw me they looked at the floor or pretended to be busy. I felt like an outcast, devastated.
I REPORT ALL THIS TO MY FATHER, TRANCE-LIKE, AS IF HE WERE ANOTHER INTERROGATOR.

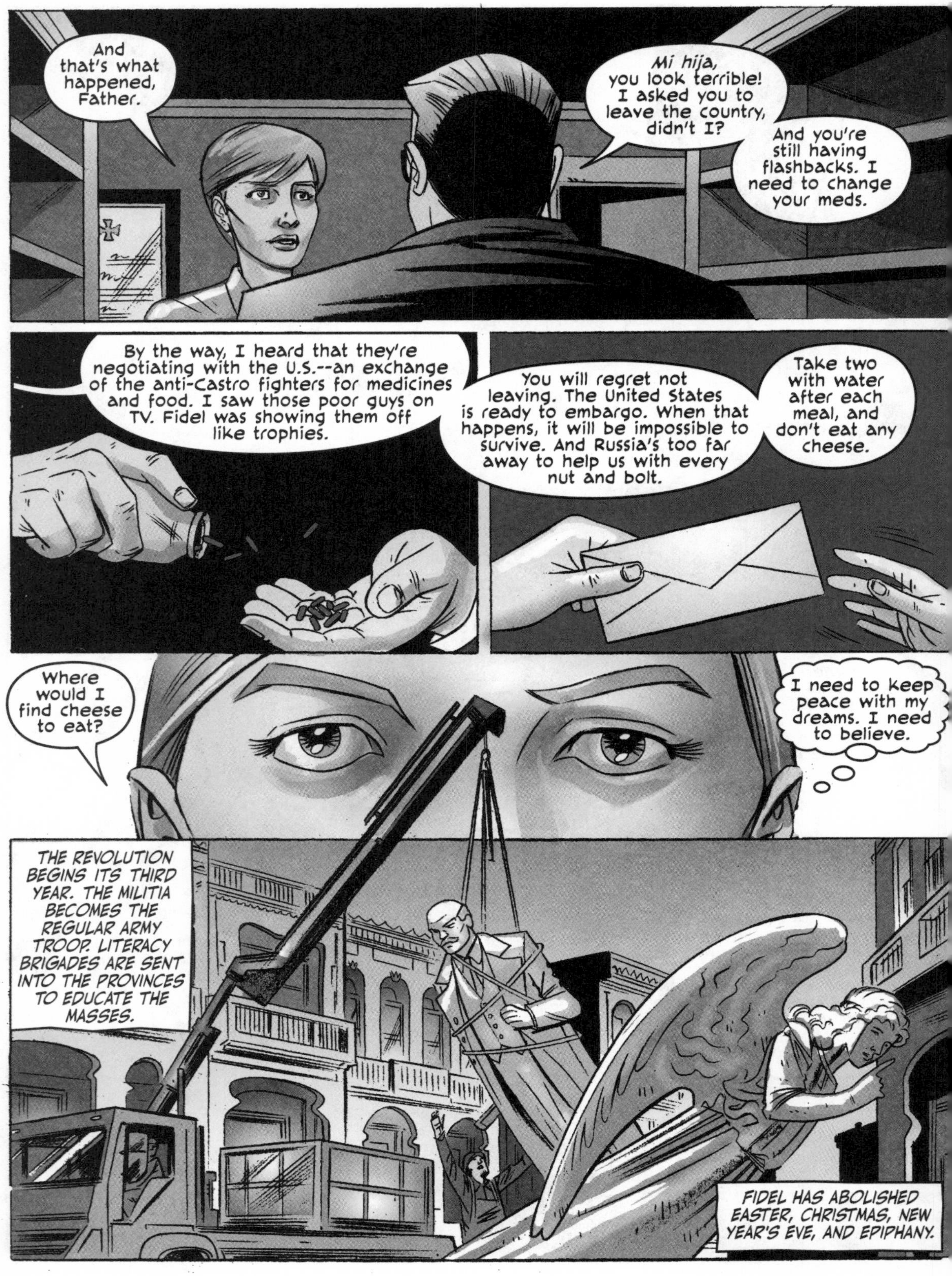

And that's what happened, Father.
Mi hija, you look terrible! I asked you to leave the country, didn't I?
And you're still having flashbacks. I need to change your meds.
By the way, I heard that they're negotiating with the U.S.--an exchange of the anti-Castro fighters for medicines and food. I saw those poor guys on TV. Fidel was showing them off like trophies.
You will regret not leaving. The United States is ready to embargo. When that happens, it will be impossible to survive. And Russia's too far away to help us with every nut and bolt.
Take two with water after each meal, and don't eat any cheese.
Where would I find cheese to eat?
I need to keep peace with my dreams. I need to believe.
THE REVOLUTION BEGINS ITS THIRD YEAR. THE MILITIA BECOMES THE REGULAR ARMY TROOP. LITERACY BRIGADES ARE SENT INTO THE PROVINCES TO EDUCATE THE MASSES.
FIDEL HAS ABOLISHED EASTER, CHRISTMAS, NEW YEAR'S EVE, AND EPIPHANY.

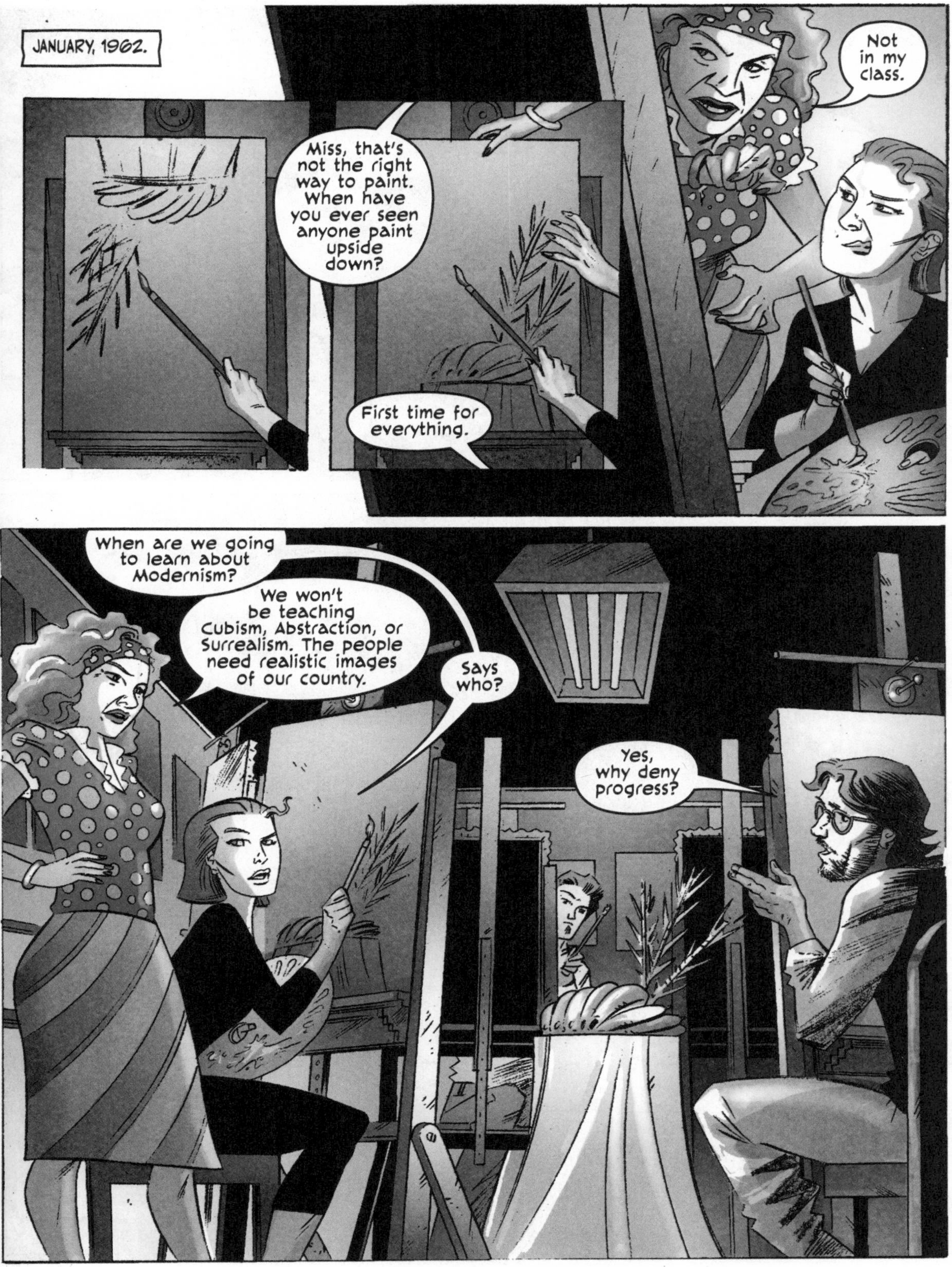
JANUARY, 1962.
Miss, that's not the right way to paint. When have you ever seen anyone paint upside down?
First time for everything.
Not in my class.
When are we going to learn about Modernism?
We won't be teaching Cubism, Abstraction, or Surrealism. The people need realistic images of our country.
Says who?
Yes, why deny progress?

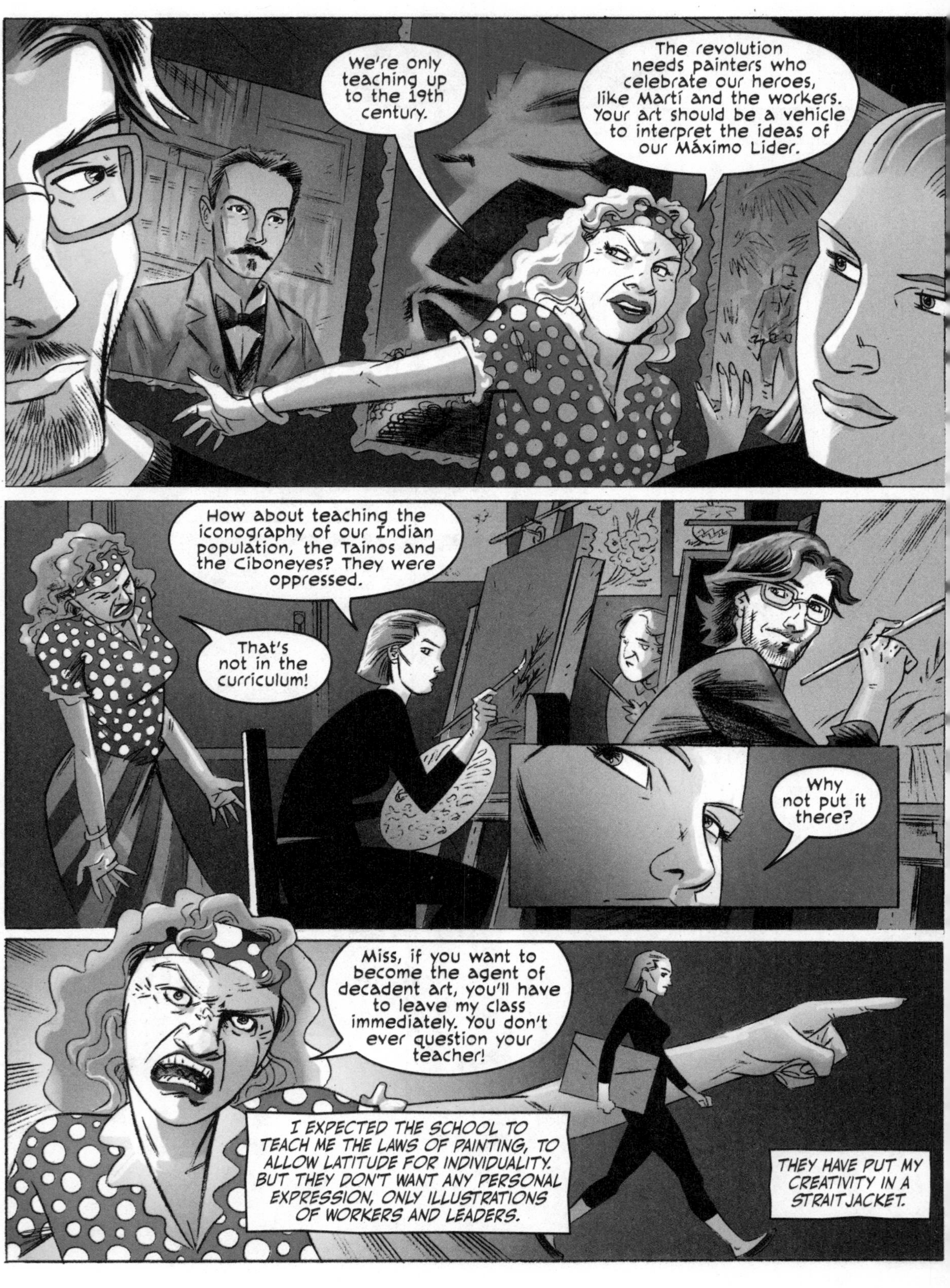
We're only teaching up to the 19th century.
The revolution needs painters who celebrate our heroes, like Martí and the workers. Your art should be a vehicle to interpret the ideas of our Máximo Lider.
How about teaching the iconography of our Indian population, the Tainos and the Ciboneyes? They were oppressed.
That's not in the curriculum!
Why not put it there?
Miss, if you want to become the agent of decadent art, you'll have to leave my class immediately. You don't ever question your teacher!
I EXPECTED THE SCHOOL TO TEACH ME THE LAWS OF PAINTING, TO ALLOW LATITUDE FOR INDIVIDUALITY. BUT THEY DON'T WANT ANY PERSONAL EXPRESSION, ONLY ILLUSTRATIONS OF WORKERS AND LEADERS.
THEY HAVE PUT MY CREATIVITY IN A STRAITJACKET.

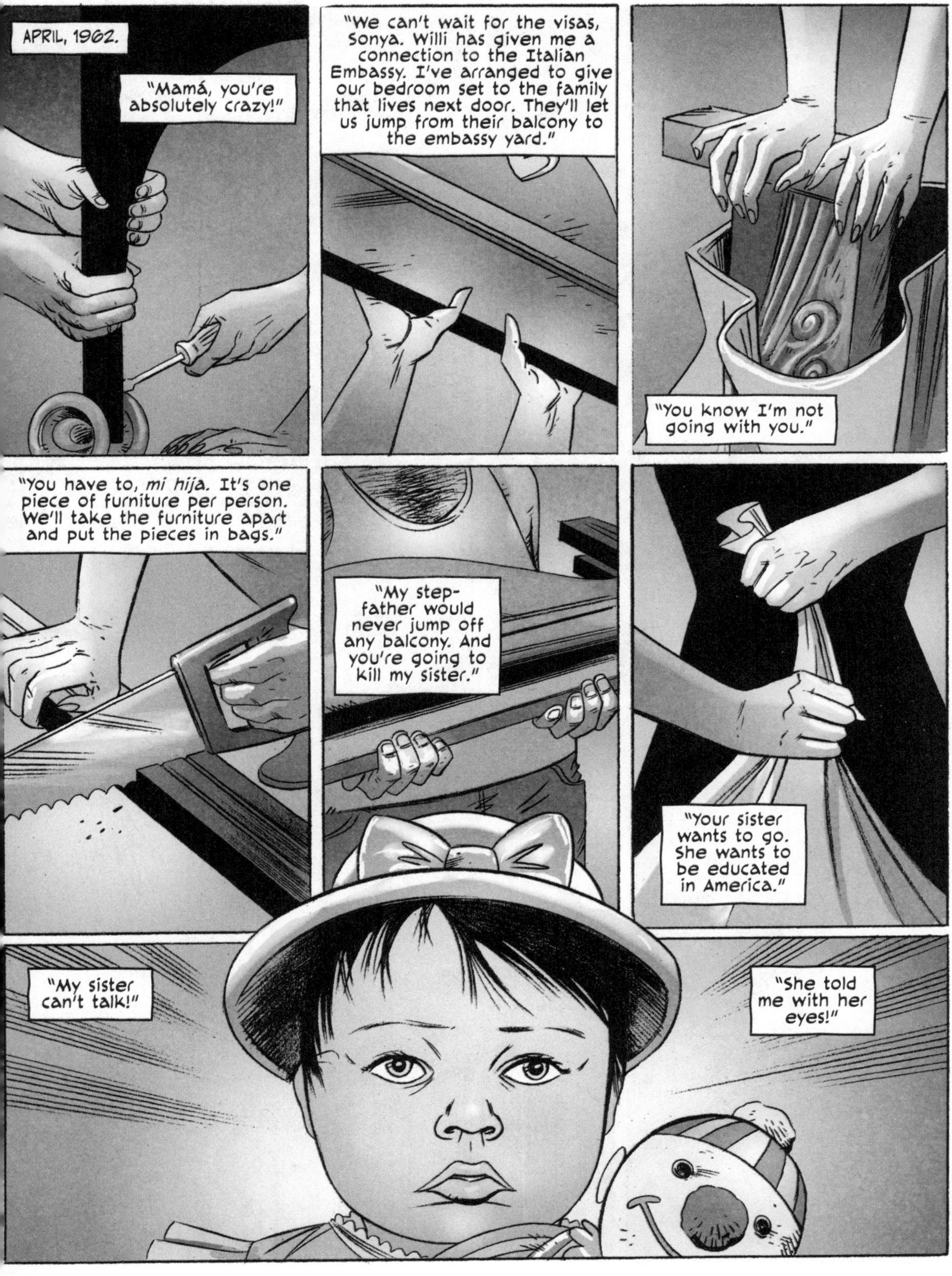
APRIL, 1962.
"Mamá, you're absolutely crazy!"
"We can't wait for the visas, Sonya. Willi has given me a connection to the Italian Embassy. I've arranged to give our bedroom set to the family that lives next door. They'll let us jump from their balcony to the embassy yard."
"You know I'm not going with you."
"You have to, *mi hija*. It's one piece of furniture per person. We'll take the furniture apart and put the pieces in bags."
"My step-father would never jump off any balcony. And you're going to kill my sister."
"Your sister wants to go. She wants to be educated in America."
"My sister can't talk!"
"She told me with her eyes!"

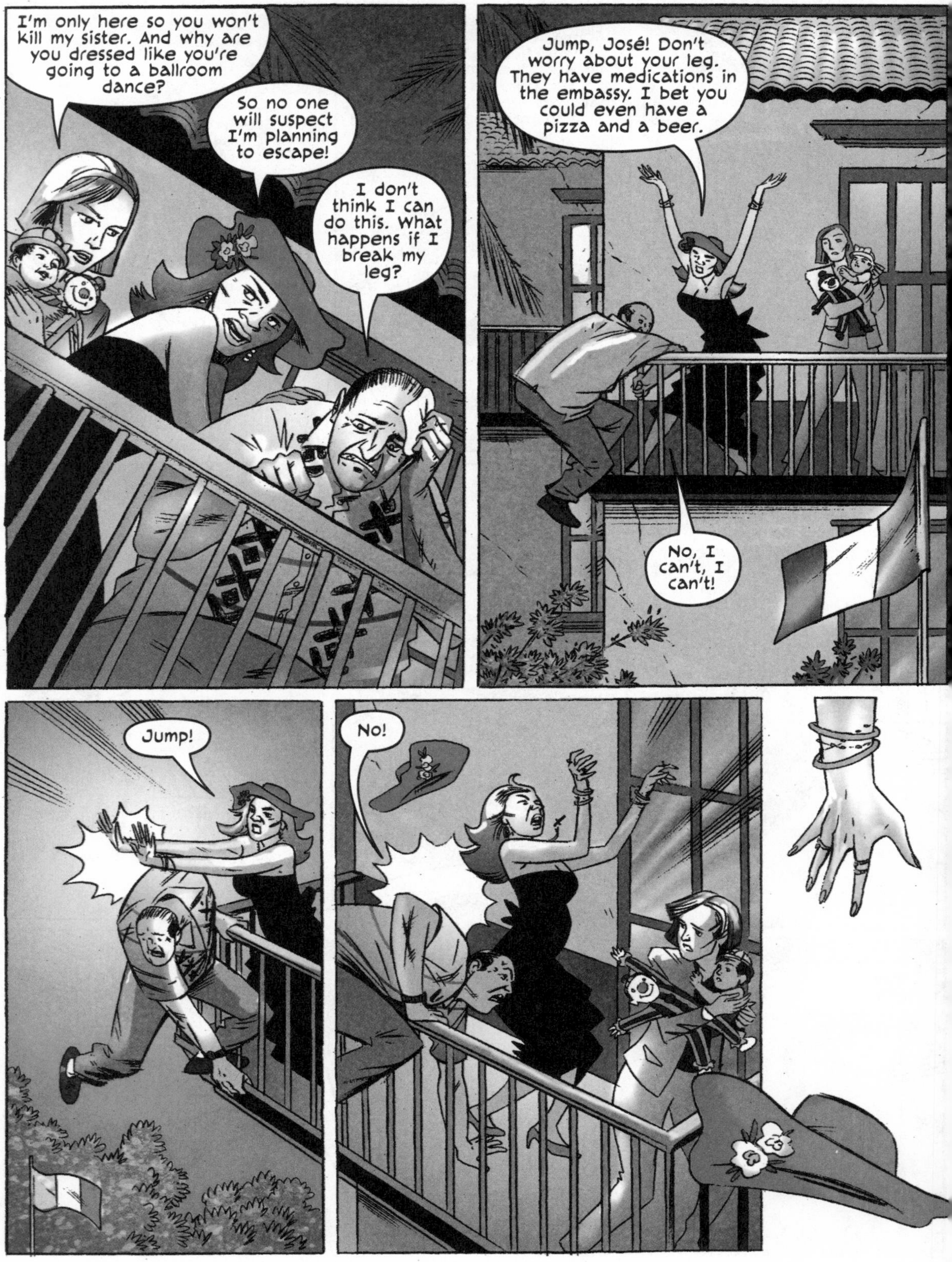
I'm only here so you won't kill my sister. And why are you dressed like you're going to a ballroom dance?
So no one will suspect I'm planning to escape!
I don't think I can do this. What happens if I break my leg?
Jump, José! Don't worry about your leg. They have medications in the embassy. I bet you could even have a pizza and a beer.
No, I can't, I can't!
Jump!
No!

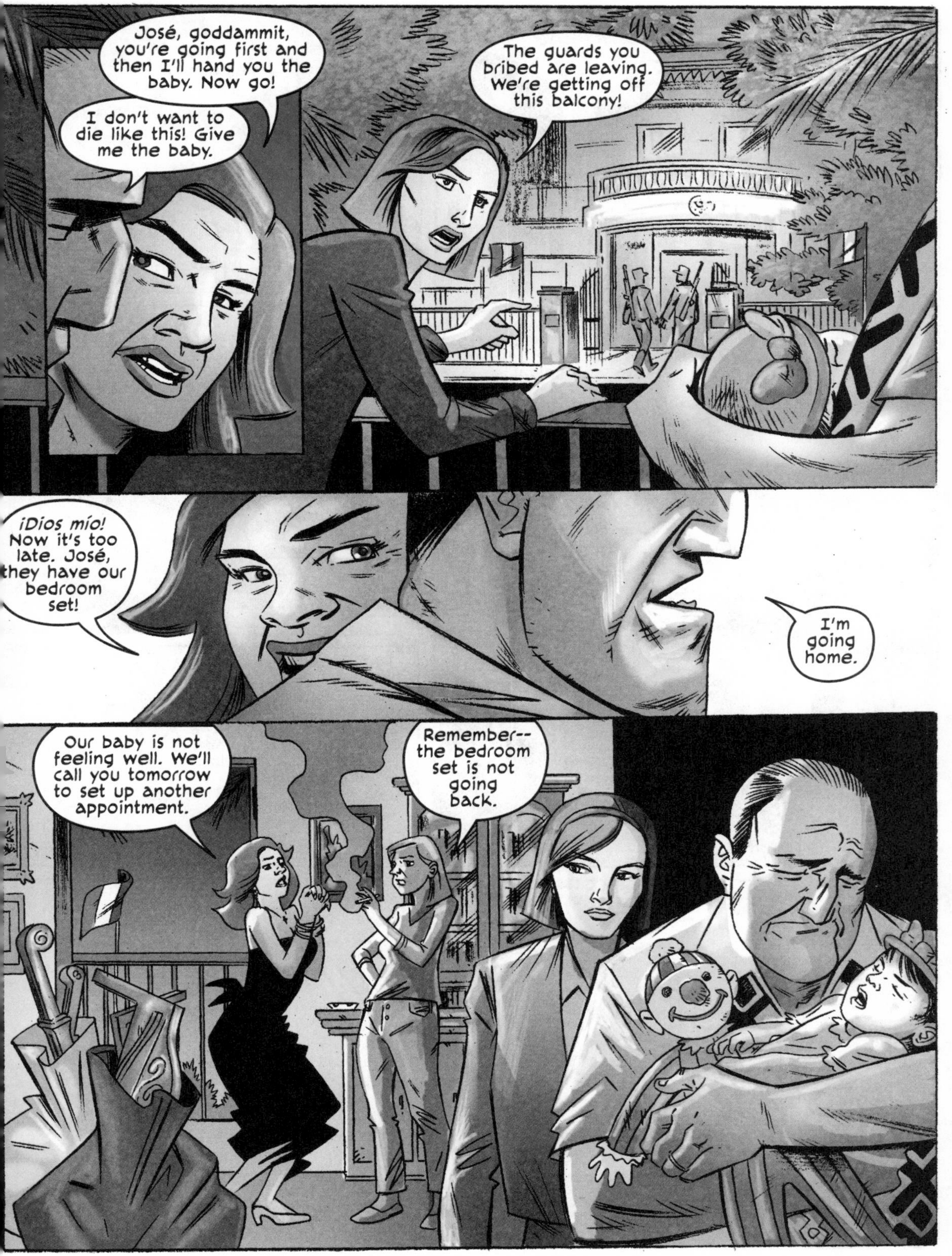
José, goddammit, you're going first and then I'll hand you the baby. Now go!
I don't want to die like this! Give me the baby.
The guards you bribed are leaving. We're getting off this balcony!
¡Dios mío! Now it's too late. José, they have our bedroom set!
I'm going home.
Our baby is not feeling well. We'll call you tomorrow to set up another appointment.
Remember-- the bedroom set is not going back.

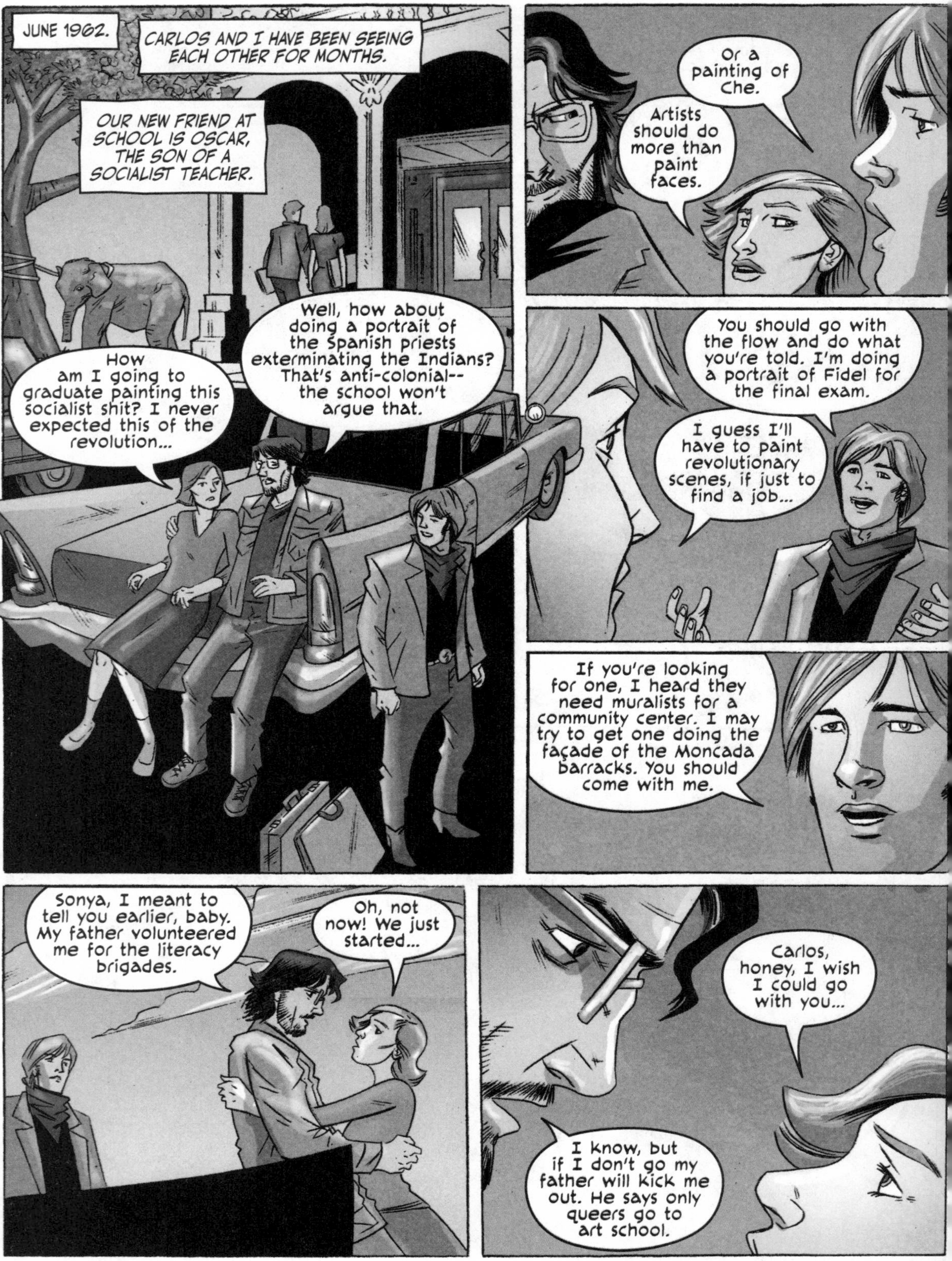
JUNE 1962.
CARLOS AND I HAVE BEEN SEEING EACH OTHER FOR MONTHS.
OUR NEW FRIEND AT SCHOOL IS OSCAR, THE SON OF A SOCIALIST TEACHER.
How am I going to graduate painting this socialist shit? I never expected this of the revolution...
Well, how about doing a portrait of the Spanish priests exterminating the Indians? That's anti-colonial-- the school won't argue that.
Or a painting of Che.
Artists should do more than paint faces.
You should go with the flow and do what you're told. I'm doing a portrait of Fidel for the final exam.
I guess I'll have to paint revolutionary scenes, if just to find a job...
If you're looking for one, I heard they need muralists for a community center. I may try to get one doing the façade of the Moncada barracks. You should come with me.
Sonya, I meant to tell you earlier, baby. My father volunteered me for the literacy brigades.
Oh, not now! We just started...
Carlos, honey, I wish I could go with you...
I know, but if I don't go my father will kick me out. He says only queers go to art school.

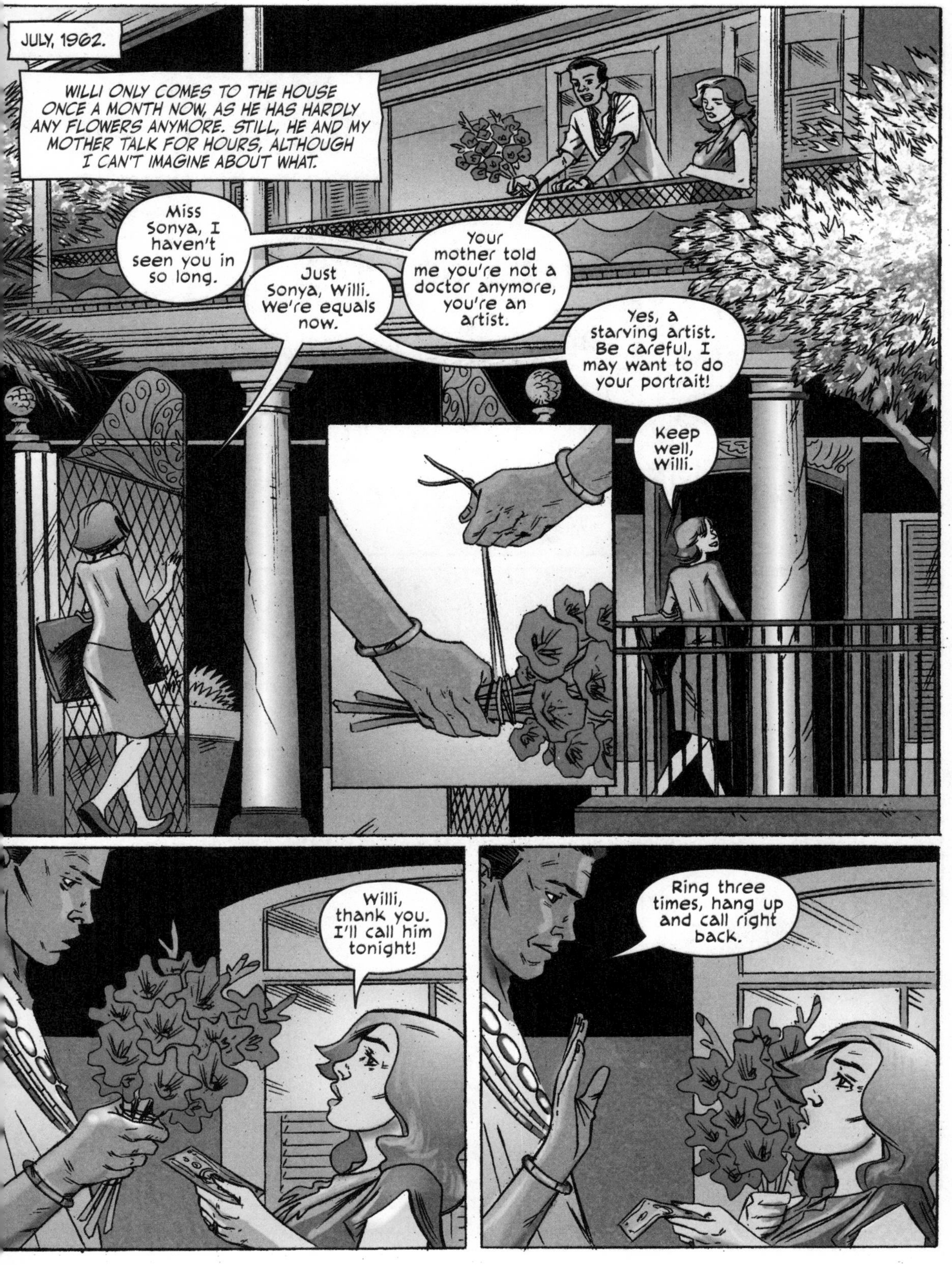
JULY, 1962.
WILLI ONLY COMES TO THE HOUSE ONCE A MONTH NOW, AS HE HAS HARDLY ANY FLOWERS ANYMORE. STILL, HE AND MY MOTHER TALK FOR HOURS, ALTHOUGH I CAN'T IMAGINE ABOUT WHAT.
Miss Sonya, I haven't seen you in so long.
Your mother told me you're not a doctor anymore, you're an artist.
Just Sonya, Willi. We're equals now.
Yes, a starving artist. Be careful, I may want to do your portrait!
Keep well, Willi.
Willi, thank you. I'll call him tonight!
Ring three times, hang up and call right back.

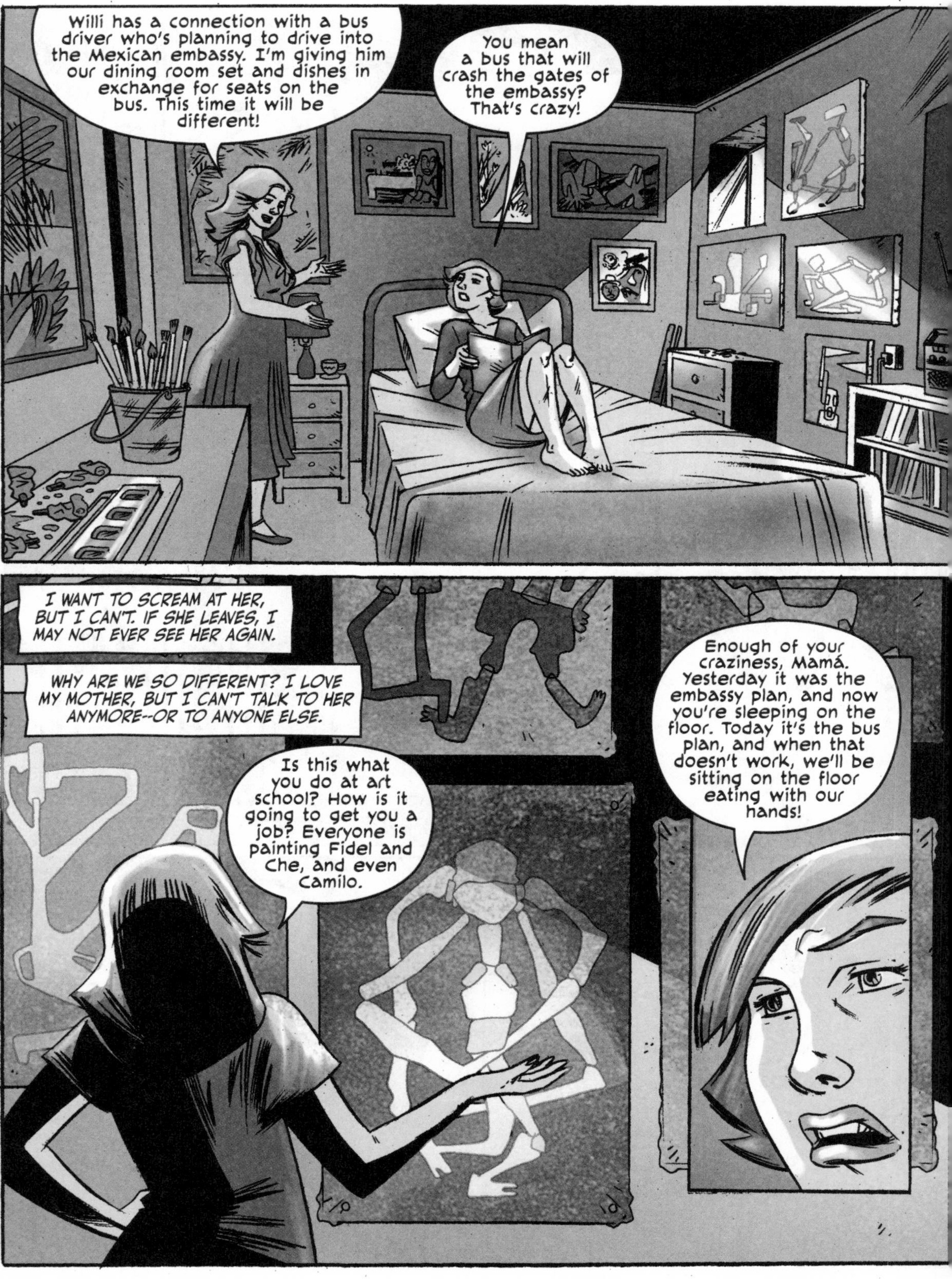
Willi has a connection with a bus driver who's planning to drive into the Mexican embassy. I'm giving him our dining room set and dishes in exchange for seats on the bus. This time it will be different!
You mean a bus that will crash the gates of the embassy? That's crazy!
I WANT TO SCREAM AT HER, BUT I CAN'T. IF SHE LEAVES, I MAY NOT EVER SEE HER AGAIN.
WHY ARE WE SO DIFFERENT? I LOVE MY MOTHER, BUT I CAN'T TALK TO HER ANYMORE--OR TO ANYONE ELSE.
Is this what you do at art school? How is it going to get you a job? Everyone is painting Fidel and Che, and even Camilo.
Enough of your craziness, Mamá. Yesterday it was the embassy plan, and now you're sleeping on the floor. Today it's the bus plan, and when that doesn't work, we'll be sitting on the floor eating with our hands!

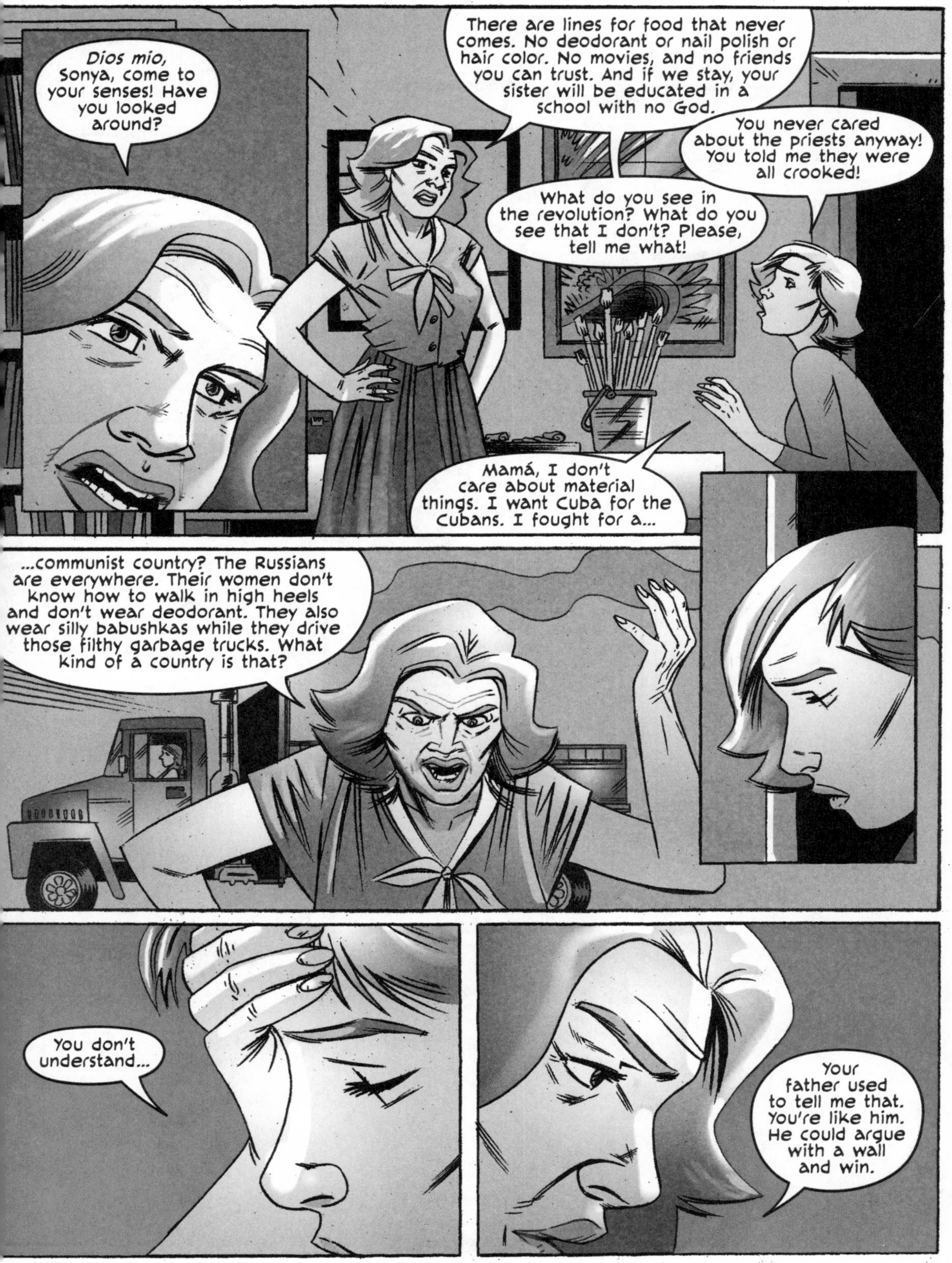

Dios mio, Sonya, come to your senses! Have you looked around?
There are lines for food that never comes. No deodorant or nail polish or hair color. No movies, and no friends you can trust. And if we stay, your sister will be educated in a school with no God.
You never cared about the priests anyway! You told me they were all crooked!
What do you see in the revolution? What do you see that I don't? Please, tell me what!
Mamá, I don't care about material things. I want Cuba for the Cubans. I fought for a...
...communist country? The Russians are everywhere. Their women don't know how to walk in high heels and don't wear deodorant. They also wear silly babushkas while they drive those filthy garbage trucks. What kind of a country is that?
You don't understand...
Your father used to tell me that. You're like him. He could argue with a wall and win.

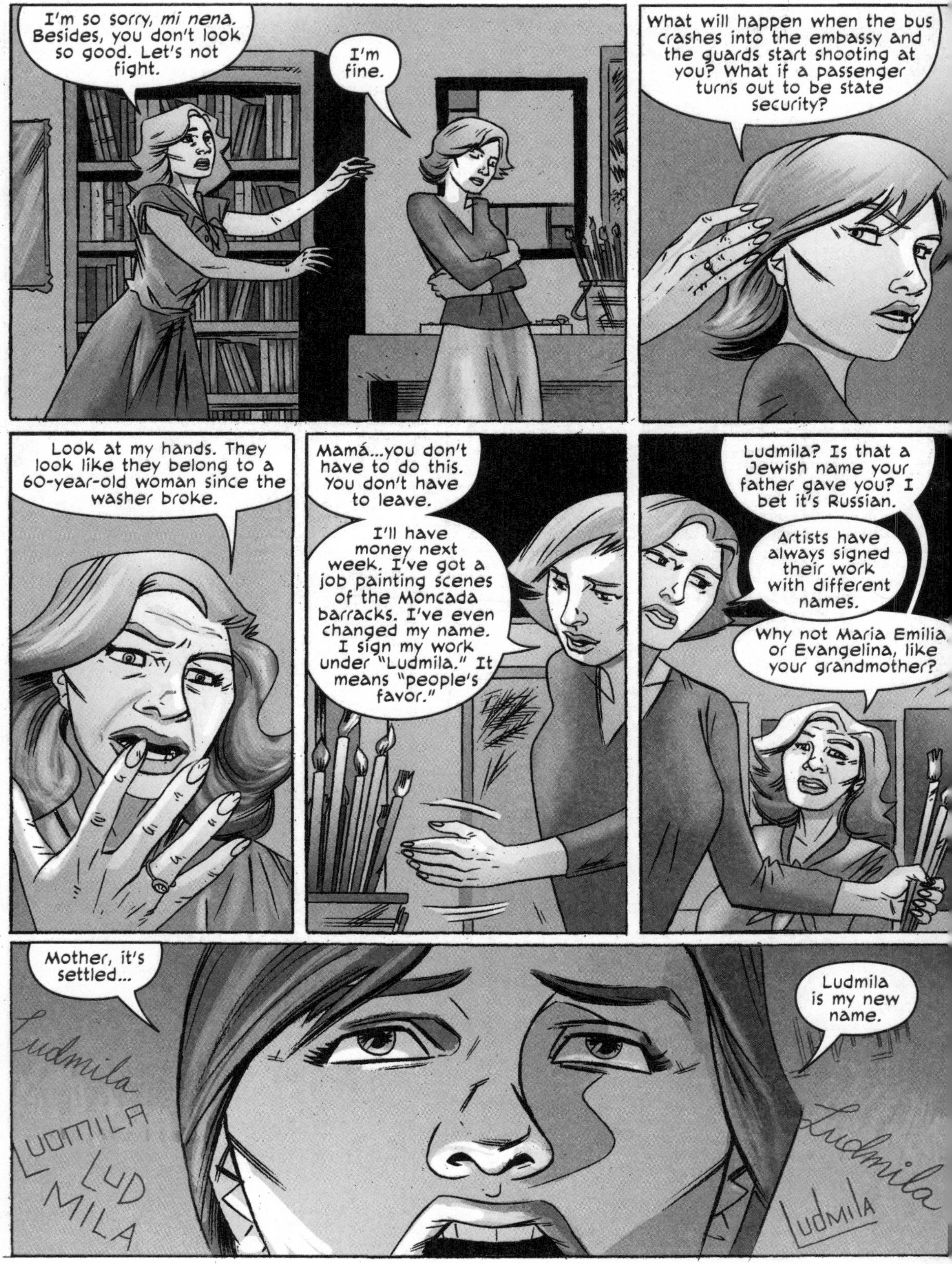
I'm so sorry, *mi nena*. Besides, you don't look so good. Let's not fight.
I'm fine.
What will happen when the bus crashes into the embassy and the guards start shooting at you? What if a passenger turns out to be state security?
Look at my hands. They look like they belong to a 60-year-old woman since the washer broke.
Mamá...you don't have to do this. You don't have to leave.
I'll have money next week. I've got a job painting scenes of the Moncada barracks. I've even changed my name. I sign my work under "Ludmila." It means "people's favor."
Ludmila? Is that a Jewish name your father gave you? I bet it's Russian.
Artists have always signed their work with different names.
Why not Maria Emilia or Evangelina, like your grandmother?
Mother, it's settled...
Ludmila is my new name.
Ludmila
LUDMILA
LUD
MILA
Ludmila
LUDMILA

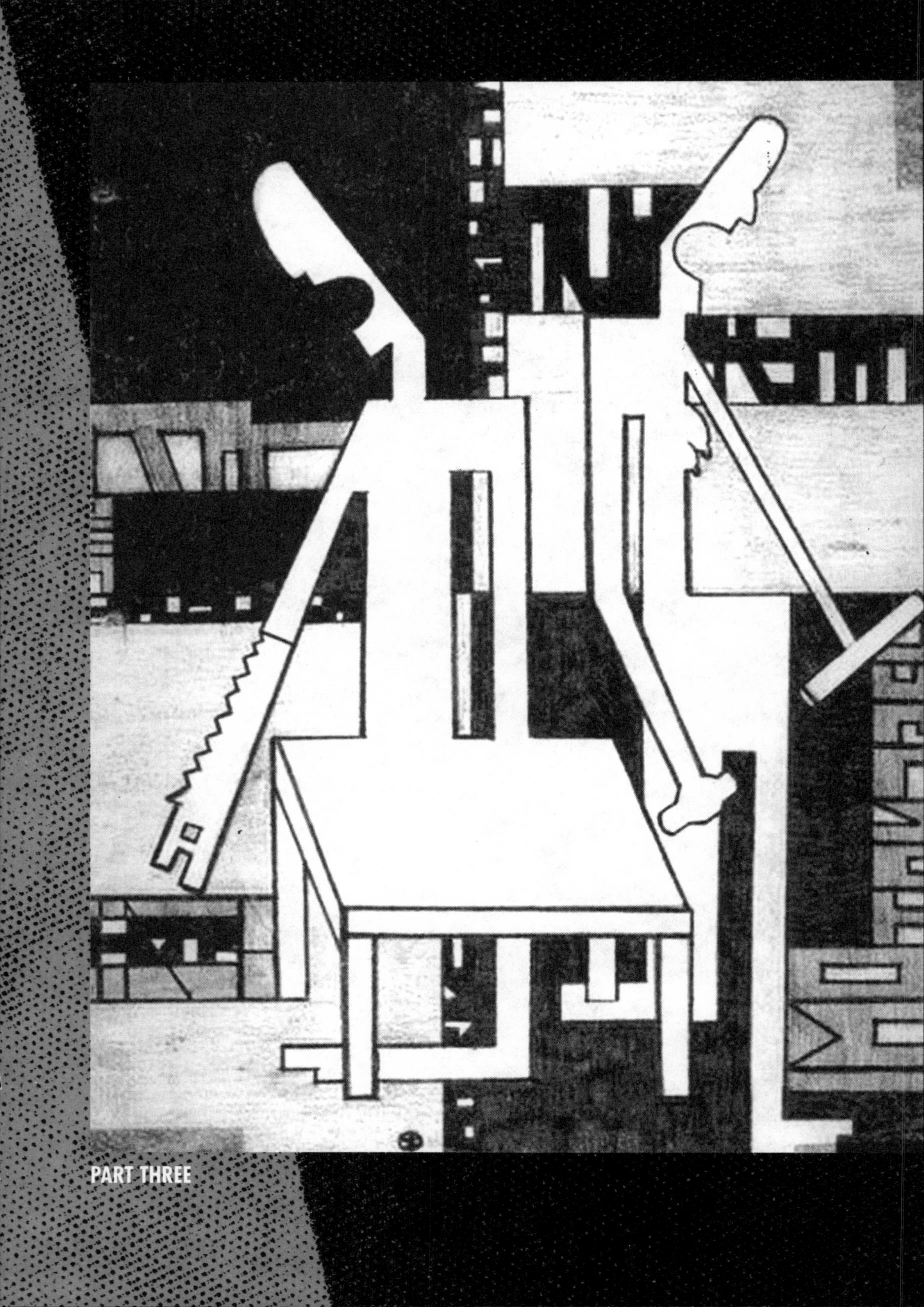

PART THREE

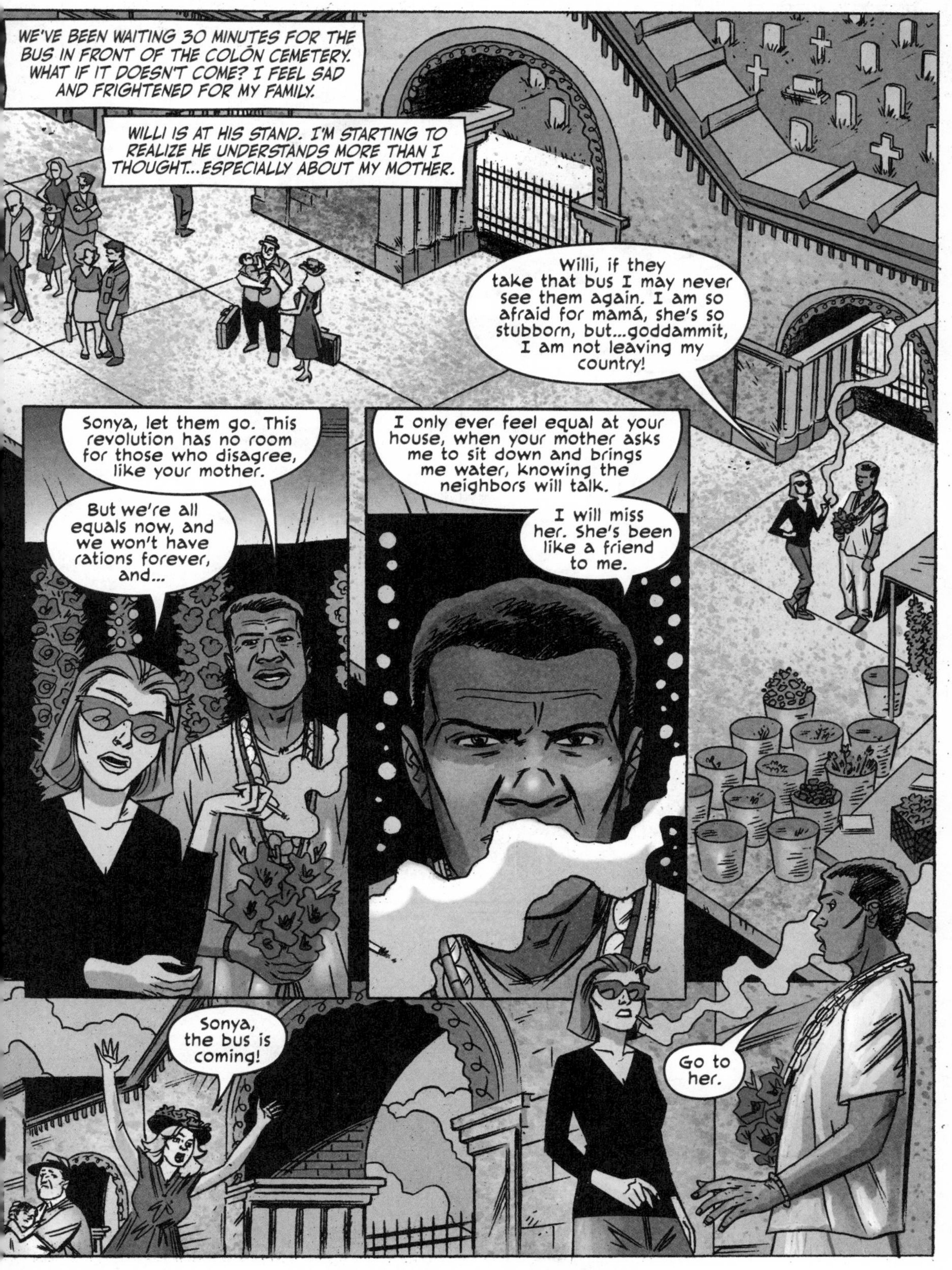
WE'VE BEEN WAITING 30 MINUTES FOR THE BUS IN FRONT OF THE COLÓN CEMETERY. WHAT IF IT DOESN'T COME? I FEEL SAD AND FRIGHTENED FOR MY FAMILY.
WILLI IS AT HIS STAND. I'M STARTING TO REALIZE HE UNDERSTANDS MORE THAN I THOUGHT...ESPECIALLY ABOUT MY MOTHER.
Willi, if they take that bus I may never see them again. I am so afraid for mamá, she's so stubborn, but...goddammit, I am not leaving my country!
Sonya, let them go. This revolution has no room for those who disagree, like your mother.
But we're all equals now, and we won't have rations forever, and...
I only ever feel equal at your house, when your mother asks me to sit down and brings me water, knowing the neighbors will talk.
I will miss her. She's been like a friend to me.
Sonya, the bus is coming!
Go to her.

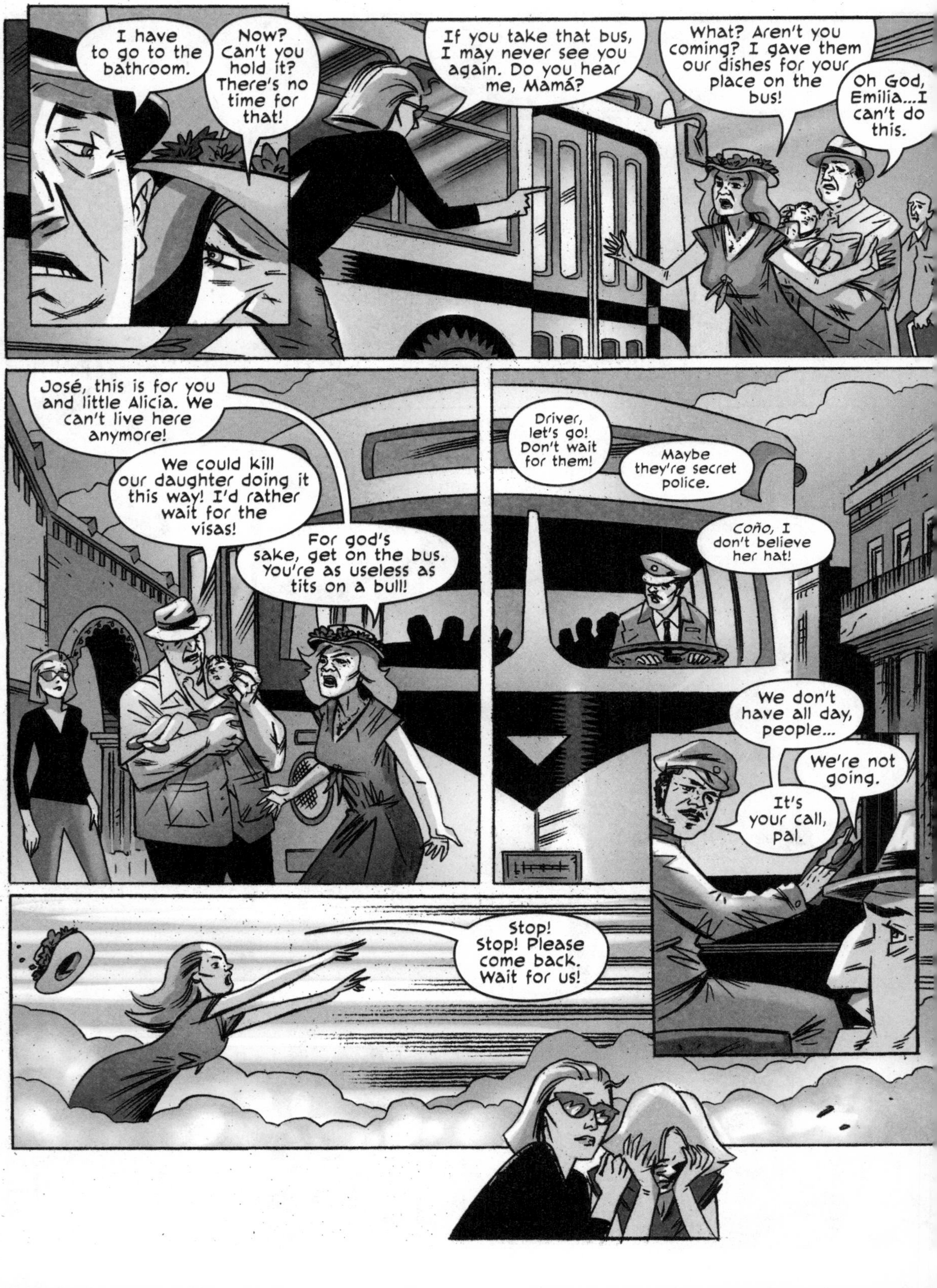

I have to go to the bathroom.
Now? Can't you hold it? There's no time for that!
If you take that bus, I may never see you again. Do you hear me, Mamá?
What? Aren't you coming? I gave them our dishes for your place on the bus!
Oh God, Emilia...I can't do this.
José, this is for you and little Alicia. We can't live here anymore!
We could kill our daughter doing it this way! I'd rather wait for the visas!
For god's sake, get on the bus. You're as useless as tits on a bull!
Driver, let's go! Don't wait for them!
Maybe they're secret police.
Coño, I don't believe her hat!
We don't have all day, people...
We're not going.
It's your call, pal.
Stop! Stop! Please come back. Wait for us!

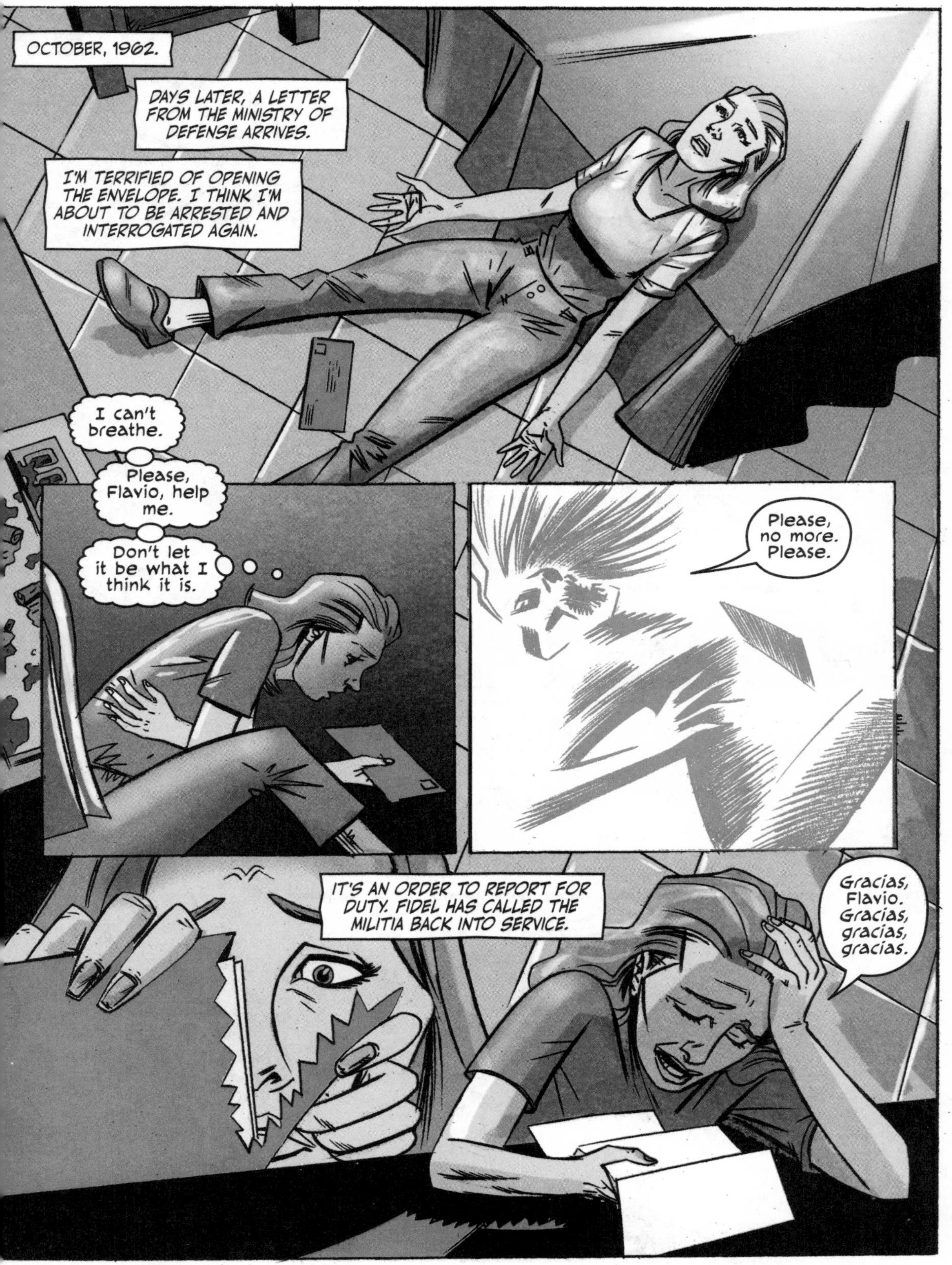
OCTOBER, 1962.
DAYS LATER, A LETTER FROM THE MINISTRY OF DEFENSE ARRIVES.
I'M TERRIFIED OF OPENING THE ENVELOPE. I THINK I'M ABOUT TO BE ARRESTED AND INTERROGATED AGAIN.
I can't breathe.
Please, Flavio, help me.
Don't let it be what I think it is.
Please, no more. Please.
IT'S AN ORDER TO REPORT FOR DUTY. FIDEL HAS CALLED THE MILITIA BACK INTO SERVICE.
Gracias, Flavio. Gracias, gracias, gracias.

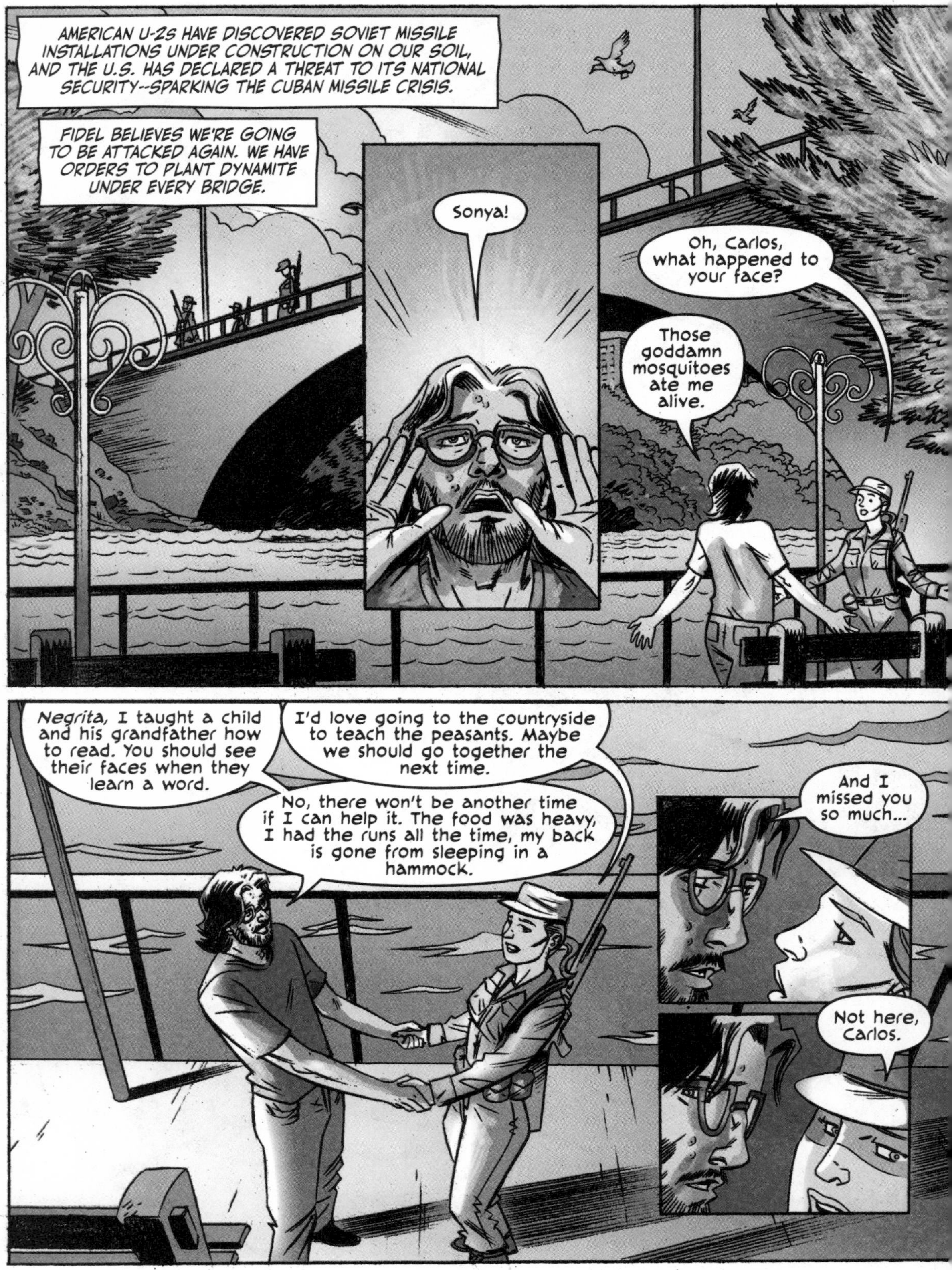
AMERICAN U-2S HAVE DISCOVERED SOVIET MISSILE INSTALLATIONS UNDER CONSTRUCTION ON OUR SOIL, AND THE U.S. HAS DECLARED A THREAT TO ITS NATIONAL SECURITY--SPARKING THE CUBAN MISSILE CRISIS.
FIDEL BELIEVES WE'RE GOING TO BE ATTACKED AGAIN. WE HAVE ORDERS TO PLANT DYNAMITE UNDER EVERY BRIDGE.
Sonya!
Oh, Carlos, what happened to your face?
Those goddamn mosquitoes ate me alive.
Negrita, I taught a child and his grandfather how to read. You should see their faces when they learn a word.
I'd love going to the countryside to teach the peasants. Maybe we should go together the next time.
No, there won't be another time if I can help it. The food was heavy, I had the runs all the time, my back is gone from sleeping in a hammock.
And I missed you so much...
Not here, Carlos.

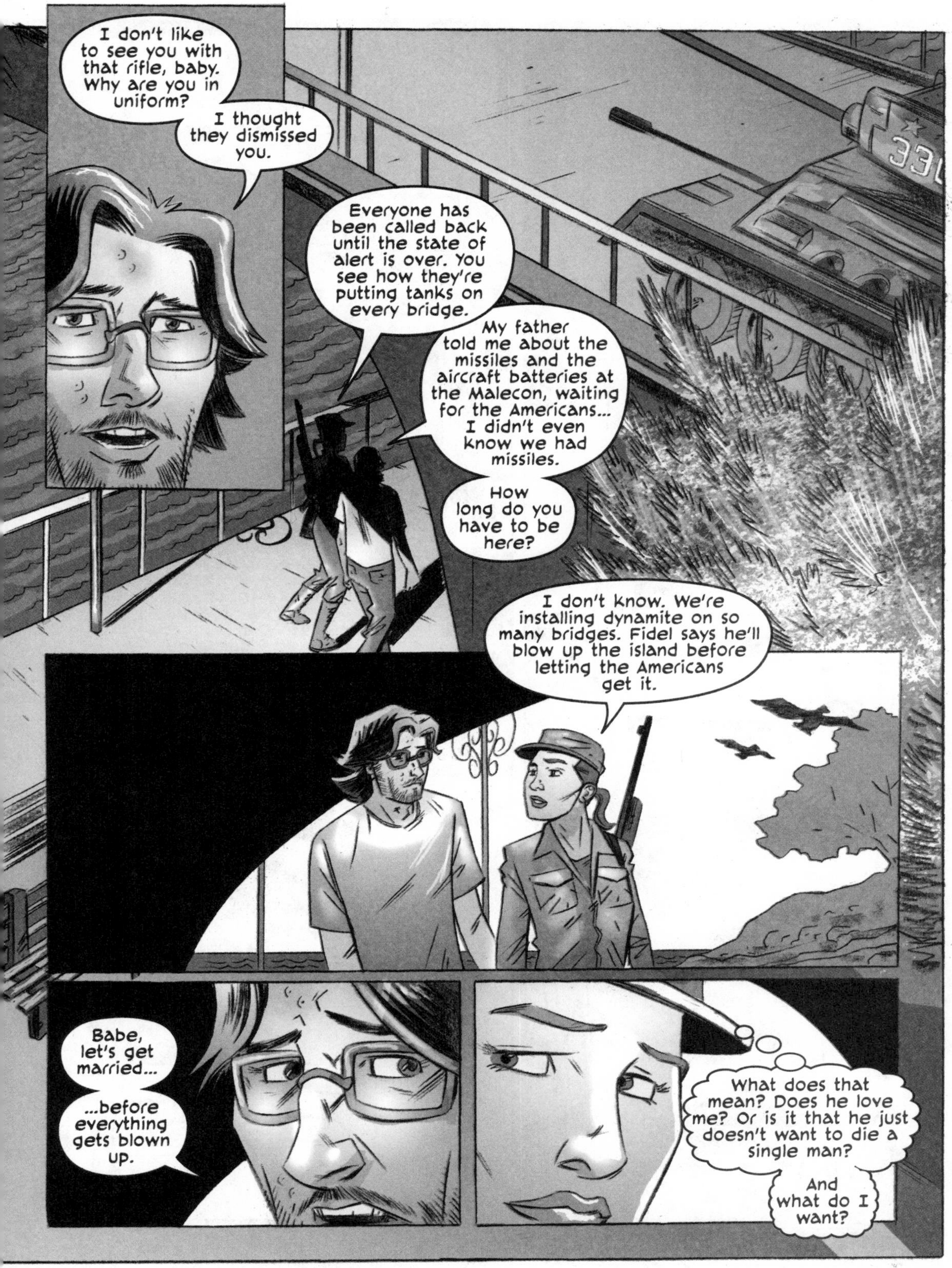
I don't like to see you with that rifle, baby. Why are you in uniform?
I thought they dismissed you.
Everyone has been called back until the state of alert is over. You see how they're putting tanks on every bridge.
My father told me about the missiles and the aircraft batteries at the Malecon, waiting for the Americans... I didn't even know we had missiles.
How long do you have to be here?
I don't know. We're installing dynamite on so many bridges. Fidel says he'll blow up the island before letting the Americans get it.
Babe, let's get married...
...before everything gets blown up.
What does that mean? Does he love me? Or is it that he just doesn't want to die a single man?
And what do I want?

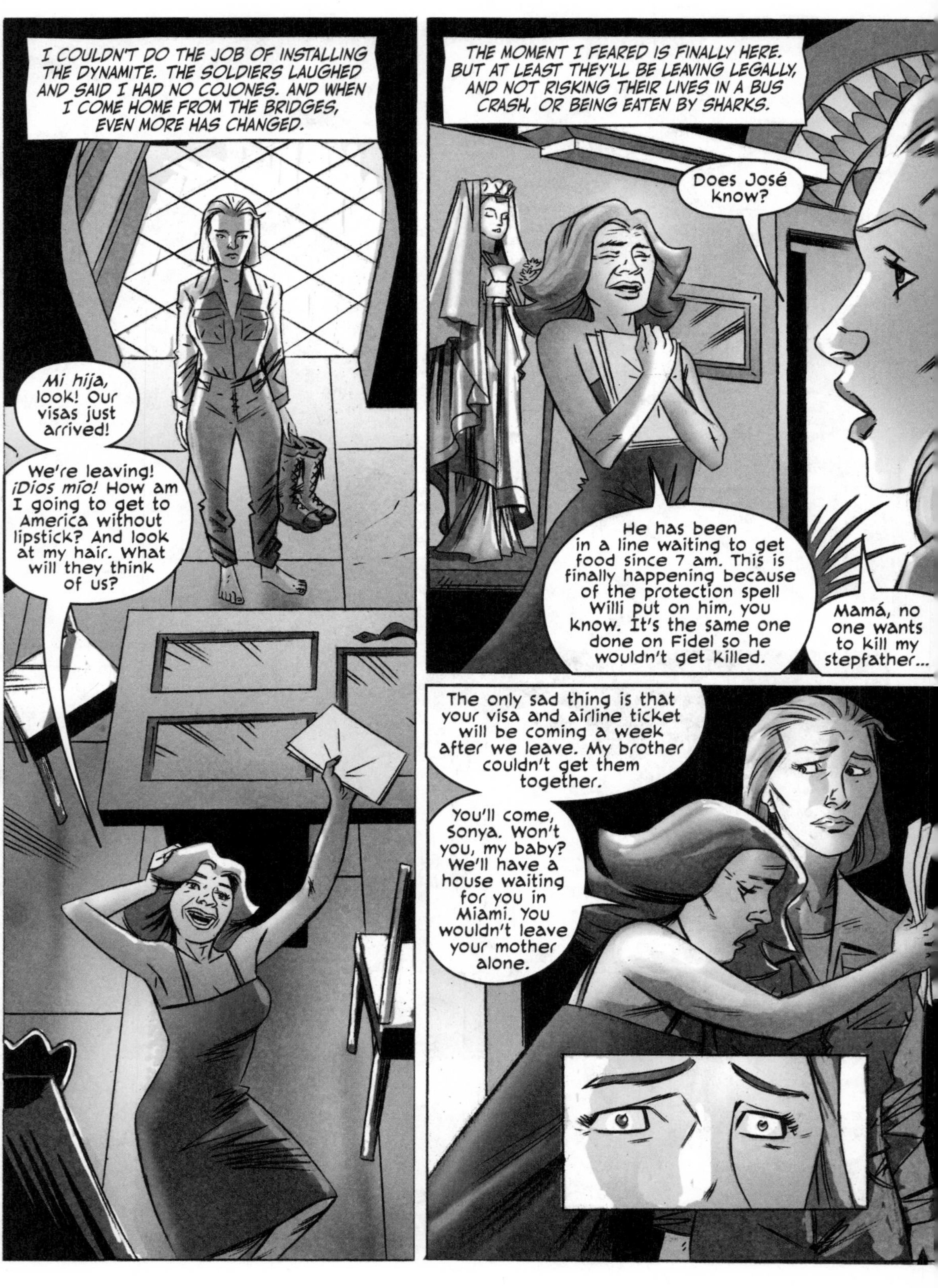
I COULDN'T DO THE JOB OF INSTALLING THE DYNAMITE. THE SOLDIERS LAUGHED AND SAID I HAD NO COJONES. AND WHEN I COME HOME FROM THE BRIDGES, EVEN MORE HAS CHANGED.
Mi hija, look! Our visas just arrived!
We're leaving! ¡Dios mío! How am I going to get to America without lipstick? And look at my hair. What will they think of us?
THE MOMENT I FEARED IS FINALLY HERE. BUT AT LEAST THEY'LL BE LEAVING LEGALLY, AND NOT RISKING THEIR LIVES IN A BUS CRASH, OR BEING EATEN BY SHARKS.
Does José know?
He has been in a line waiting to get food since 7 am. This is finally happening because of the protection spell Willi put on him, you know. It's the same one done on Fidel so he wouldn't get killed.
Mamá, no one wants to kill my stepfather...
The only sad thing is that your visa and airline ticket will be coming a week after we leave. My brother couldn't get them together.
You'll come, Sonya. Won't you, my baby? We'll have a house waiting for you in Miami. You wouldn't leave your mother alone.

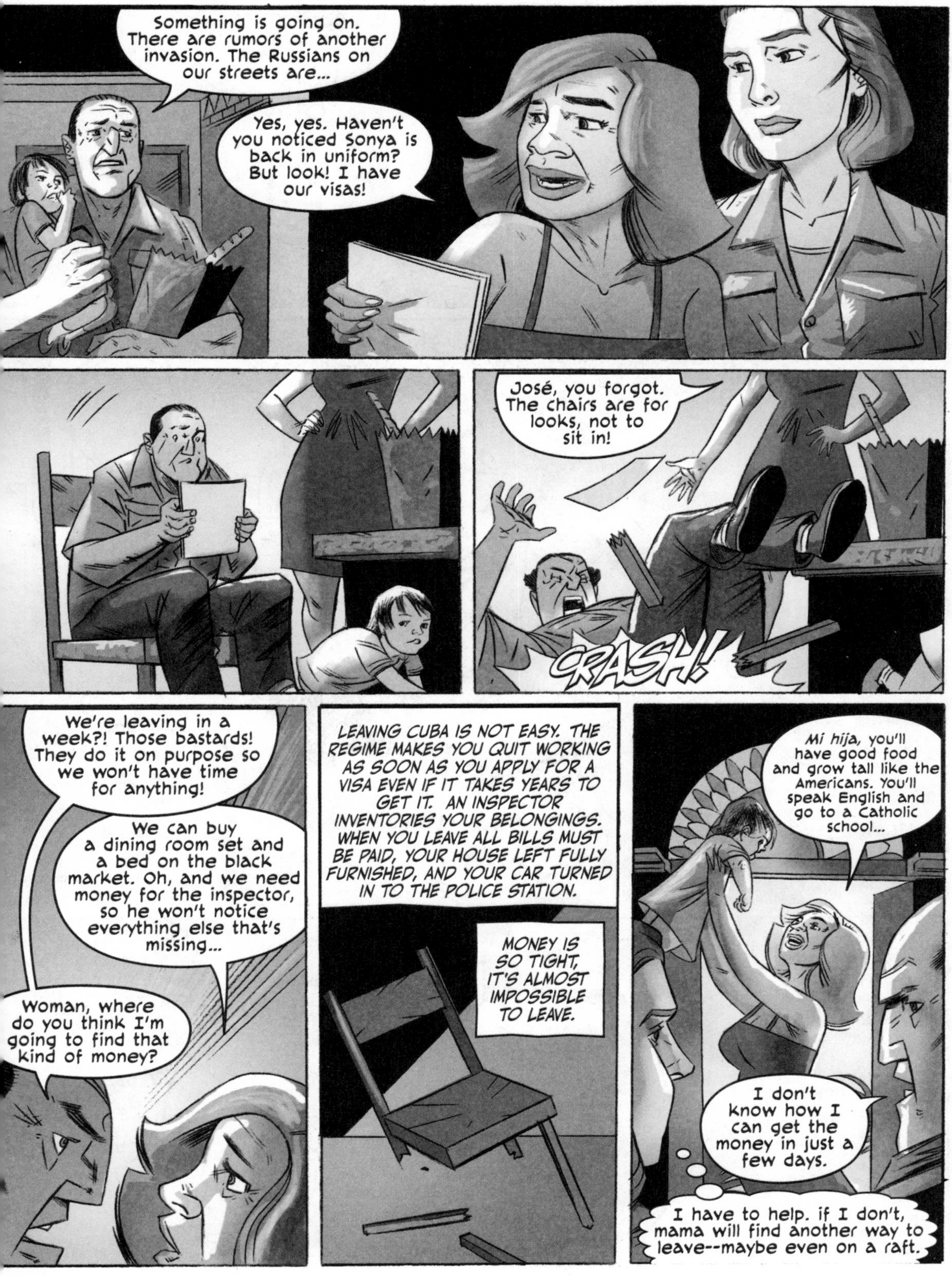

Something is going on. There are rumors of another invasion. The Russians on our streets are...
Yes, yes. Haven't you noticed Sonya is back in uniform? But look! I have our visas!
José, you forgot. The chairs are for looks, not to sit in!
CRASH!
We're leaving in a week?! Those bastards! They do it on purpose so we won't have time for anything!
We can buy a dining room set and a bed on the black market. Oh, and we need money for the inspector, so he won't notice everything else that's missing...
Woman, where do you think I'm going to find that kind of money?
LEAVING CUBA IS NOT EASY. THE REGIME MAKES YOU QUIT WORKING AS SOON AS YOU APPLY FOR A VISA EVEN IF IT TAKES YEARS TO GET IT. AN INSPECTOR INVENTORIES YOUR BELONGINGS. WHEN YOU LEAVE ALL BILLS MUST BE PAID, YOUR HOUSE LEFT FULLY FURNISHED, AND YOUR CAR TURNED IN TO THE POLICE STATION.
MONEY IS SO TIGHT, IT'S ALMOST IMPOSSIBLE TO LEAVE.
Mi hija, you'll have good food and grow tall like the Americans. You'll speak English and go to a Catholic school...
I don't know how I can get the money in just a few days.
I have to help. if I don't, mama will find another way to leave--maybe even on a raft.

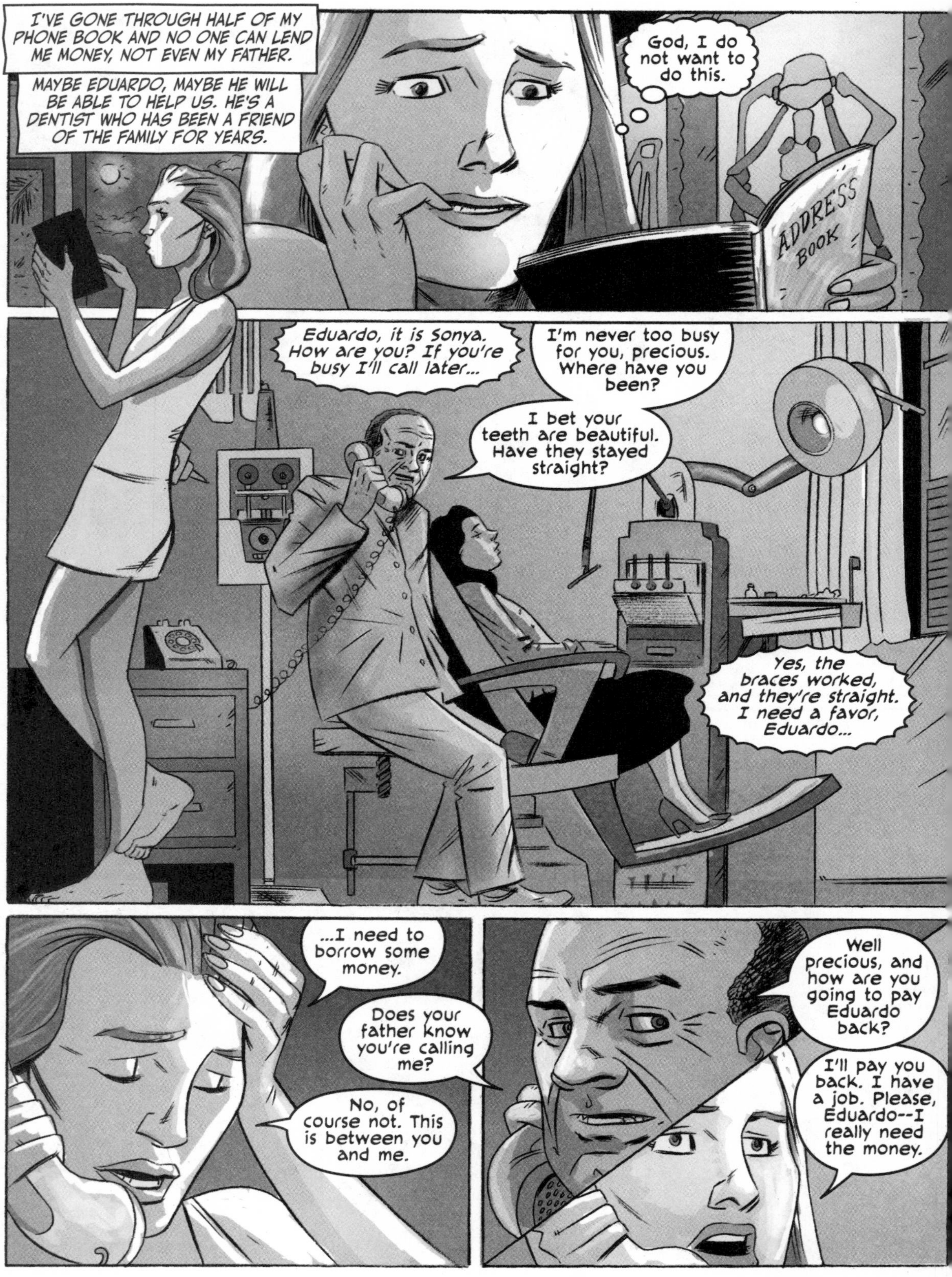
I'VE GONE THROUGH HALF OF MY PHONE BOOK AND NO ONE CAN LEND ME MONEY, NOT EVEN MY FATHER.
MAYBE EDUARDO, MAYBE HE WILL BE ABLE TO HELP US. HE'S A DENTIST WHO HAS BEEN A FRIEND OF THE FAMILY FOR YEARS.
God, I do not want to do this.
ADDRESS BOOK
Eduardo, it is Sonya. How are you? If you're busy I'll call later...
I'm never too busy for you, precious. Where have you been?
I bet your teeth are beautiful. Have they stayed straight?
Yes, the braces worked, and they're straight. I need a favor, Eduardo...
...I need to borrow some money.
Does your father know you're calling me?
No, of course not. This is between you and me.
Well precious, and how are you going to pay Eduardo back?
I'll pay you back. I have a job. Please, Eduardo--I really need the money.

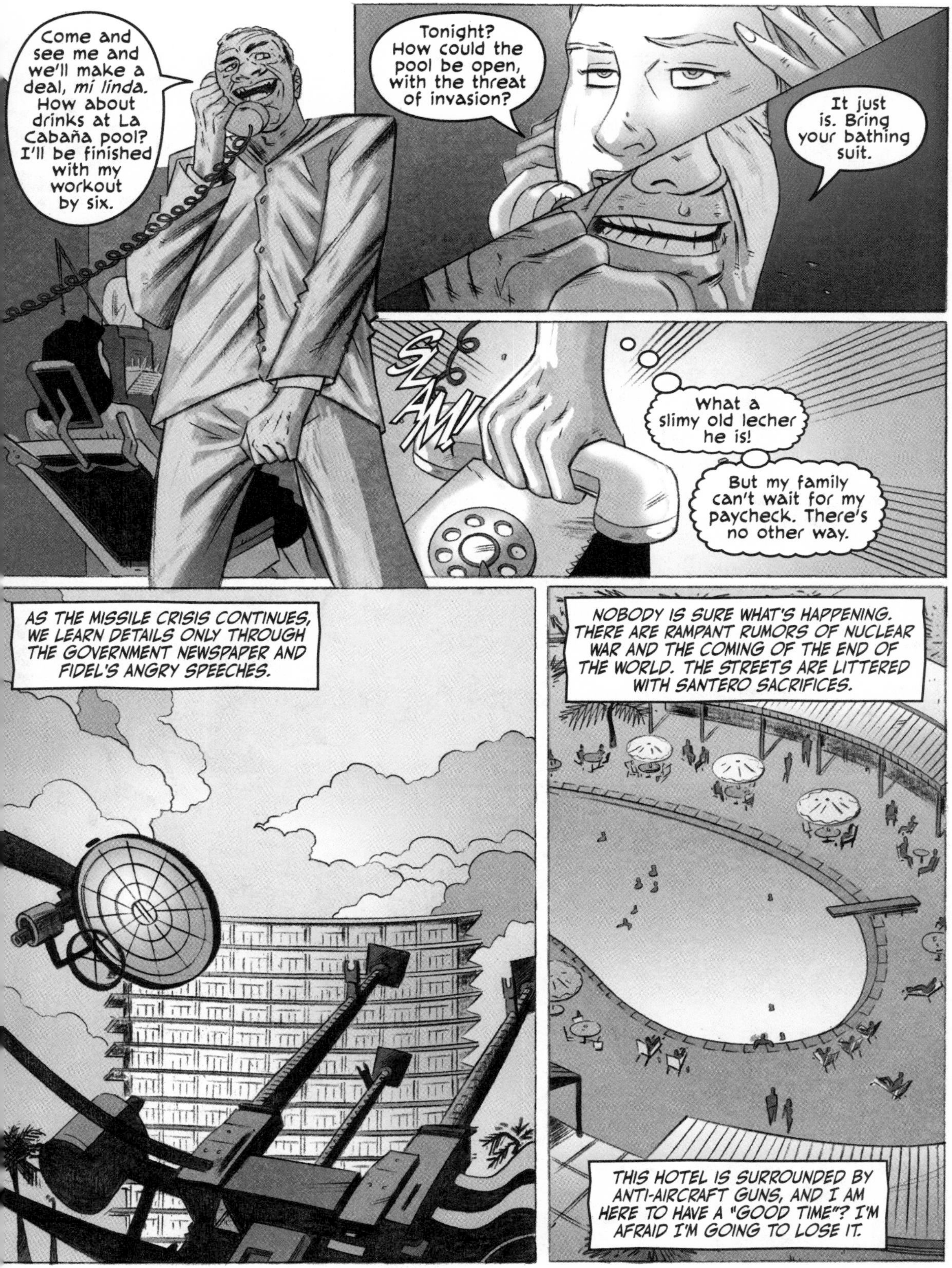

Come and see me and we'll make a deal, *mi linda.* How about drinks at La Cabaña pool? I'll be finished with my workout by six.
Tonight? How could the pool be open, with the threat of invasion?
It just is. Bring your bathing suit.
SLAM!
What a slimy old lecher he is!
But my family can't wait for my paycheck. There's no other way.
AS THE MISSILE CRISIS CONTINUES, WE LEARN DETAILS ONLY THROUGH THE GOVERNMENT NEWSPAPER AND FIDEL'S ANGRY SPEECHES.
NOBODY IS SURE WHAT'S HAPPENING. THERE ARE RAMPANT RUMORS OF NUCLEAR WAR AND THE COMING OF THE END OF THE WORLD. THE STREETS ARE LITTERED WITH SANTERO SACRIFICES.
THIS HOTEL IS SURROUNDED BY ANTI-AIRCRAFT GUNS, AND I AM HERE TO HAVE A "GOOD TIME"? I'M AFRAID I'M GOING TO LOSE IT.

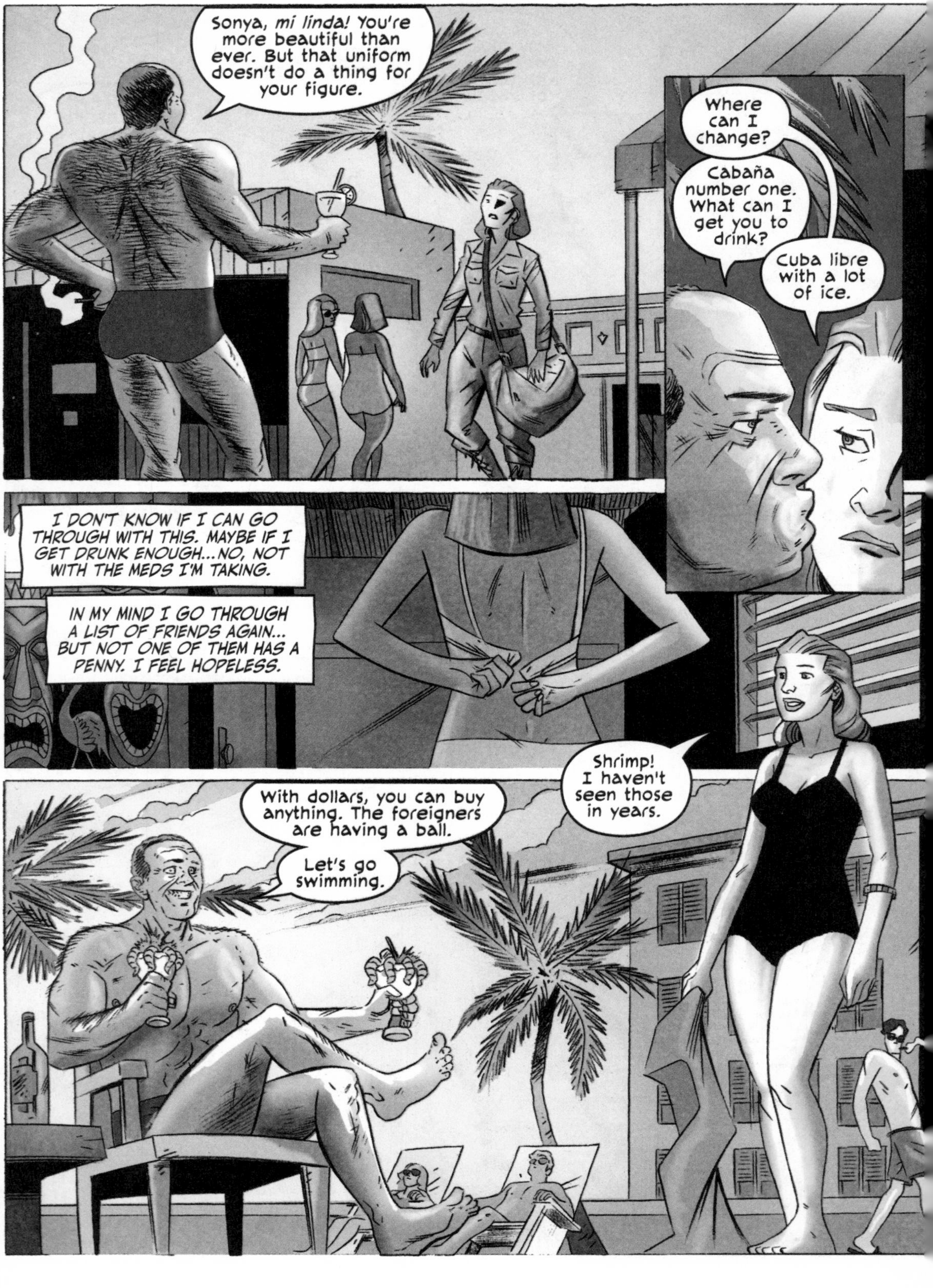
Sonya, *mi linda!* You're more beautiful than ever. But that uniform doesn't do a thing for your figure.
Where can I change?
Cabaña number one. What can I get you to drink?
Cuba libre with a lot of ice.
I DON'T KNOW IF I CAN GO THROUGH WITH THIS. MAYBE IF I GET DRUNK ENOUGH...NO, NOT WITH THE MEDS I'M TAKING.
IN MY MIND I GO THROUGH A LIST OF FRIENDS AGAIN... BUT NOT ONE OF THEM HAS A PENNY. I FEEL HOPELESS.
Shrimp! I haven't seen those in years.
With dollars, you can buy anything. The foreigners are having a ball.
Let's go swimming.

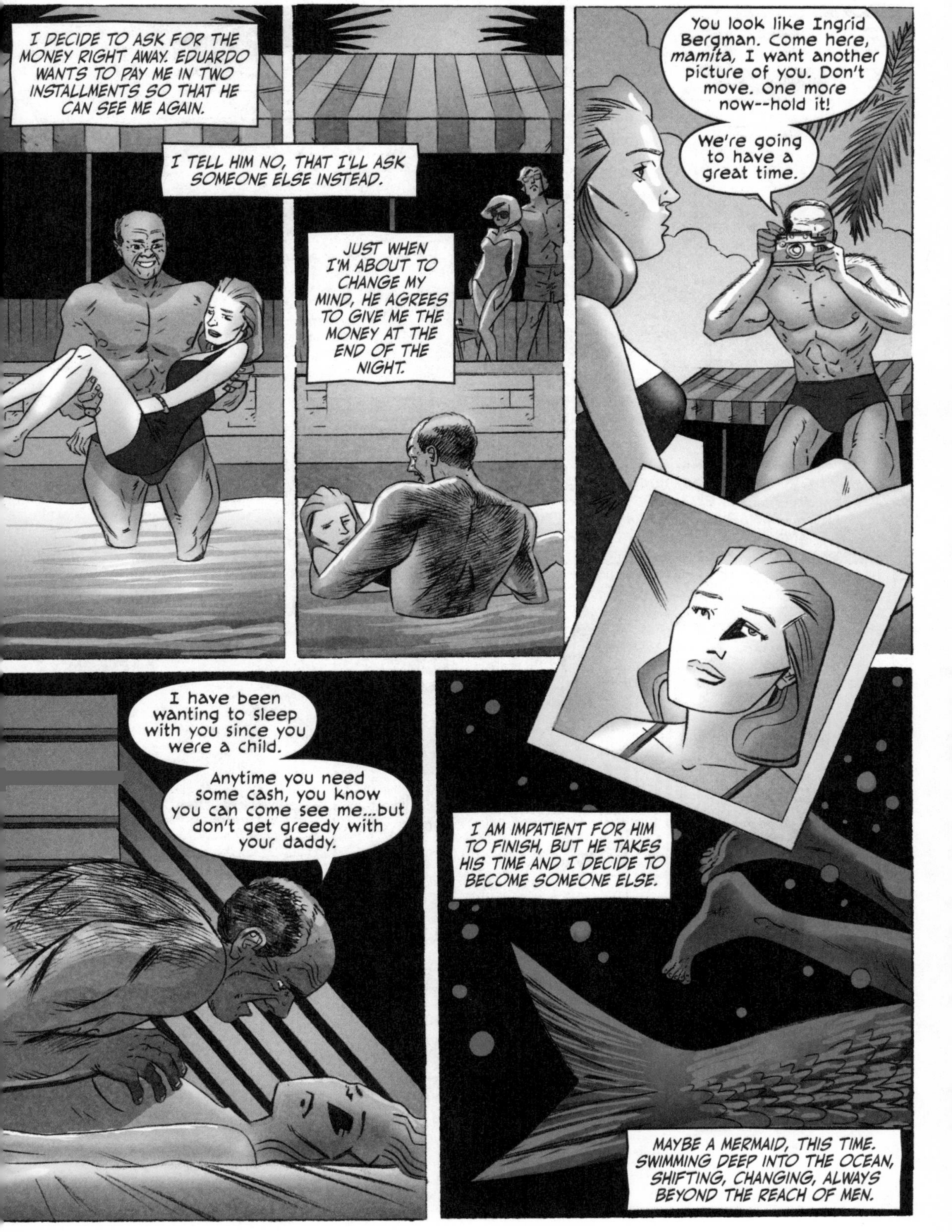
I DECIDE TO ASK FOR THE MONEY RIGHT AWAY. EDUARDO WANTS TO PAY ME IN TWO INSTALLMENTS SO THAT HE CAN SEE ME AGAIN.
I TELL HIM NO, THAT I'LL ASK SOMEONE ELSE INSTEAD.
JUST WHEN I'M ABOUT TO CHANGE MY MIND, HE AGREES TO GIVE ME THE MONEY AT THE END OF THE NIGHT.
You look like Ingrid Bergman. Come here, *mamita*, I want another picture of you. Don't move. One more now--hold it!
We're going to have a great time.
I have been wanting to sleep with you since you were a child.
Anytime you need some cash, you know you can come see me...but don't get greedy with your daddy.
I AM IMPATIENT FOR HIM TO FINISH, BUT HE TAKES HIS TIME AND I DECIDE TO BECOME SOMEONE ELSE.
MAYBE A MERMAID, THIS TIME. SWIMMING DEEP INTO THE OCEAN, SHIFTING, CHANGING, ALWAYS BEYOND THE REACH OF MEN.

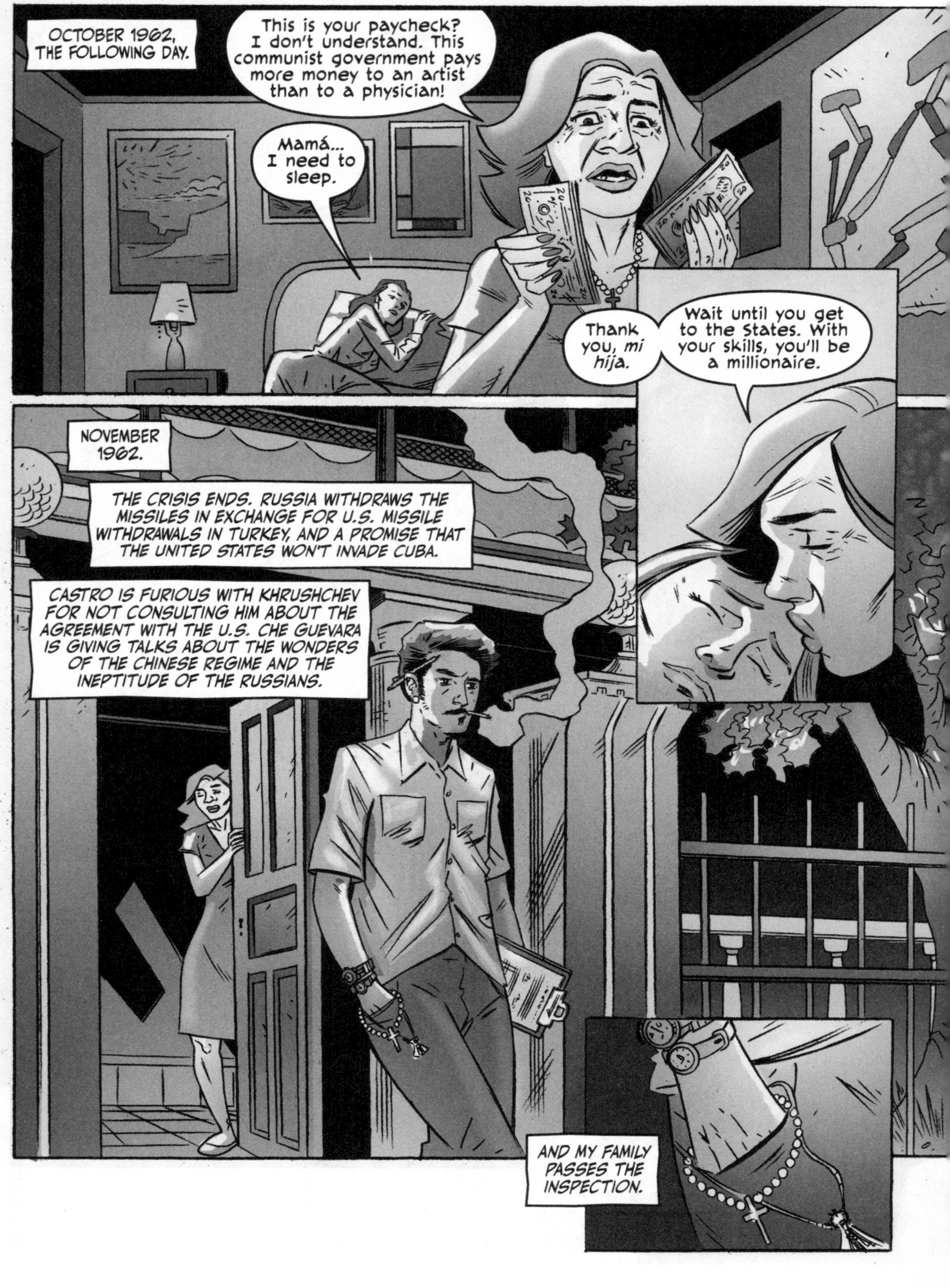
OCTOBER 1962, THE FOLLOWING DAY.
This is your paycheck? I don't understand. This communist government pays more money to an artist than to a physician!
Mamá... I need to sleep.
Wait until you get to the States. With your skills, you'll be a millionaire.
Thank you, *mi hija.*
NOVEMBER 1962.
THE CRISIS ENDS. RUSSIA WITHDRAWS THE MISSILES IN EXCHANGE FOR U.S. MISSILE WITHDRAWALS IN TURKEY, AND A PROMISE THAT THE UNITED STATES WON'T INVADE CUBA.
CASTRO IS FURIOUS WITH KHRUSHCHEV FOR NOT CONSULTING HIM ABOUT THE AGREEMENT WITH THE U.S. CHE GUEVARA IS GIVING TALKS ABOUT THE WONDERS OF THE CHINESE REGIME AND THE INEPTITUDE OF THE RUSSIANS.
AND MY FAMILY PASSES THE INSPECTION.

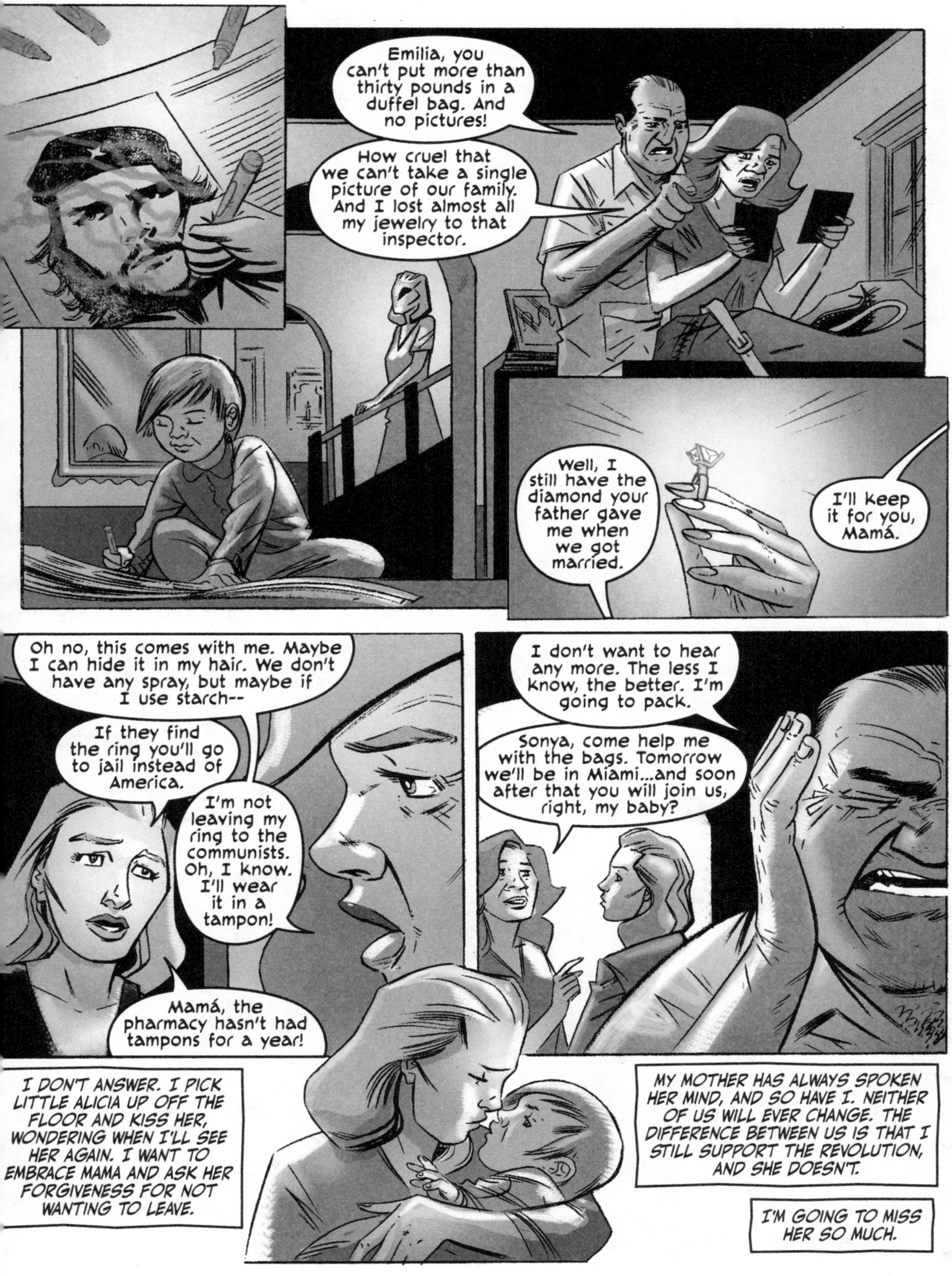

Emilia, you can't put more than thirty pounds in a duffel bag. And no pictures!
How cruel that we can't take a single picture of our family. And I lost almost all my jewelry to that inspector.
Well, I still have the diamond your father gave me when we got married.
I'll keep it for you, Mamá.
Oh no, this comes with me. Maybe I can hide it in my hair. We don't have any spray, but maybe if I use starch--
If they find the ring you'll go to jail instead of America.
I'm not leaving my ring to the communists. Oh, I know. I'll wear it in a tampon!
Mamá, the pharmacy hasn't had tampons for a year!
I don't want to hear any more. The less I know, the better. I'm going to pack.
Sonya, come help me with the bags. Tomorrow we'll be in Miami...and soon after that you will join us, right, my baby?
I DON'T ANSWER. I PICK LITTLE ALICIA UP OFF THE FLOOR AND KISS HER, WONDERING WHEN I'LL SEE HER AGAIN. I WANT TO EMBRACE MAMA AND ASK HER FORGIVENESS FOR NOT WANTING TO LEAVE.
MY MOTHER HAS ALWAYS SPOKEN HER MIND, AND SO HAVE I. NEITHER OF US WILL EVER CHANGE. THE DIFFERENCE BETWEEN US IS THAT I STILL SUPPORT THE REVOLUTION, AND SHE DOESN'T.
I'M GOING TO MISS HER SO MUCH.

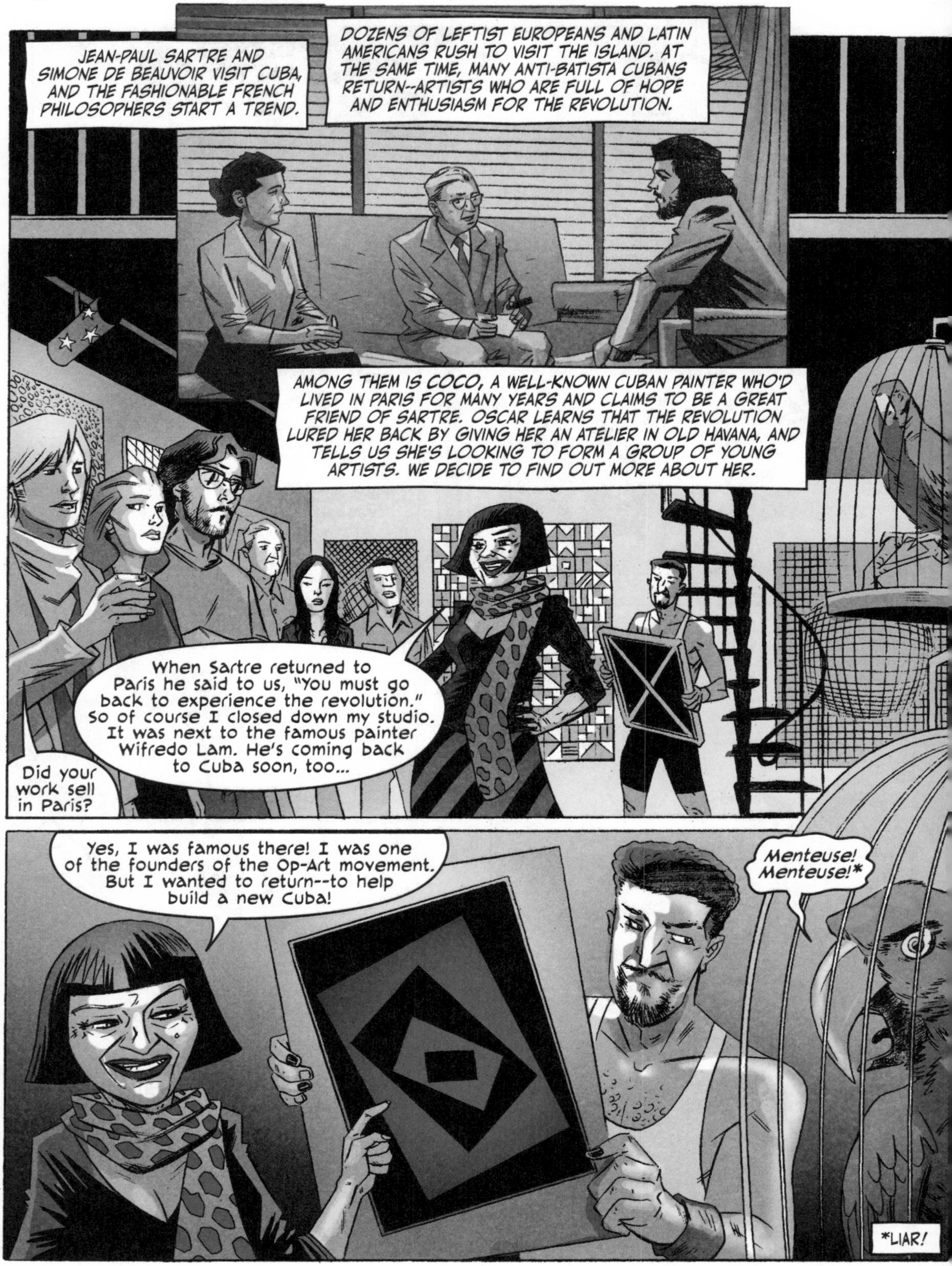

JEAN-PAUL SARTRE AND SIMONE DE BEAUVOIR VISIT CUBA, AND THE FASHIONABLE FRENCH PHILOSOPHERS START A TREND.
DOZENS OF LEFTIST EUROPEANS AND LATIN AMERICANS RUSH TO VISIT THE ISLAND. AT THE SAME TIME, MANY ANTI-BATISTA CUBANS RETURN--ARTISTS WHO ARE FULL OF HOPE AND ENTHUSIASM FOR THE REVOLUTION.
AMONG THEM IS COCO, A WELL-KNOWN CUBAN PAINTER WHO'D LIVED IN PARIS FOR MANY YEARS AND CLAIMS TO BE A GREAT FRIEND OF SARTRE. OSCAR LEARNS THAT THE REVOLUTION LURED HER BACK BY GIVING HER AN ATELIER IN OLD HAVANA, AND TELLS US SHE'S LOOKING TO FORM A GROUP OF YOUNG ARTISTS. WE DECIDE TO FIND OUT MORE ABOUT HER.
When Sartre returned to Paris he said to us, "You must go back to experience the revolution." So of course I closed down my studio. It was next to the famous painter Wifredo Lam. He's coming back to Cuba soon, too...
Did your work sell in Paris?
Yes, I was famous there! I was one of the founders of the Op-Art movement. But I wanted to return--to help build a new Cuba!
Menteuse! Menteuse!*
*LIAR!

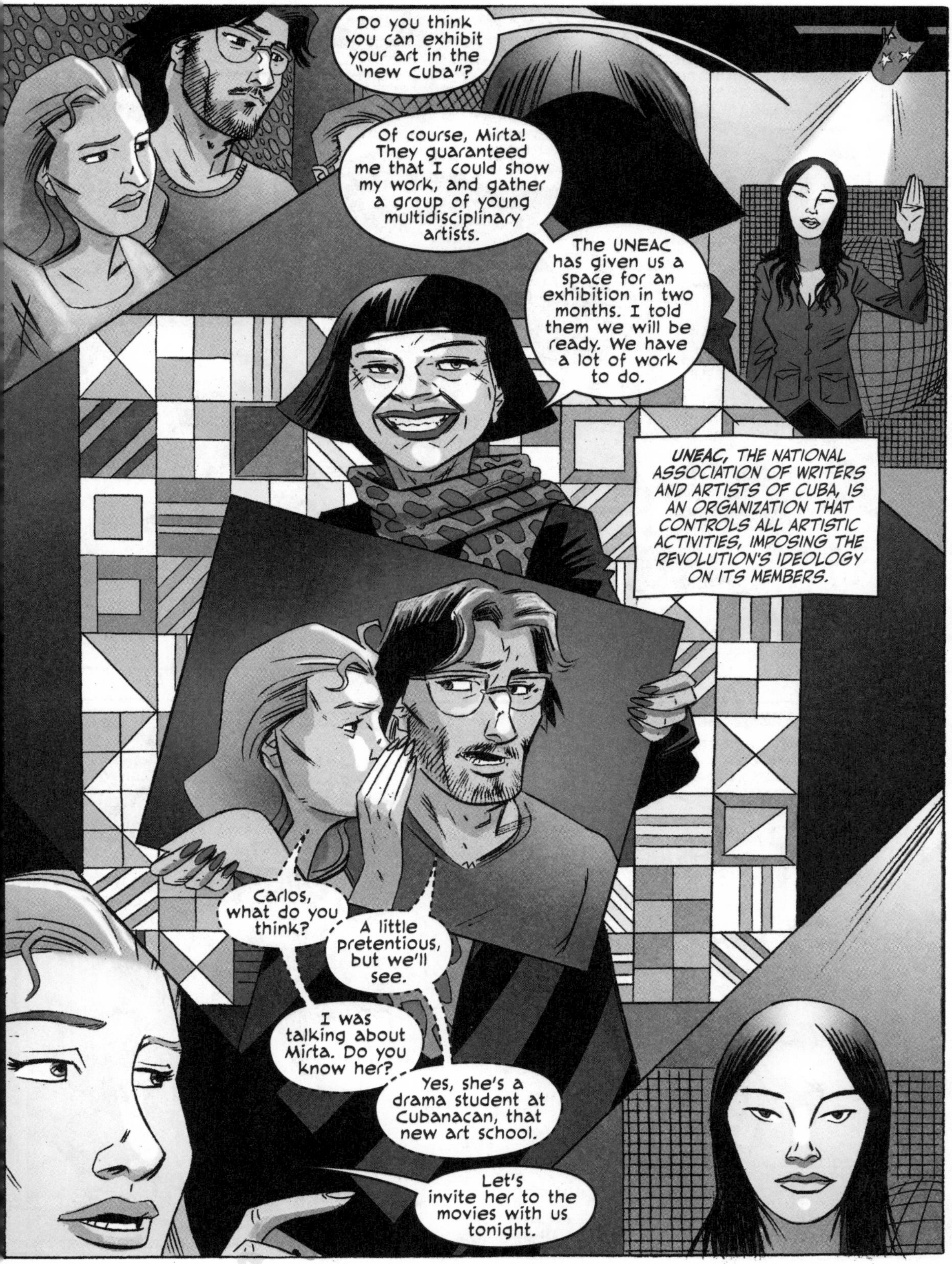
Do you think you can exhibit your art in the "new Cuba"?
Of course, Mirta! They guaranteed me that I could show my work, and gather a group of young multidisciplinary artists.
The UNEAC has given us a space for an exhibition in two months. I told them we will be ready. We have a lot of work to do.
UNEAC, THE NATIONAL ASSOCIATION OF WRITERS AND ARTISTS OF CUBA, IS AN ORGANIZATION THAT CONTROLS ALL ARTISTIC ACTIVITIES, IMPOSING THE REVOLUTION'S IDEOLOGY ON ITS MEMBERS.
Carlos, what do you think?
A little pretentious, but we'll see.
I was talking about Mirta. Do you know her?
Yes, she's a drama student at Cubanacan, that new art school.
Let's invite her to the movies with us tonight.

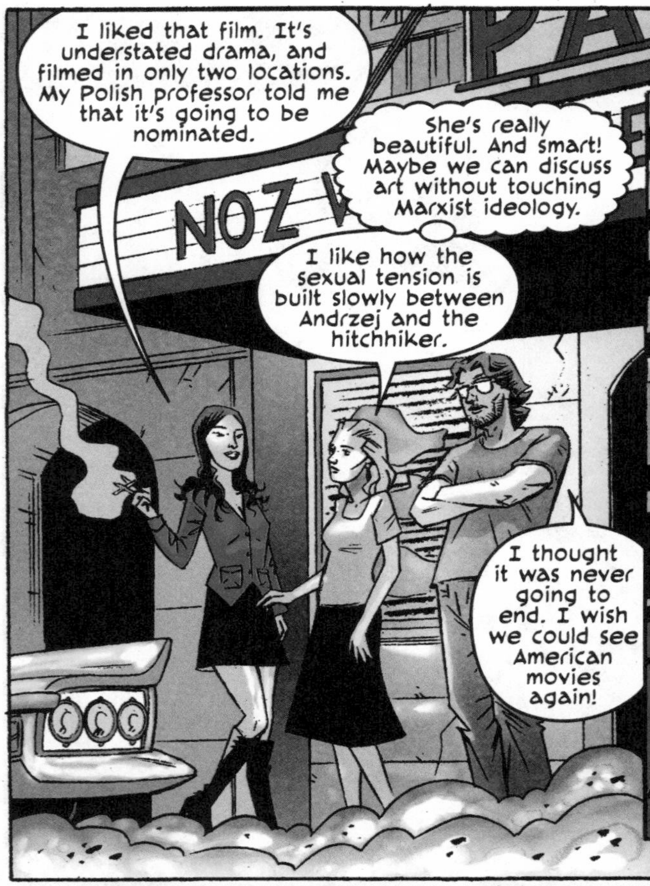

I liked that film. It's understated drama, and filmed in only two locations. My Polish professor told me that it's going to be nominated.
She's really beautiful. And smart! Maybe we can discuss art without touching Marxist ideology.
I like how the sexual tension is built slowly between Andrzej and the hitchhiker.
I thought it was never going to end. I wish we could see American movies again!
NOZ

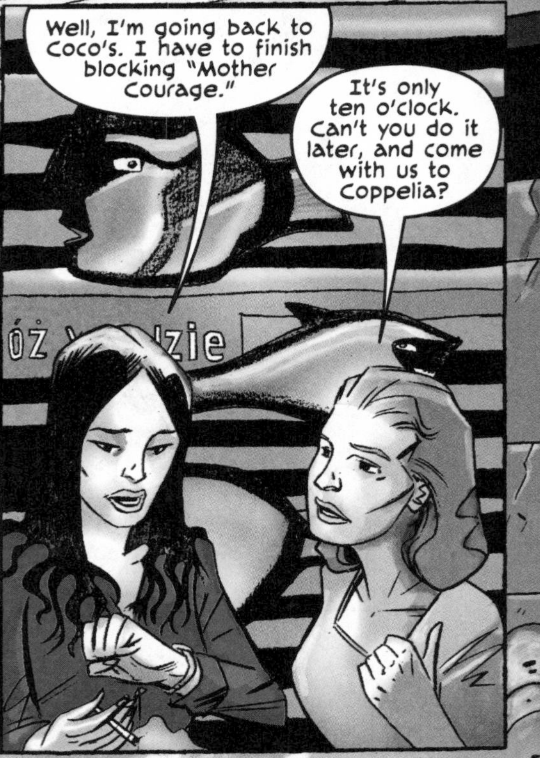

Well, I'm going back to Coco's. I have to finish blocking "Mother Courage."
It's only ten o'clock. Can't you do it later, and come with us to Coppelia?

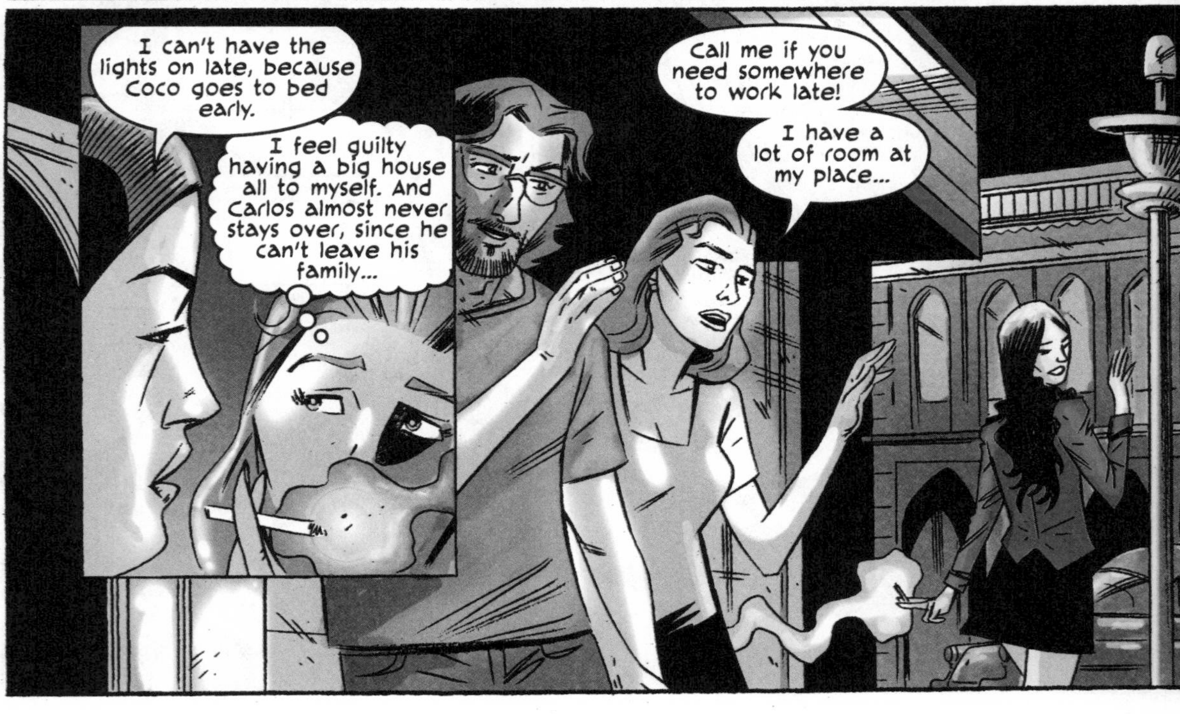

I can't have the lights on late, because Coco goes to bed early.
I feel guilty having a big house all to myself. And Carlos almost never stays over, since he can't leave his family...
Call me if you need somewhere to work late!
I have a lot of room at my place...

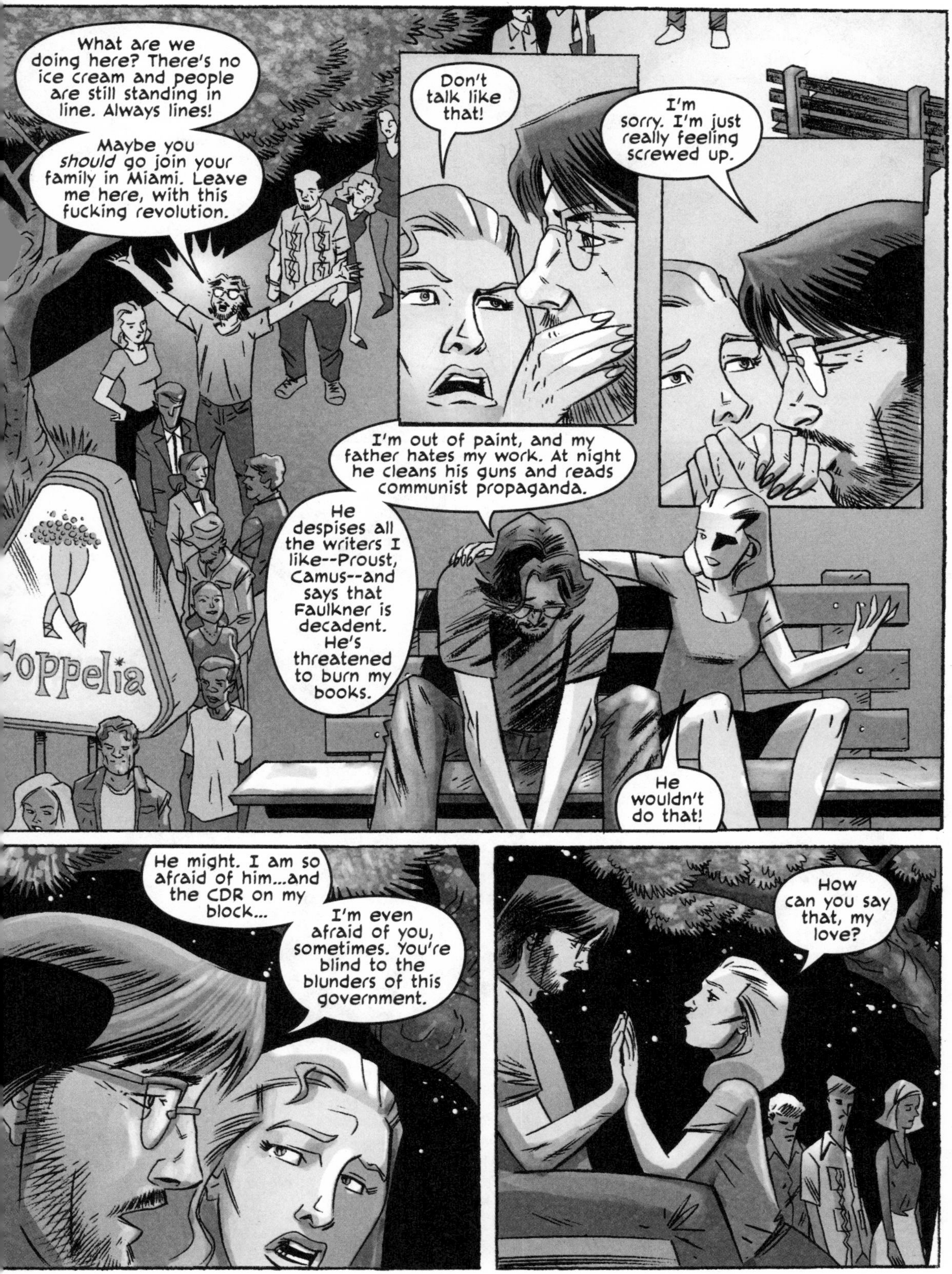
What are we doing here? There's no ice cream and people are still standing in line. Always lines!
Maybe you *should* go join your family in Miami. Leave me here, with this fucking revolution.
Coppelia
Don't talk like that!
I'm sorry. I'm just really feeling screwed up.
I'm out of paint, and my father hates my work. At night he cleans his guns and reads communist propaganda.
He despises all the writers I like--Proust, Camus--and says that Faulkner is decadent. He's threatened to burn my books.
He wouldn't do that!
He might. I am so afraid of him...and the CDR on my block...
I'm even afraid of you, sometimes. You're blind to the blunders of this government.
How can you say that, my love?

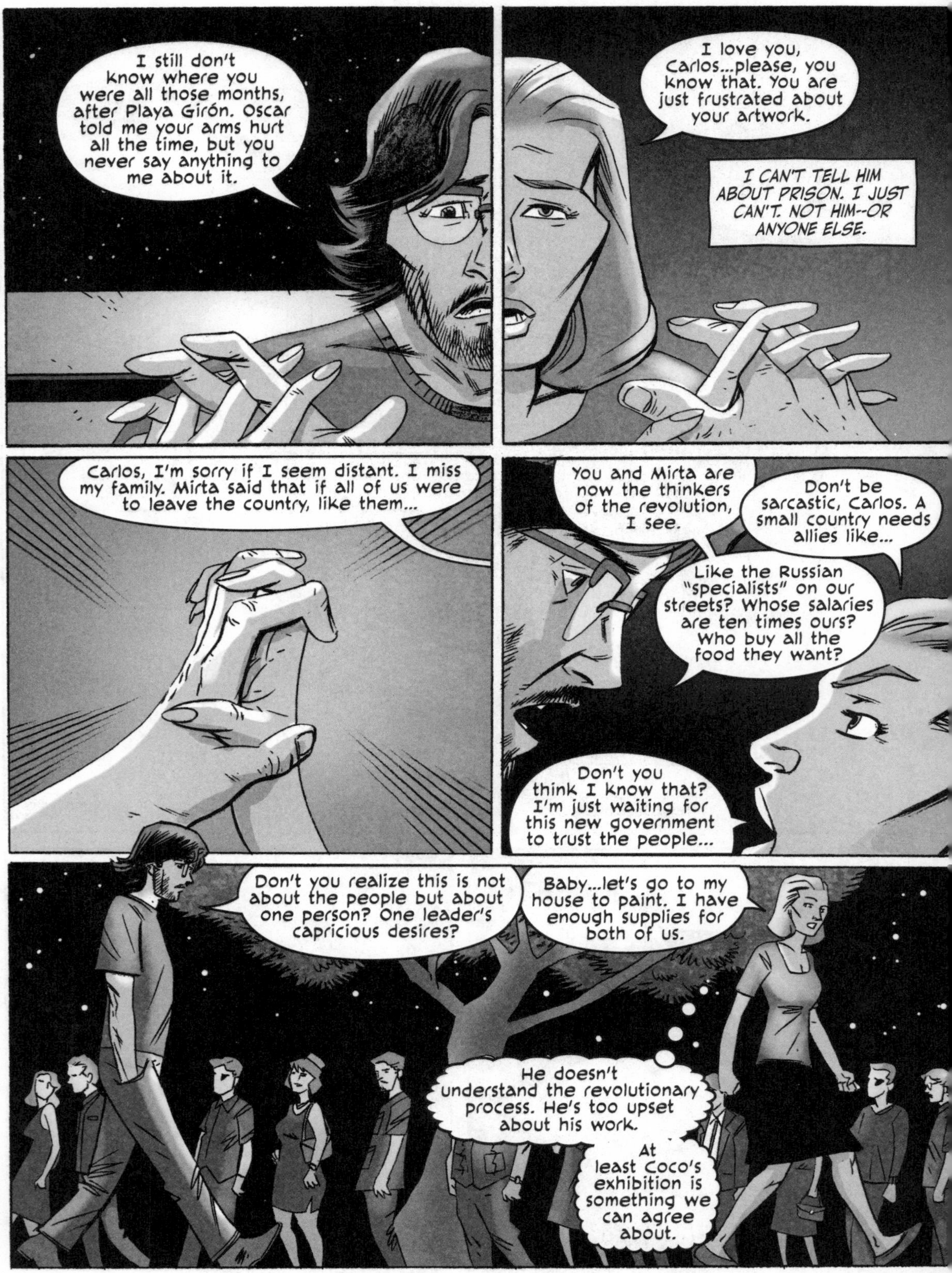
I still don't know where you were all those months, after Playa Girón. Oscar told me your arms hurt all the time, but you never say anything to me about it.
I love you, Carlos...please, you know that. You are just frustrated about your artwork.
I CAN'T TELL HIM ABOUT PRISON. I JUST CAN'T. NOT HIM--OR ANYONE ELSE.
Carlos, I'm sorry if I seem distant. I miss my family. Mirta said that if all of us were to leave the country, like them...
You and Mirta are now the thinkers of the revolution, I see.
Don't be sarcastic, Carlos. A small country needs allies like...
Like the Russian "specialists" on our streets? Whose salaries are ten times ours? Who buy all the food they want?
Don't you think I know that? I'm just waiting for this new government to trust the people...
Don't you realize this is not about the people but about one person? One leader's capricious desires?
Baby...let's go to my house to paint. I have enough supplies for both of us.
He doesn't understand the revolutionary process. He's too upset about his work.
At least Coco's exhibition is something we can agree about.

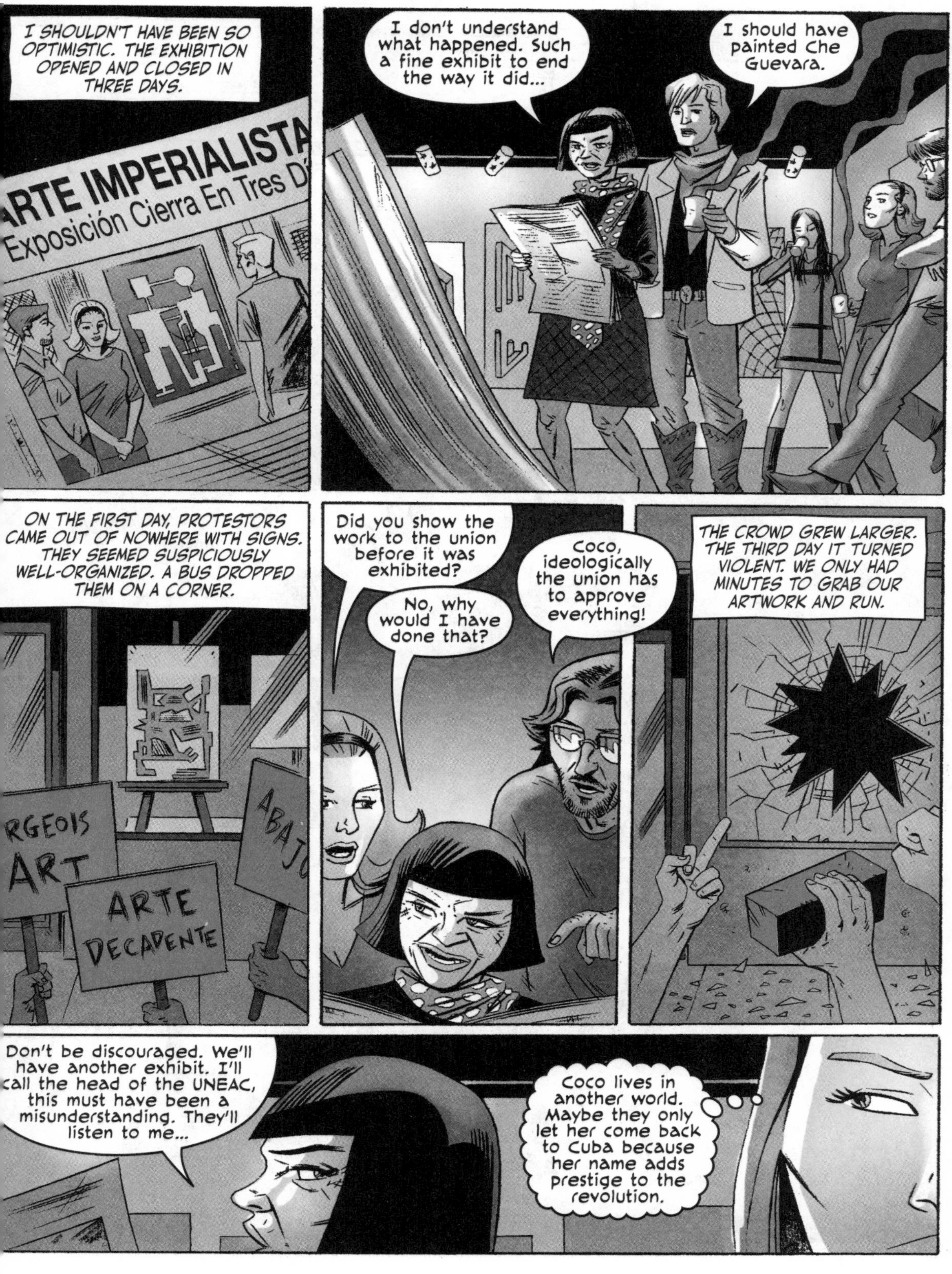

I SHOULDN'T HAVE BEEN SO OPTIMISTIC. THE EXHIBITION OPENED AND CLOSED IN THREE DAYS.
ARTE IMPERIALISTA
Exposición Cierra En Tres D
I don't understand what happened. Such a fine exhibit to end the way it did...
I should have painted Che Guevara.
ON THE FIRST DAY, PROTESTORS CAME OUT OF NOWHERE WITH SIGNS. THEY SEEMED SUSPICIOUSLY WELL-ORGANIZED. A BUS DROPPED THEM ON A CORNER.
RGEOIS ART
ABAJO
ARTE DECADENTE
Did you show the work to the union before it was exhibited?
No, why would I have done that?
Coco, ideologically the union has to approve everything!
THE CROWD GREW LARGER. THE THIRD DAY IT TURNED VIOLENT. WE ONLY HAD MINUTES TO GRAB OUR ARTWORK AND RUN.
Don't be discouraged. We'll have another exhibit. I'll call the head of the UNEAC, this must have been a misunderstanding. They'll listen to me...
Coco lives in another world. Maybe they only let her come back to Cuba because her name adds prestige to the revolution.

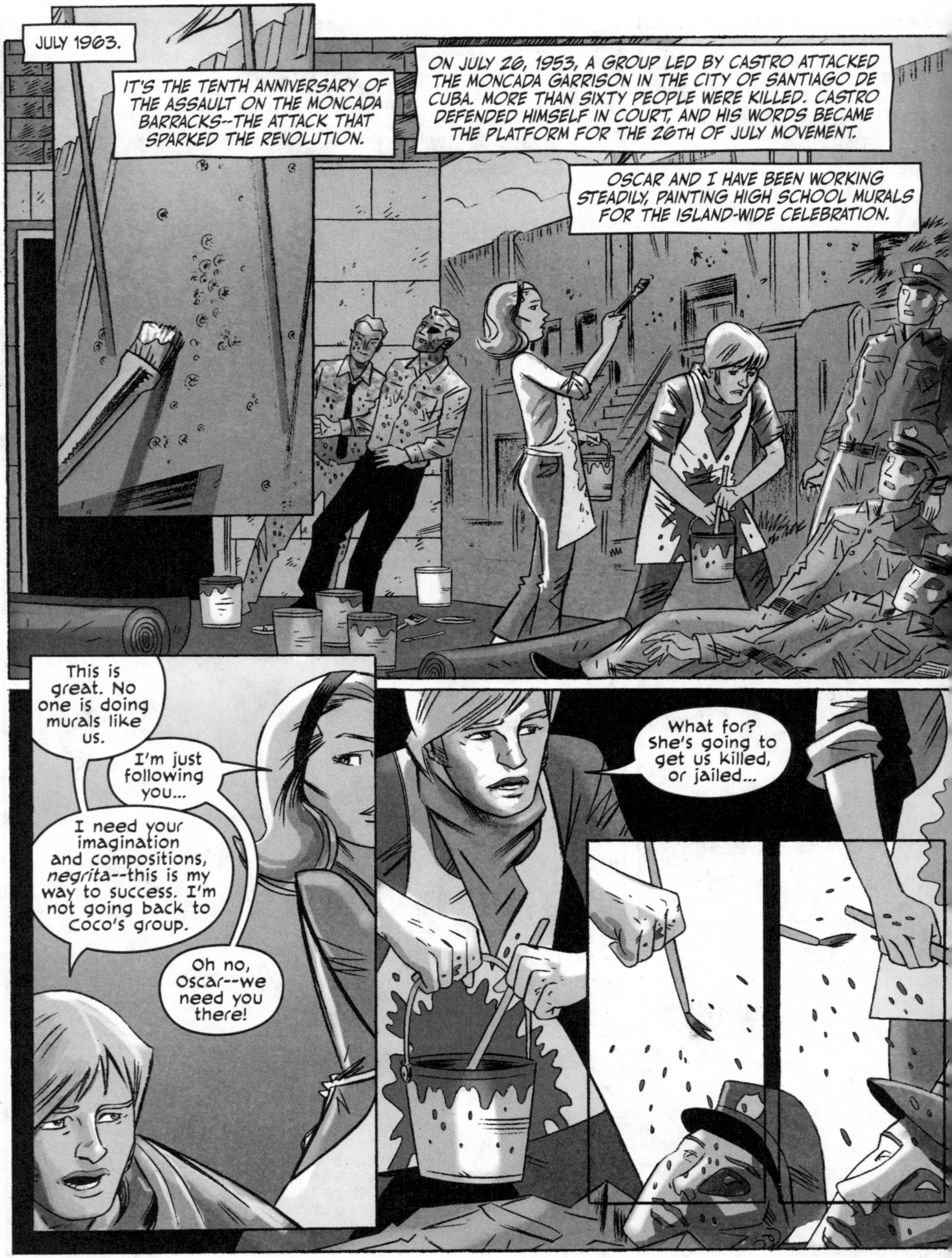
JULY 1963.
IT'S THE TENTH ANNIVERSARY OF THE ASSAULT ON THE MONCADA BARRACKS--THE ATTACK THAT SPARKED THE REVOLUTION.
ON JULY 26, 1953, A GROUP LED BY CASTRO ATTACKED THE MONCADA GARRISON IN THE CITY OF SANTIAGO DE CUBA. MORE THAN SIXTY PEOPLE WERE KILLED. CASTRO DEFENDED HIMSELF IN COURT, AND HIS WORDS BECAME THE PLATFORM FOR THE 26TH OF JULY MOVEMENT.
OSCAR AND I HAVE BEEN WORKING STEADILY, PAINTING HIGH SCHOOL MURALS FOR THE ISLAND-WIDE CELEBRATION.
This is great. No one is doing murals like us.
I'm just following you...
I need your imagination and compositions, *negrita*--this is my way to success. I'm not going back to Coco's group.
Oh no, Oscar--we need you there!
What for? She's going to get us killed, or jailed...

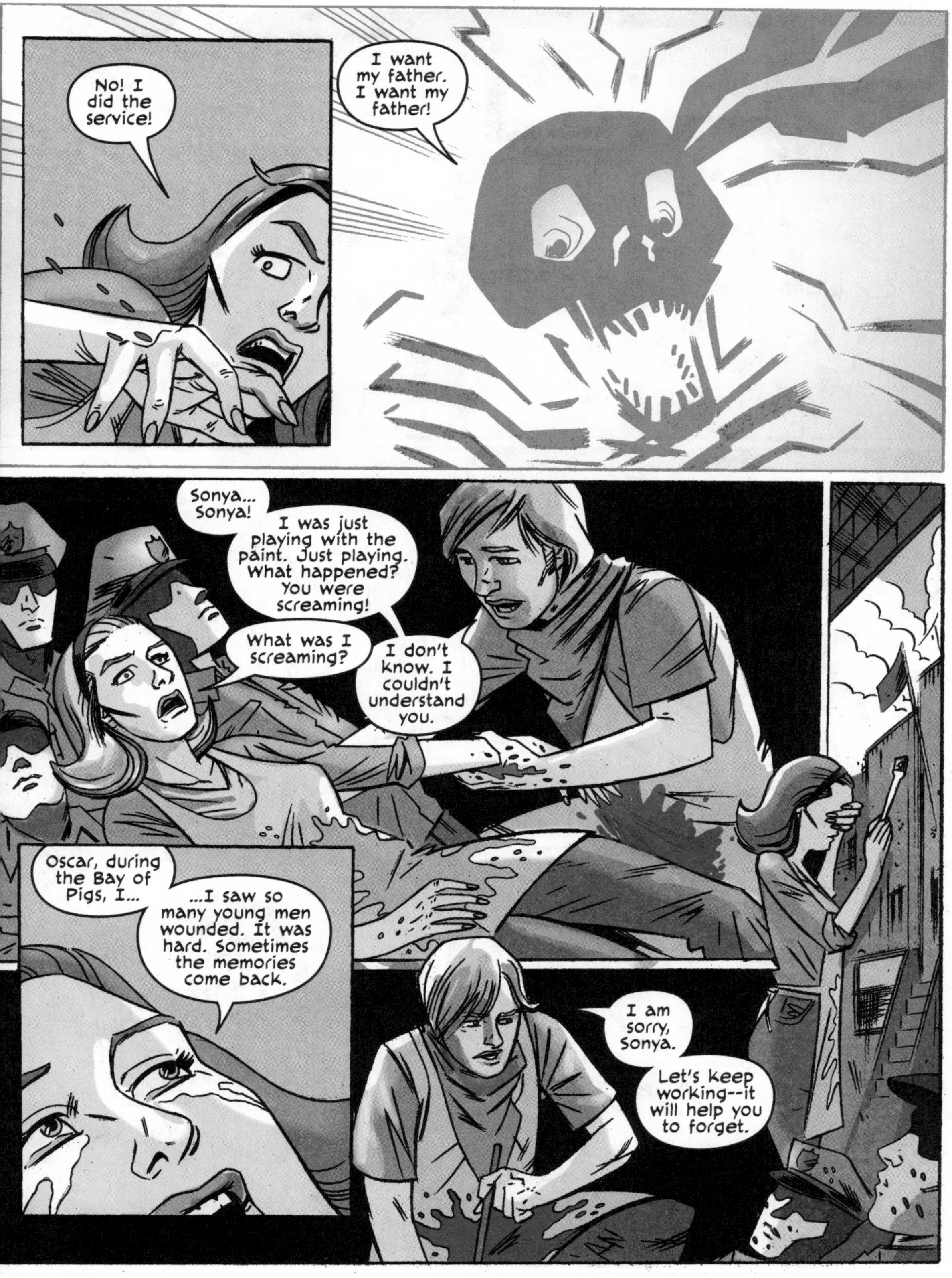
No! I did the service!
I want my father. I want my father!
Sonya... Sonya!
I was just playing with the paint. Just playing. What happened? You were screaming!
What was I screaming?
I don't know. I couldn't understand you.
Oscar, during the Bay of Pigs, I...
...I saw so many young men wounded. It was hard. Sometimes the memories come back.
I am sorry, Sonya.
Let's keep working--it will help you to forget.

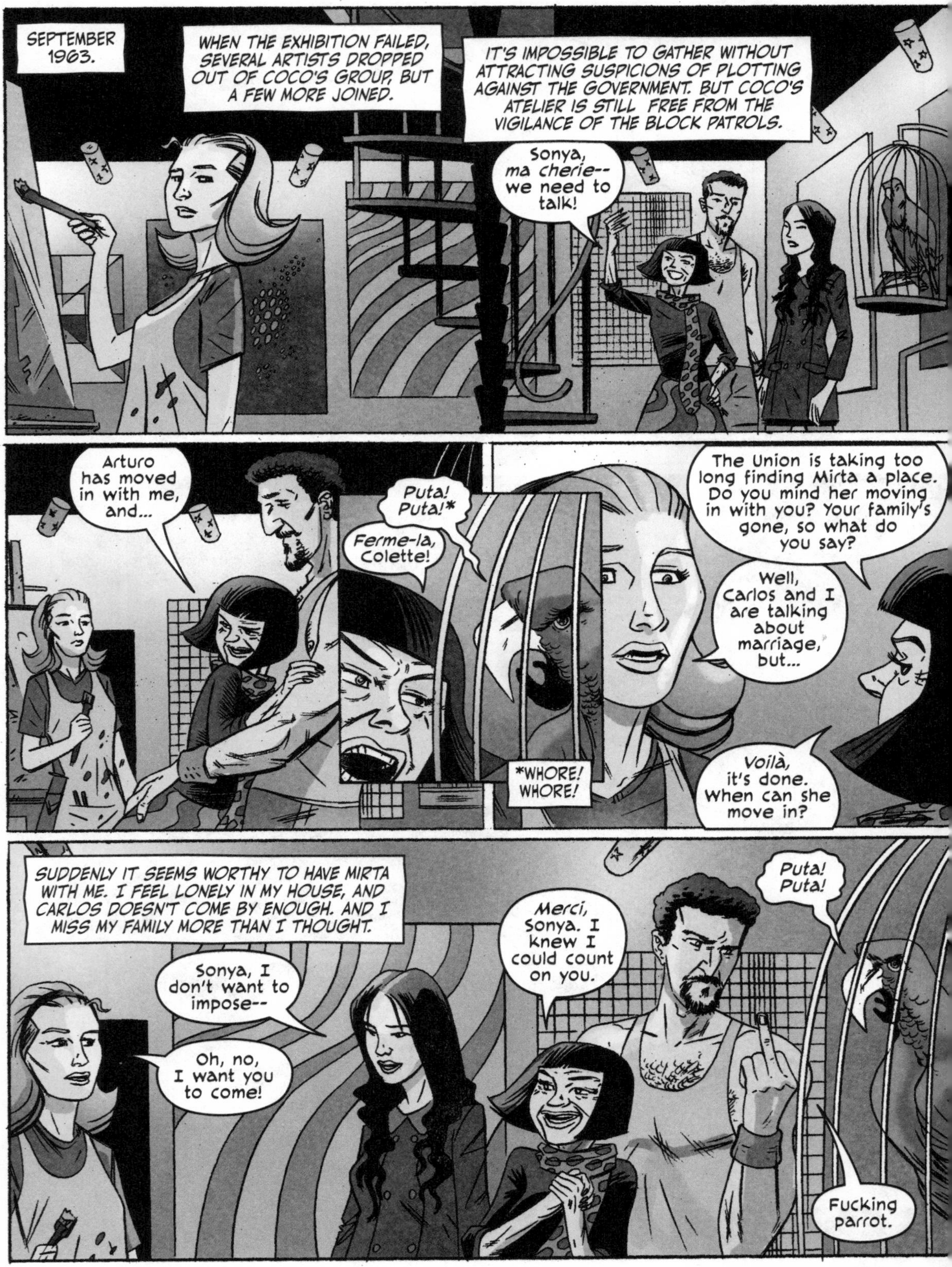

SEPTEMBER 1963.
WHEN THE EXHIBITION FAILED, SEVERAL ARTISTS DROPPED OUT OF COCO'S GROUP, BUT A FEW MORE JOINED.
IT'S IMPOSSIBLE TO GATHER WITHOUT ATTRACTING SUSPICIONS OF PLOTTING AGAINST THE GOVERNMENT. BUT COCO'S ATELIER IS STILL FREE FROM THE VIGILANCE OF THE BLOCK PATROLS.
Sonya, ma cherie-- we need to talk!
Arturo has moved in with me, and...
Puta! Puta!*
Ferme-la, Colette!
*WHORE! WHORE!
The Union is taking too long finding Mirta a place. Do you mind her moving in with you? Your family's gone, so what do you say?
Well, Carlos and I are talking about marriage, but...
Voilà, it's done. When can she move in?
SUDDENLY IT SEEMS WORTHY TO HAVE MIRTA WITH ME. I FEEL LONELY IN MY HOUSE, AND CARLOS DOESN'T COME BY ENOUGH. AND I MISS MY FAMILY MORE THAN I THOUGHT.
Sonya, I don't want to impose--
Oh, no, I want you to come!
Merci, Sonya. I knew I could count on you.
Puta! Puta!
Fucking parrot.

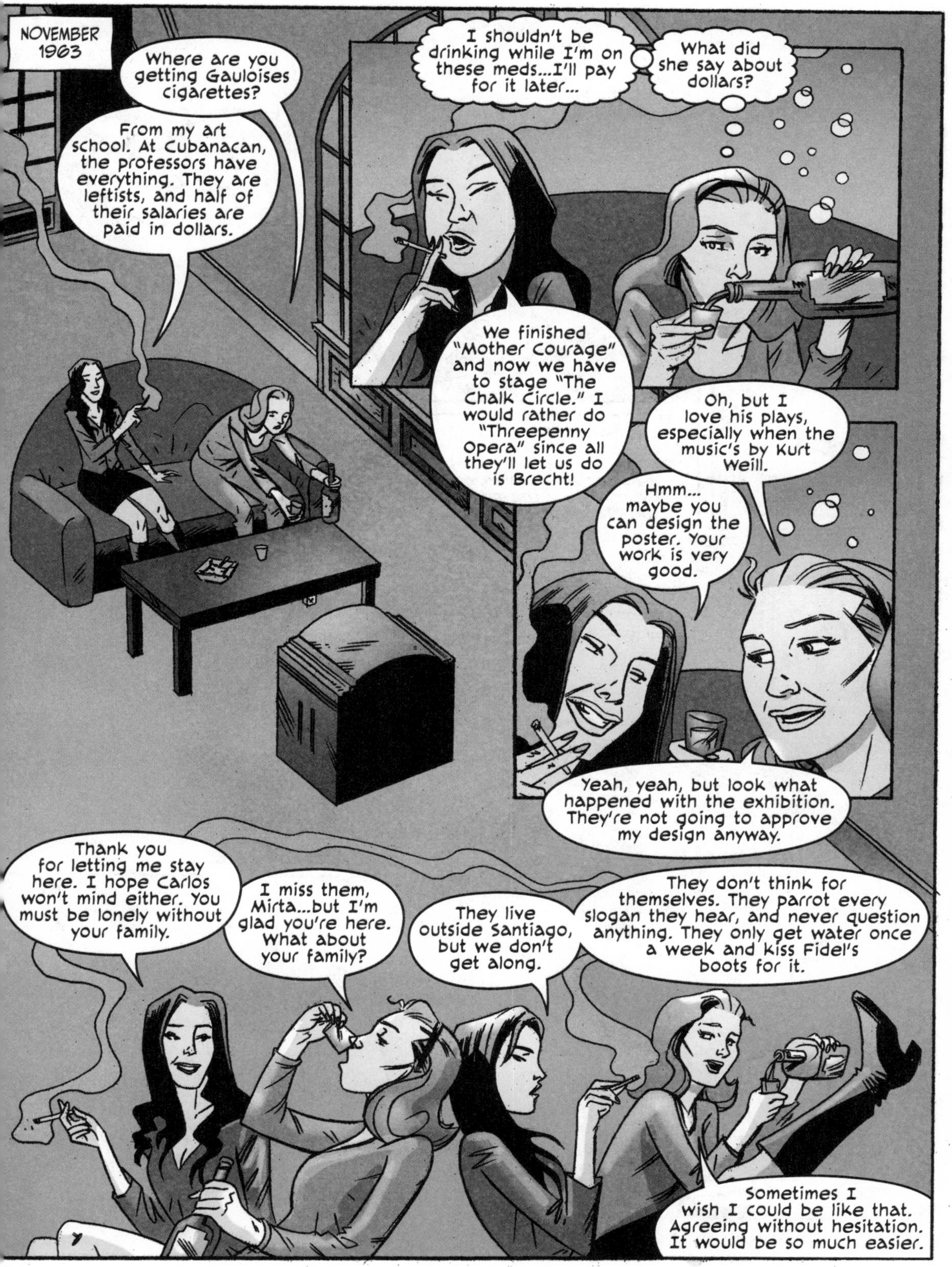
NOVEMBER 1963
Where are you getting Gauloises cigarettes?
From my art school. At Cubanacan, the professors have everything. They are leftists, and half of their salaries are paid in dollars.
I shouldn't be drinking while I'm on these meds...I'll pay for it later...
What did she say about dollars?
We finished "Mother Courage" and now we have to stage "The Chalk Circle." I would rather do "Threepenny Opera" since all they'll let us do is Brecht!
Oh, but I love his plays, especially when the music's by Kurt Weill.
Hmm... maybe you can design the poster. Your work is very good.
Yeah, yeah, but look what happened with the exhibition. They're not going to approve my design anyway.
Thank you for letting me stay here. I hope Carlos won't mind either. You must be lonely without your family.
I miss them, Mirta...but I'm glad you're here. What about your family?
They live outside Santiago, but we don't get along.
They don't think for themselves. They parrot every slogan they hear, and never question anything. They only get water once a week and kiss Fidel's boots for it.
Sometimes I wish I could be like that. Agreeing without hesitation. It would be so much easier.

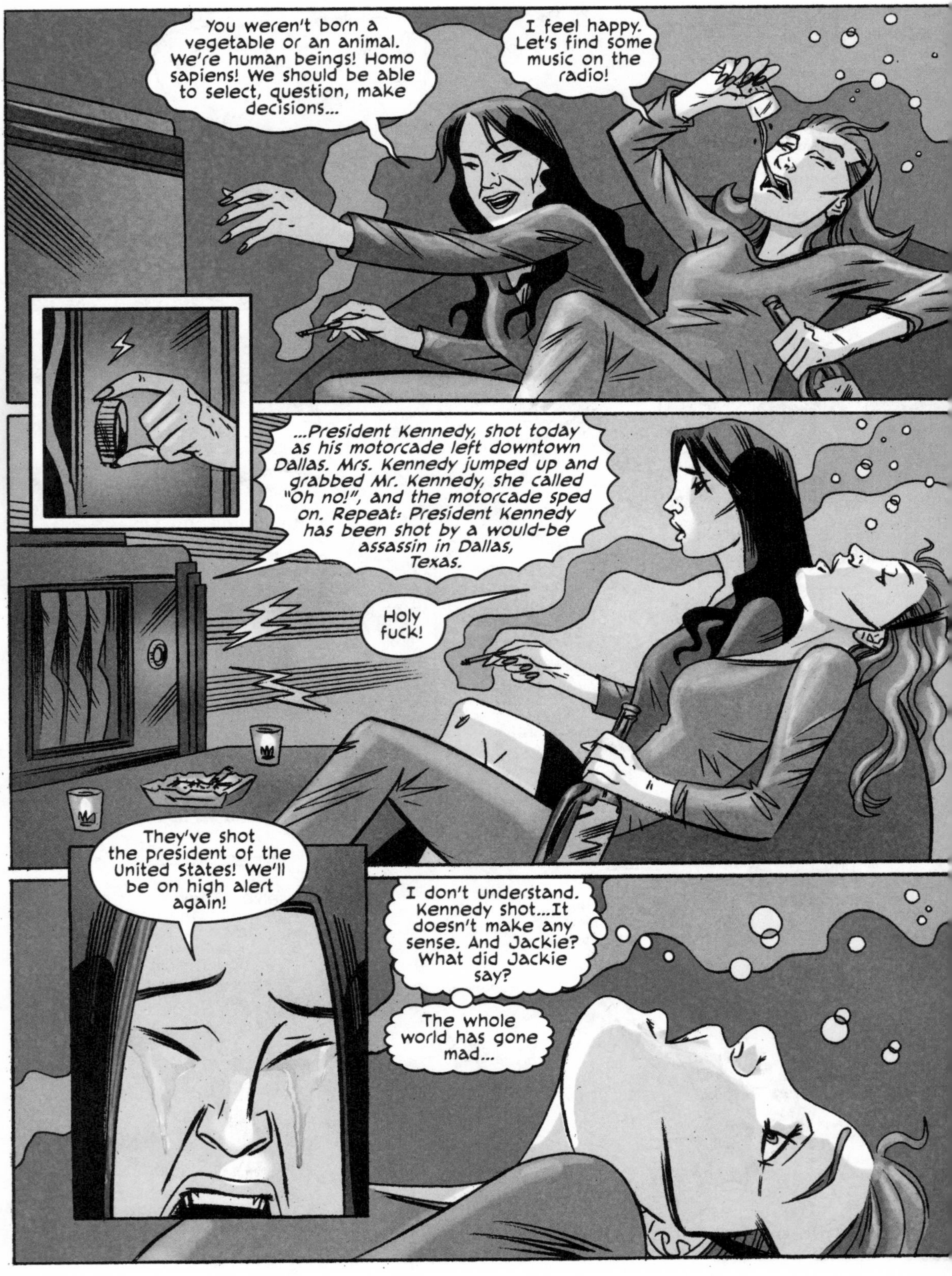
You weren't born a vegetable or an animal. We're human beings! Homo sapiens! We should be able to select, question, make decisions...
I feel happy. Let's find some music on the radio!
...President Kennedy, shot today as his motorcade left downtown Dallas. Mrs. Kennedy jumped up and grabbed Mr. Kennedy, she called "Oh no!", and the motorcade sped on. Repeat: President Kennedy has been shot by a would-be assassin in Dallas, Texas.
Holy fuck!
They've shot the president of the United States! We'll be on high alert again!
I don't understand. Kennedy shot...It doesn't make any sense. And Jackie? What did Jackie say?
The whole world has gone mad...

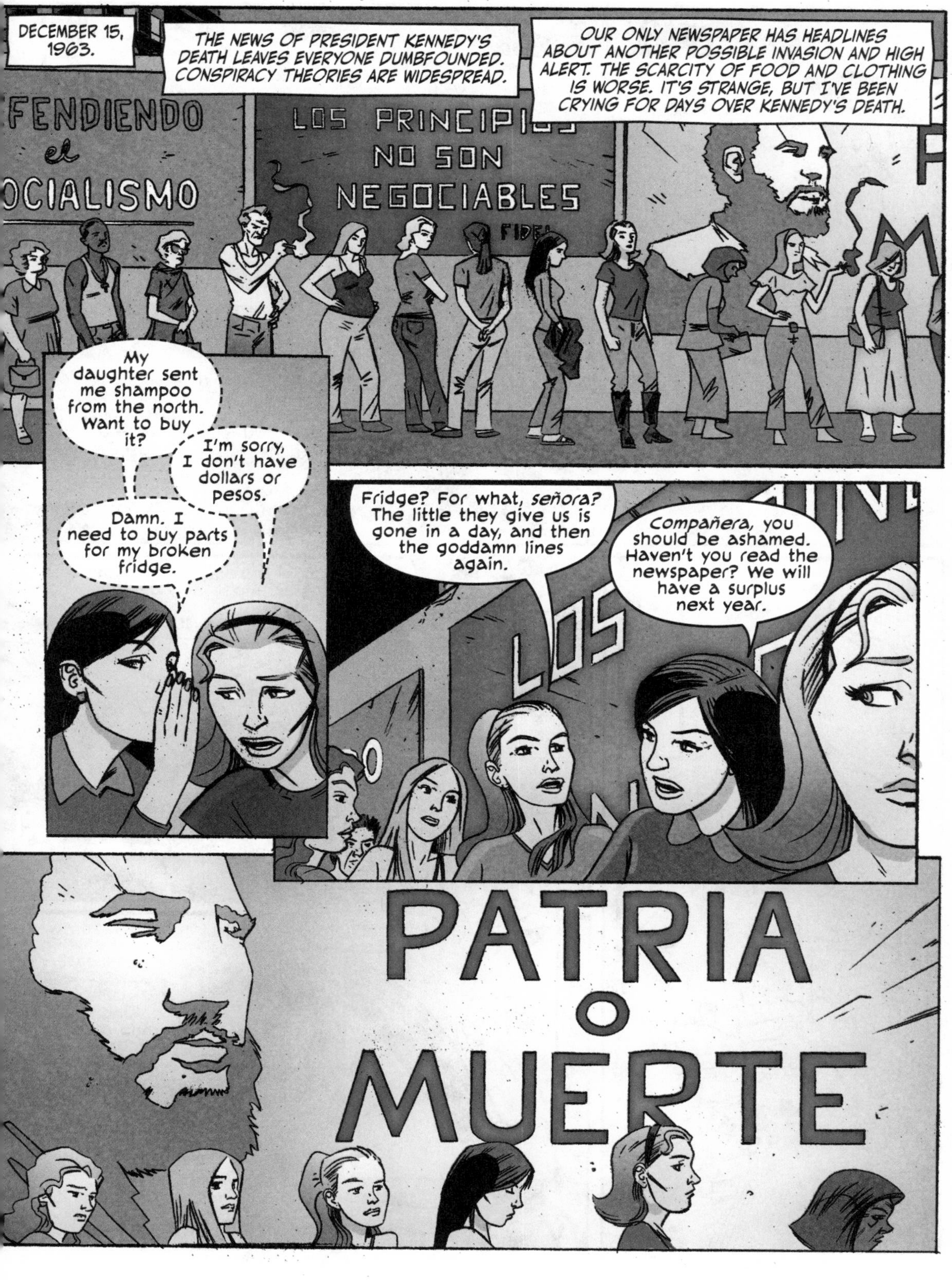
DECEMBER 15, 1963.
THE NEWS OF PRESIDENT KENNEDY'S DEATH LEAVES EVERYONE DUMBFOUNDED. CONSPIRACY THEORIES ARE WIDESPREAD.
OUR ONLY NEWSPAPER HAS HEADLINES ABOUT ANOTHER POSSIBLE INVASION AND HIGH ALERT. THE SCARCITY OF FOOD AND CLOTHING IS WORSE. IT'S STRANGE, BUT I'VE BEEN CRYING FOR DAYS OVER KENNEDY'S DEATH.
FENDIENDO el OCIALISMO
LOS PRINCIPIOS NO SON NEGOCIABLES
FIDEL
My daughter sent me shampoo from the north. Want to buy it?
I'm sorry, I don't have dollars or pesos.
Damn. I need to buy parts for my broken fridge.
Fridge? For what, *señora*? The little they give us is gone in a day, and then the goddamn lines again.
Compañera, you should be ashamed. Haven't you read the newspaper? We will have a surplus next year.
LOS
PATRIA O MUERTE

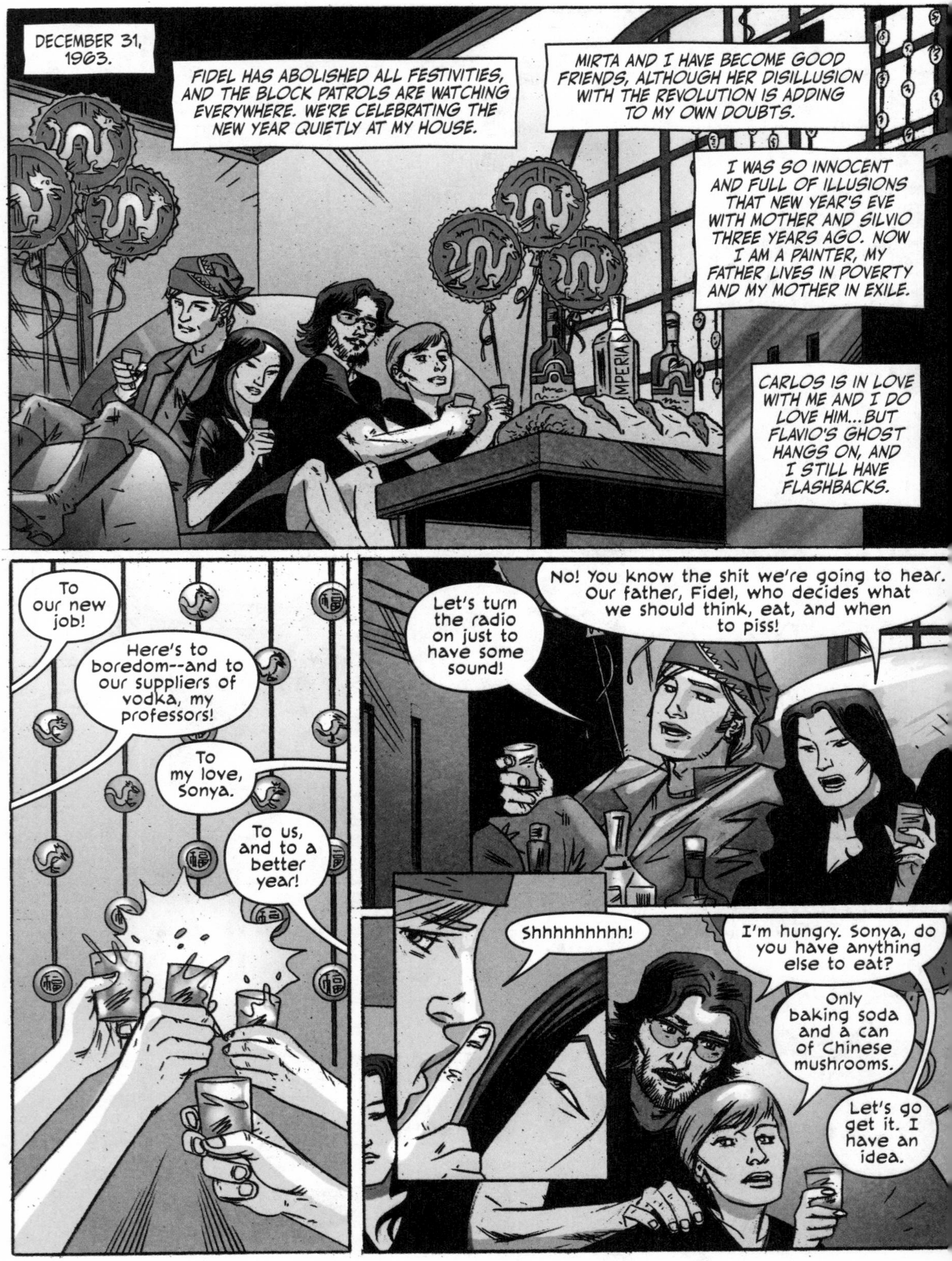
DECEMBER 31, 1963.
FIDEL HAS ABOLISHED ALL FESTIVITIES, AND THE BLOCK PATROLS ARE WATCHING EVERYWHERE. WE'RE CELEBRATING THE NEW YEAR QUIETLY AT MY HOUSE.
MIRTA AND I HAVE BECOME GOOD FRIENDS, ALTHOUGH HER DISILLUSION WITH THE REVOLUTION IS ADDING TO MY OWN DOUBTS.
I WAS SO INNOCENT AND FULL OF ILLUSIONS THAT NEW YEAR'S EVE WITH MOTHER AND SILVIO THREE YEARS AGO. NOW I AM A PAINTER, MY FATHER LIVES IN POVERTY AND MY MOTHER IN EXILE.
IMPERIAL
CARLOS IS IN LOVE WITH ME AND I DO LOVE HIM... BUT FLAVIO'S GHOST HANGS ON, AND I STILL HAVE FLASHBACKS.
To our new job!
Here's to boredom--and to our suppliers of vodka, my professors!
To my love, Sonya.
To us, and to a better year!
Let's turn the radio on just to have some sound!
No! You know the shit we're going to hear. Our father, Fidel, who decides what we should think, eat, and when to piss!
Shhhhhhhhh!
I'm hungry. Sonya, do you have anything else to eat?
Only baking soda and a can of Chinese mushrooms.
Let's go get it. I have an idea.

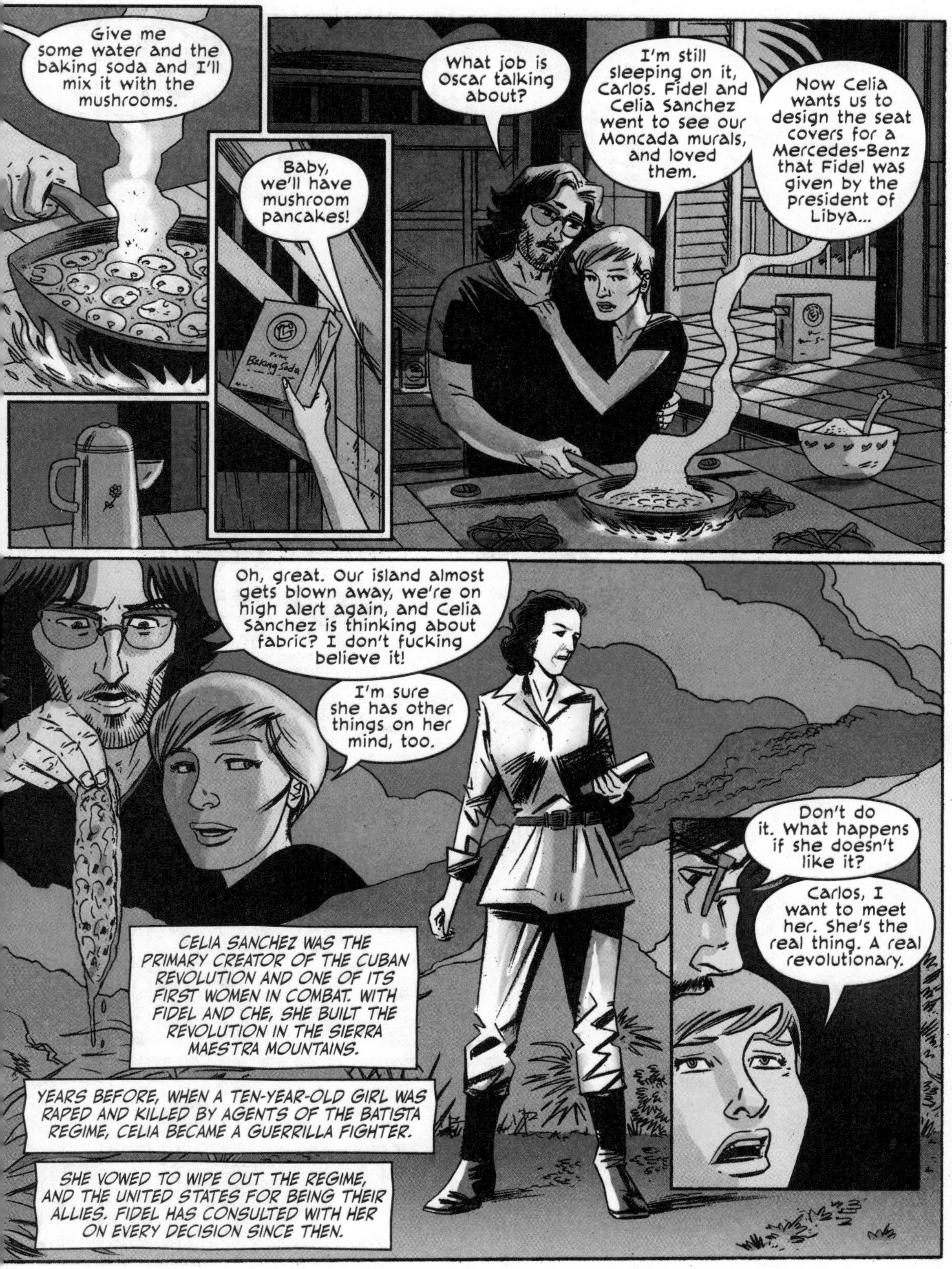

Give me some water and the baking soda and I'll mix it with the mushrooms.
Baby, we'll have mushroom pancakes!
Baking Soda
What job is Oscar talking about?
I'm still sleeping on it, Carlos. Fidel and Celia Sanchez went to see our Moncada murals, and loved them.
Now Celia wants us to design the seat covers for a Mercedes-Benz that Fidel was given by the president of Libya...
Oh, great. Our island almost gets blown away, we're on high alert again, and Celia Sanchez is thinking about fabric? I don't fucking believe it!
I'm sure she has other things on her mind, too.
CELIA SANCHEZ WAS THE PRIMARY CREATOR OF THE CUBAN REVOLUTION AND ONE OF ITS FIRST WOMEN IN COMBAT. WITH FIDEL AND CHE, SHE BUILT THE REVOLUTION IN THE SIERRA MAESTRA MOUNTAINS.
YEARS BEFORE, WHEN A TEN-YEAR-OLD GIRL WAS RAPED AND KILLED BY AGENTS OF THE BATISTA REGIME, CELIA BECAME A GUERRILLA FIGHTER.
SHE VOWED TO WIPE OUT THE REGIME, AND THE UNITED STATES FOR BEING THEIR ALLIES. FIDEL HAS CONSULTED WITH HER ON EVERY DECISION SINCE THEN.
Don't do it. What happens if she doesn't like it?
Carlos, I want to meet her. She's the real thing. A real revolutionary.

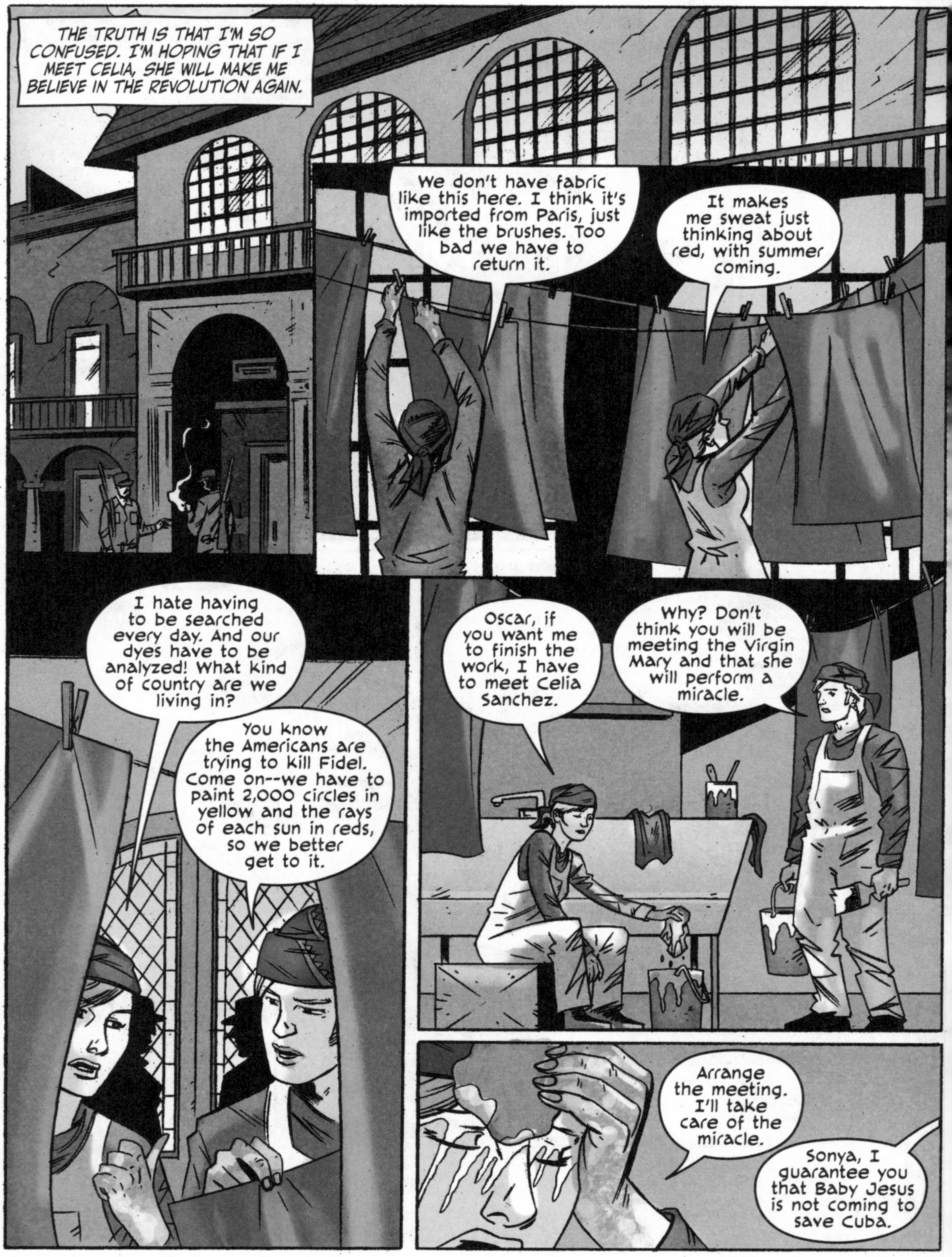
THE TRUTH IS THAT I'M SO CONFUSED. I'M HOPING THAT IF I MEET CELIA, SHE WILL MAKE ME BELIEVE IN THE REVOLUTION AGAIN.
We don't have fabric like this here. I think it's imported from Paris, just like the brushes. Too bad we have to return it.
It makes me sweat just thinking about red, with summer coming.
I hate having to be searched every day. And our dyes have to be analyzed! What kind of country are we living in?
You know the Americans are trying to kill Fidel. Come on--we have to paint 2,000 circles in yellow and the rays of each sun in reds, so we better get to it.
Oscar, if you want me to finish the work, I have to meet Celia Sanchez.
Why? Don't think you will be meeting the Virgin Mary and that she will perform a miracle.
Arrange the meeting. I'll take care of the miracle.
Sonya, I guarantee you that Baby Jesus is not coming to save Cuba.

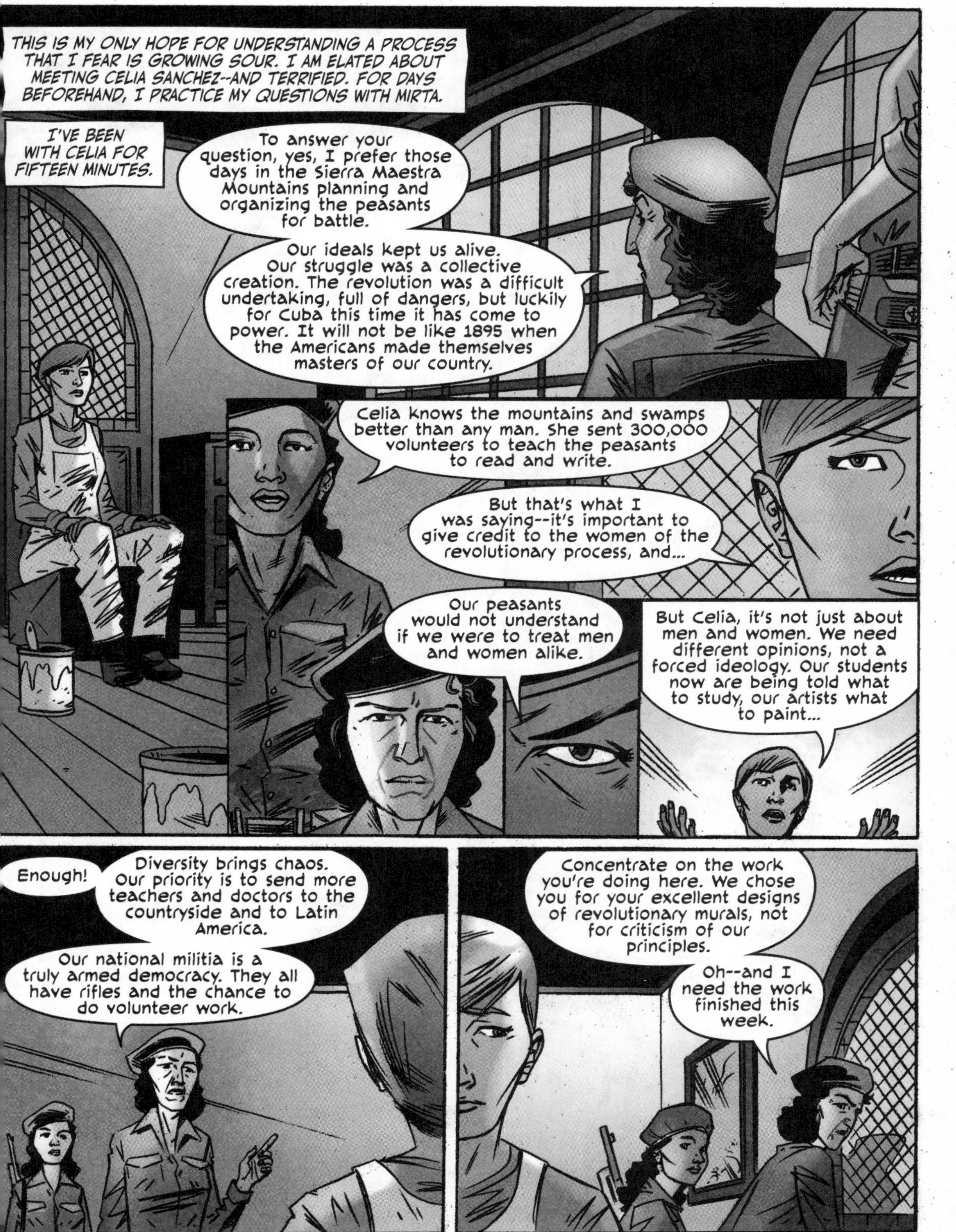
THIS IS MY ONLY HOPE FOR UNDERSTANDING A PROCESS THAT I FEAR IS GROWING SOUR. I AM ELATED ABOUT MEETING CELIA SANCHEZ--AND TERRIFIED. FOR DAYS BEFOREHAND, I PRACTICE MY QUESTIONS WITH MIRTA.
I'VE BEEN WITH CELIA FOR FIFTEEN MINUTES.
To answer your question, yes, I prefer those days in the Sierra Maestra Mountains planning and organizing the peasants for battle.
Our ideals kept us alive. Our struggle was a collective creation. The revolution was a difficult undertaking, full of dangers, but luckily for Cuba this time it has come to power. It will not be like 1895 when the Americans made themselves masters of our country.
Celia knows the mountains and swamps better than any man. She sent 300,000 volunteers to teach the peasants to read and write.
But that's what I was saying--it's important to give credit to the women of the revolutionary process, and...
Our peasants would not understand if we were to treat men and women alike.
But Celia, it's not just about men and women. We need different opinions, not a forced ideology. Our students now are being told what to study, our artists what to paint...
Enough!
Diversity brings chaos. Our priority is to send more teachers and doctors to the countryside and to Latin America.
Our national militia is a truly armed democracy. They all have rifles and the chance to do volunteer work.
Concentrate on the work you're doing here. We chose you for your excellent designs of revolutionary murals, not for criticism of our principles.
Oh--and I need the work finished this week.

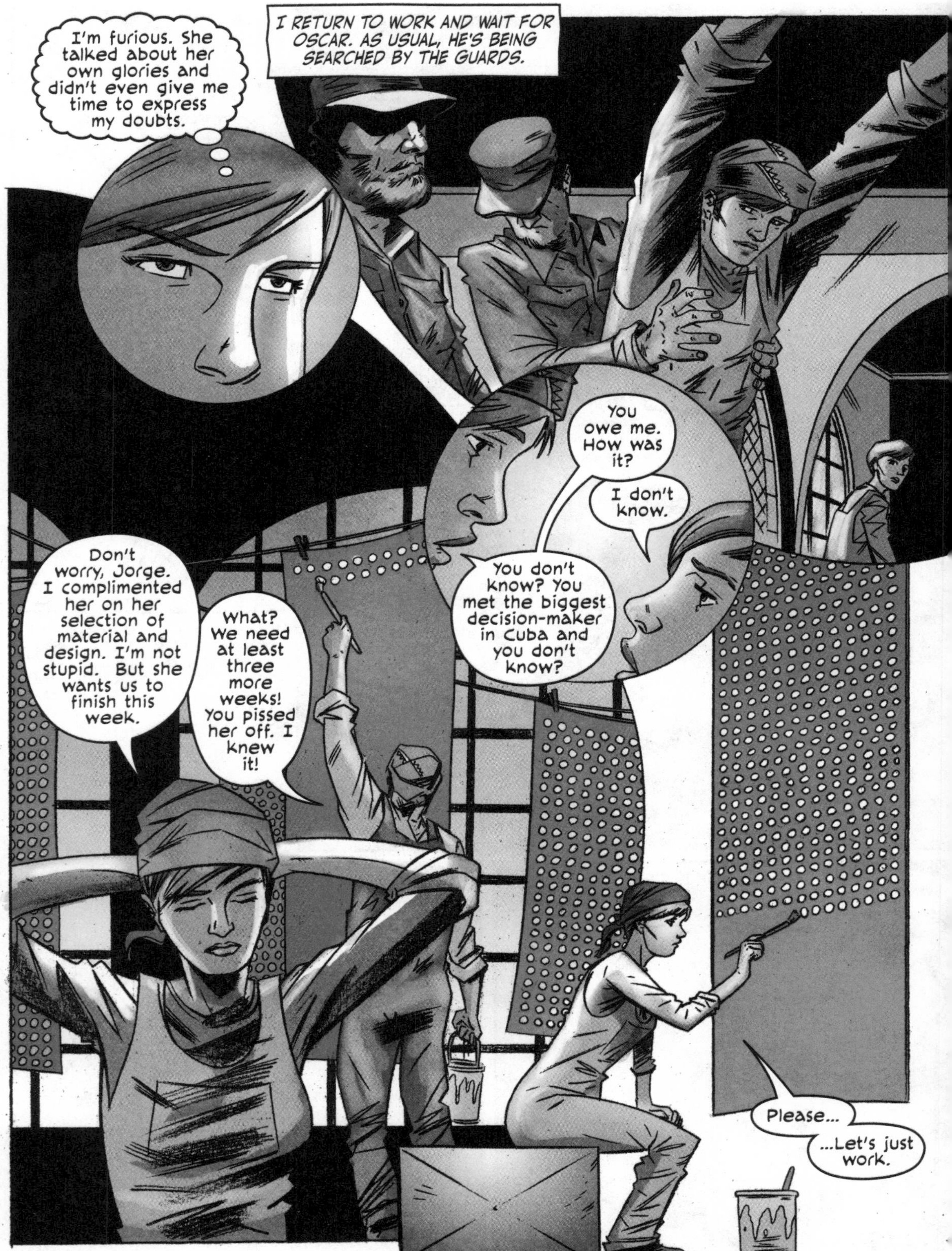
I'm furious. She talked about her own glories and didn't even give me time to express my doubts.
I RETURN TO WORK AND WAIT FOR OSCAR. AS USUAL, HE'S BEING SEARCHED BY THE GUARDS.
You owe me. How was it?
I don't know.
You don't know? You met the biggest decision-maker in Cuba and you don't know?
Don't worry, Jorge. I complimented her on her selection of material and design. I'm not stupid. But she wants us to finish this week.
What? We need at least three more weeks! You pissed her off. I knew it!
Please...
...Let's just work.

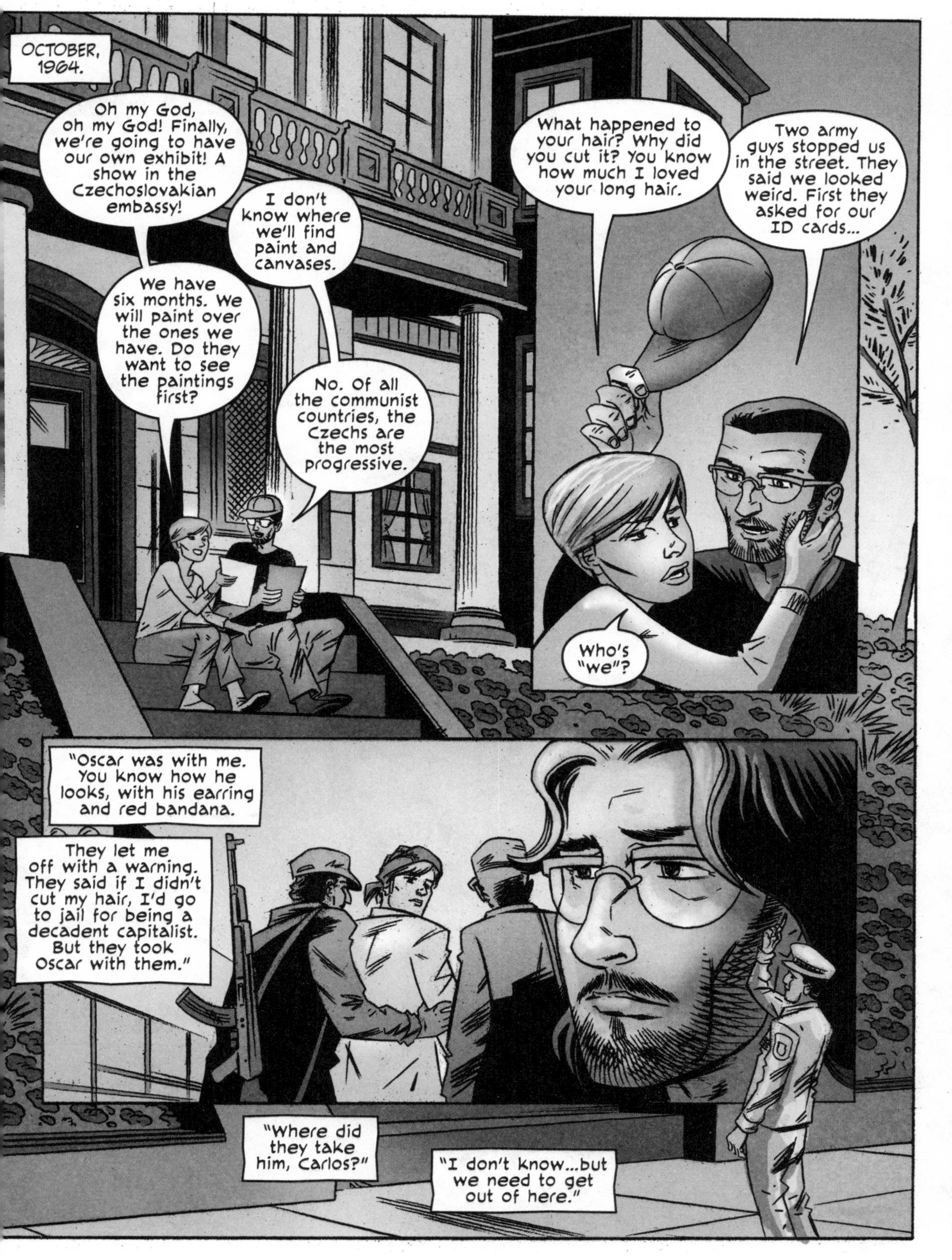
OCTOBER, 1964.
Oh my God, oh my God! Finally, we're going to have our own exhibit! A show in the Czechoslovakian embassy!
I don't know where we'll find paint and canvases.
We have six months. We will paint over the ones we have. Do they want to see the paintings first?
No. Of all the communist countries, the Czechs are the most progressive.
What happened to your hair? Why did you cut it? You know how much I loved your long hair.
Two army guys stopped us in the street. They said we looked weird. First they asked for our ID cards...
Who's "we"?
"Oscar was with me. You know how he looks, with his earring and red bandana.
They let me off with a warning. They said if I didn't cut my hair, I'd go to jail for being a decadent capitalist. But they took Oscar with them."
"Where did they take him, Carlos?"
"I don't know...but we need to get out of here."

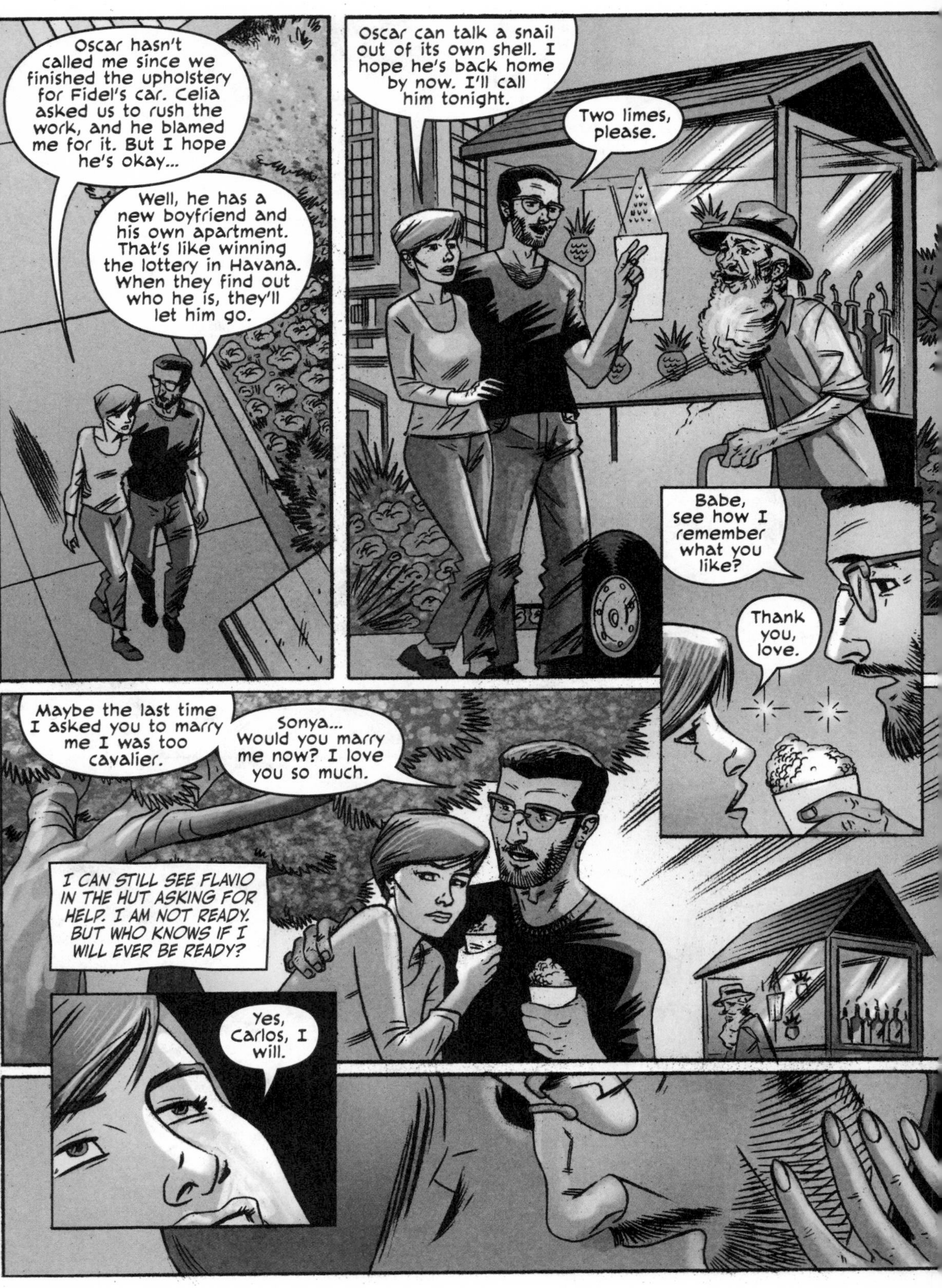
Oscar hasn't called me since we finished the upholstery for Fidel's car. Celia asked us to rush the work, and he blamed me for it. But I hope he's okay...
Well, he has a new boyfriend and his own apartment. That's like winning the lottery in Havana. When they find out who he is, they'll let him go.
Oscar can talk a snail out of its own shell. I hope he's back home by now. I'll call him tonight.
Two limes, please.
Babe, see how I remember what you like?
Thank you, love.
Maybe the last time I asked you to marry me I was too cavalier.
Sonya... Would you marry me now? I love you so much.
I CAN STILL SEE FLAVIO IN THE HUT ASKING FOR HELP. I AM NOT READY. BUT WHO KNOWS IF I WILL EVER BE READY?
Yes, Carlos, I will.

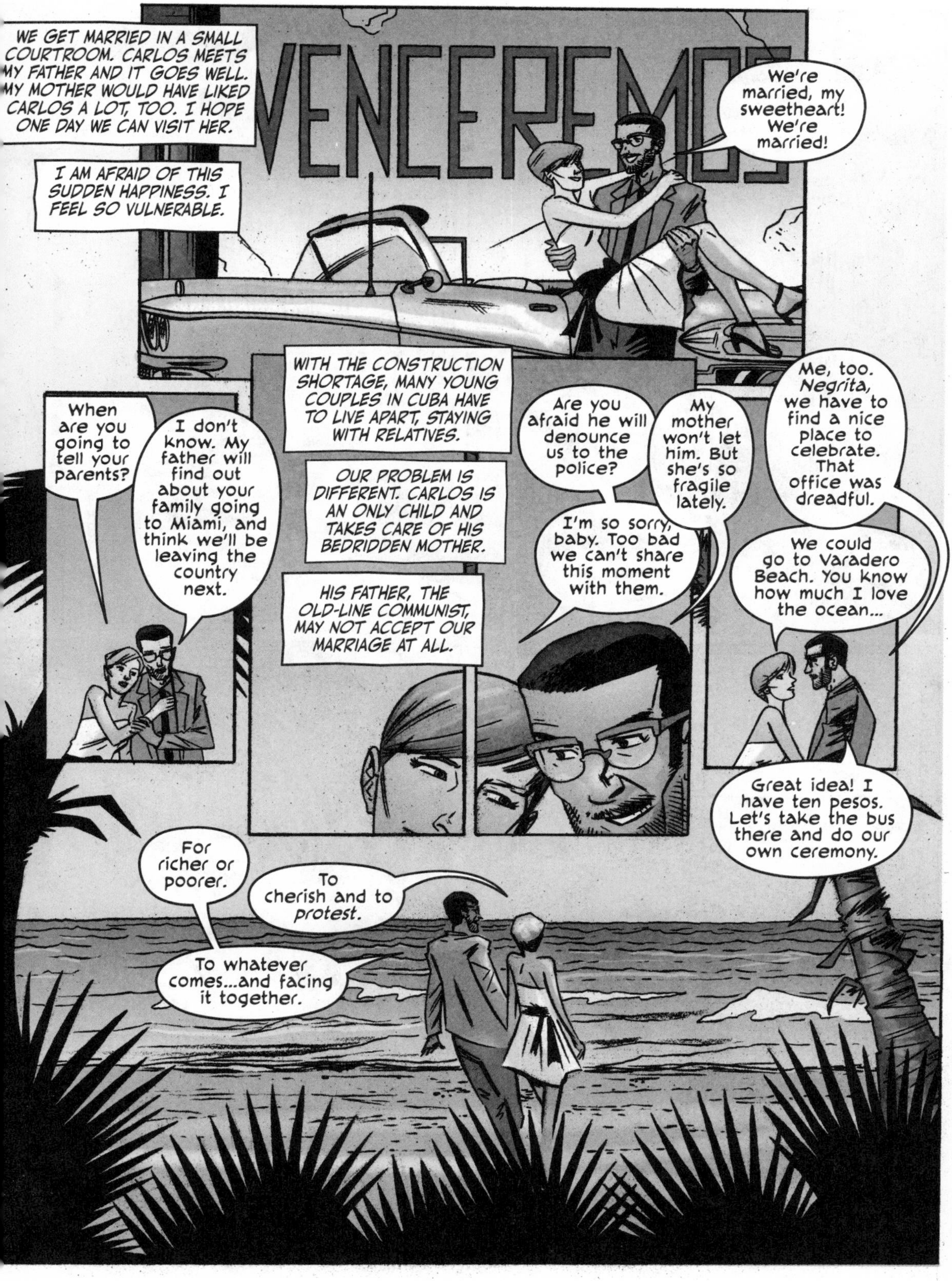
WE GET MARRIED IN A SMALL COURTROOM. CARLOS MEETS MY FATHER AND IT GOES WELL. MY MOTHER WOULD HAVE LIKED CARLOS A LOT, TOO. I HOPE ONE DAY WE CAN VISIT HER.
I AM AFRAID OF THIS SUDDEN HAPPINESS. I FEEL SO VULNERABLE.
VENCEREMOS
We're married, my sweetheart! We're married!
When are you going to tell your parents?
I don't know. My father will find out about your family going to Miami, and think we'll be leaving the country next.
WITH THE CONSTRUCTION SHORTAGE, MANY YOUNG COUPLES IN CUBA HAVE TO LIVE APART, STAYING WITH RELATIVES.
OUR PROBLEM IS DIFFERENT. CARLOS IS AN ONLY CHILD AND TAKES CARE OF HIS BEDRIDDEN MOTHER.
HIS FATHER, THE OLD-LINE COMMUNIST, MAY NOT ACCEPT OUR MARRIAGE AT ALL.
Are you afraid he will denounce us to the police?
My mother won't let him. But she's so fragile lately.
I'm so sorry, baby. Too bad we can't share this moment with them.
Me, too. *Negrita*, we have to find a nice place to celebrate. That office was dreadful.
We could go to Varadero Beach. You know how much I love the ocean...
Great idea! I have ten pesos. Let's take the bus there and do our own ceremony.
For richer or poorer.
To cherish and to *protest*.
To whatever comes...and facing it together.

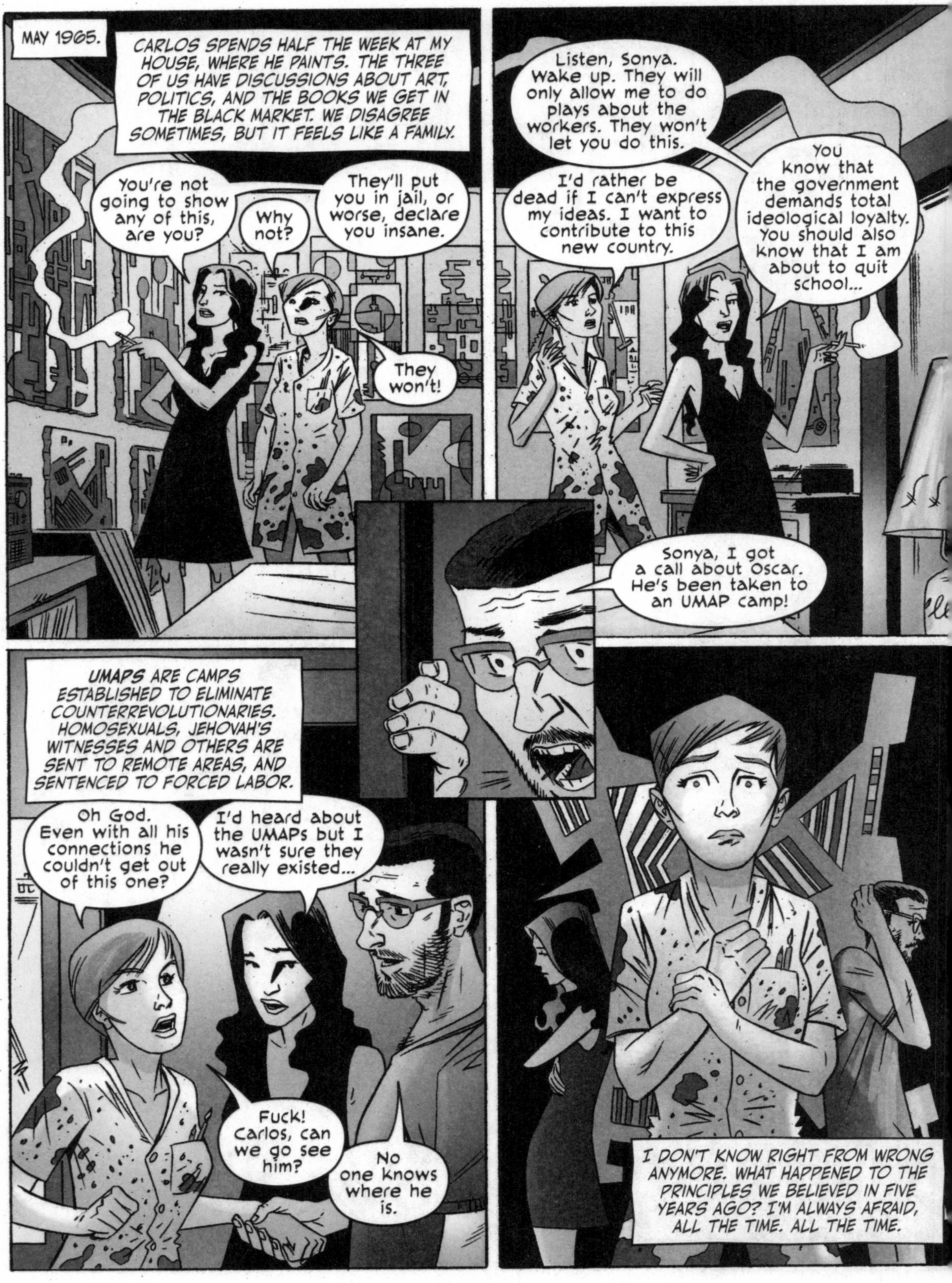

MAY 1965.
CARLOS SPENDS HALF THE WEEK AT MY HOUSE, WHERE HE PAINTS. THE THREE OF US HAVE DISCUSSIONS ABOUT ART, POLITICS, AND THE BOOKS WE GET IN THE BLACK MARKET. WE DISAGREE SOMETIMES, BUT IT FEELS LIKE A FAMILY.
You're not going to show any of this, are you?
Why not?
They'll put you in jail, or worse, declare you insane.
They won't!
Listen, Sonya. Wake up. They will only allow me to do plays about the workers. They won't let you do this.
I'd rather be dead if I can't express my ideas. I want to contribute to this new country.
You know that the government demands total ideological loyalty. You should also know that I am about to quit school...
Sonya, I got a call about Oscar. He's been taken to an UMAP camp!
UMAPS ARE CAMPS ESTABLISHED TO ELIMINATE COUNTERREVOLUTIONARIES. HOMOSEXUALS, JEHOVAH'S WITNESSES AND OTHERS ARE SENT TO REMOTE AREAS, AND SENTENCED TO FORCED LABOR.
Oh God. Even with all his connections he couldn't get out of this one?
I'd heard about the UMAPs but I wasn't sure they really existed...
Fuck! Carlos, can we go see him?
No one knows where he is.
I DON'T KNOW RIGHT FROM WRONG ANYMORE. WHAT HAPPENED TO THE PRINCIPLES WE BELIEVED IN FIVE YEARS AGO? I'M ALWAYS AFRAID, ALL THE TIME. ALL THE TIME.

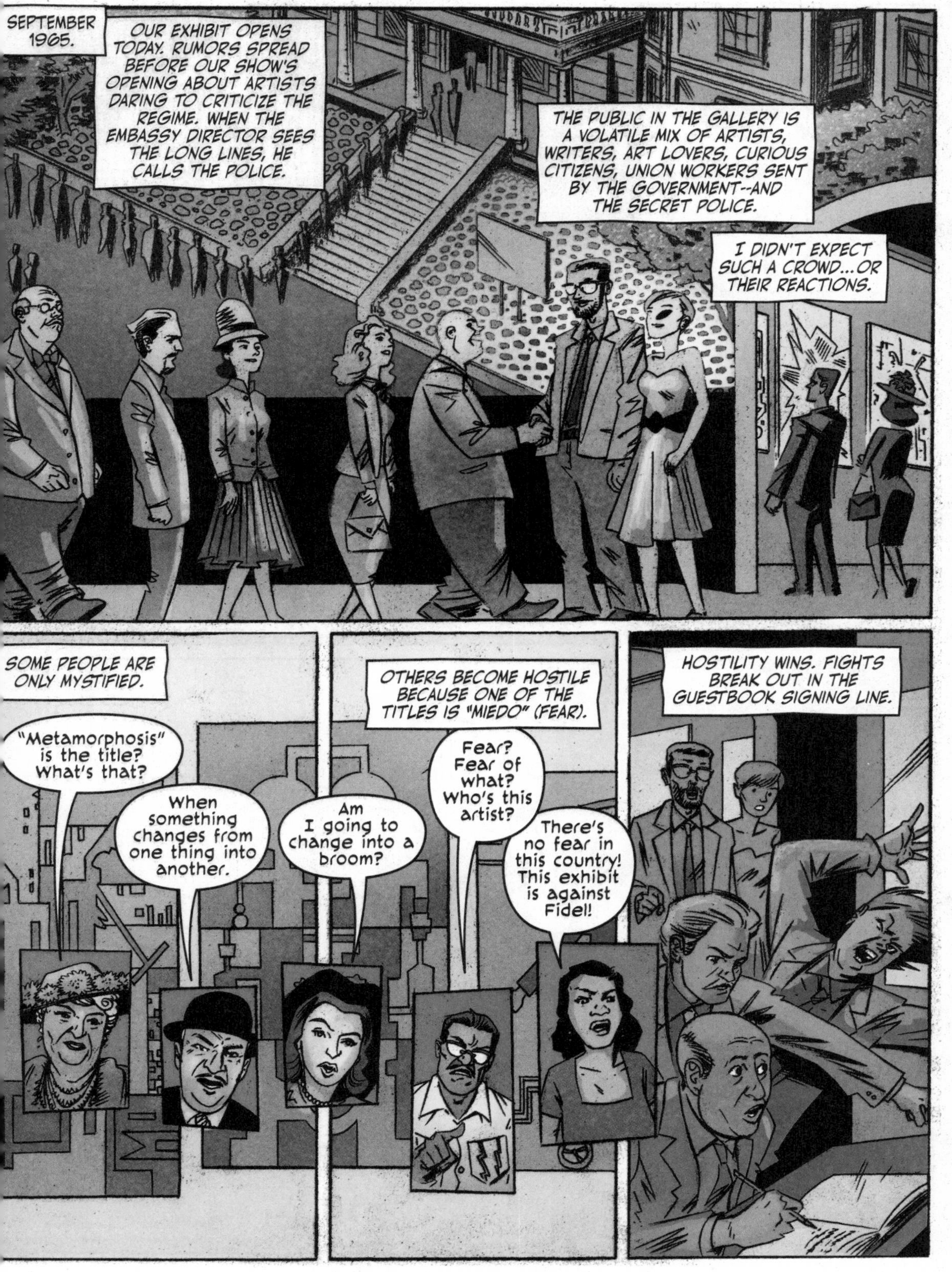
SEPTEMBER 1965.
OUR EXHIBIT OPENS TODAY. RUMORS SPREAD BEFORE OUR SHOW'S OPENING ABOUT ARTISTS DARING TO CRITICIZE THE REGIME. WHEN THE EMBASSY DIRECTOR SEES THE LONG LINES, HE CALLS THE POLICE.
THE PUBLIC IN THE GALLERY IS A VOLATILE MIX OF ARTISTS, WRITERS, ART LOVERS, CURIOUS CITIZENS, UNION WORKERS SENT BY THE GOVERNMENT--AND THE SECRET POLICE.
I DIDN'T EXPECT SUCH A CROWD...OR THEIR REACTIONS.
SOME PEOPLE ARE ONLY MYSTIFIED.
"Metamorphosis" is the title? What's that?
When something changes from one thing into another.
Am I going to change into a broom?
OTHERS BECOME HOSTILE BECAUSE ONE OF THE TITLES IS "MIEDO" (FEAR).
Fear? Fear of what? Who's this artist?
There's no fear in this country! This exhibit is against Fidel!
HOSTILITY WINS. FIGHTS BREAK OUT IN THE GUESTBOOK SIGNING LINE.

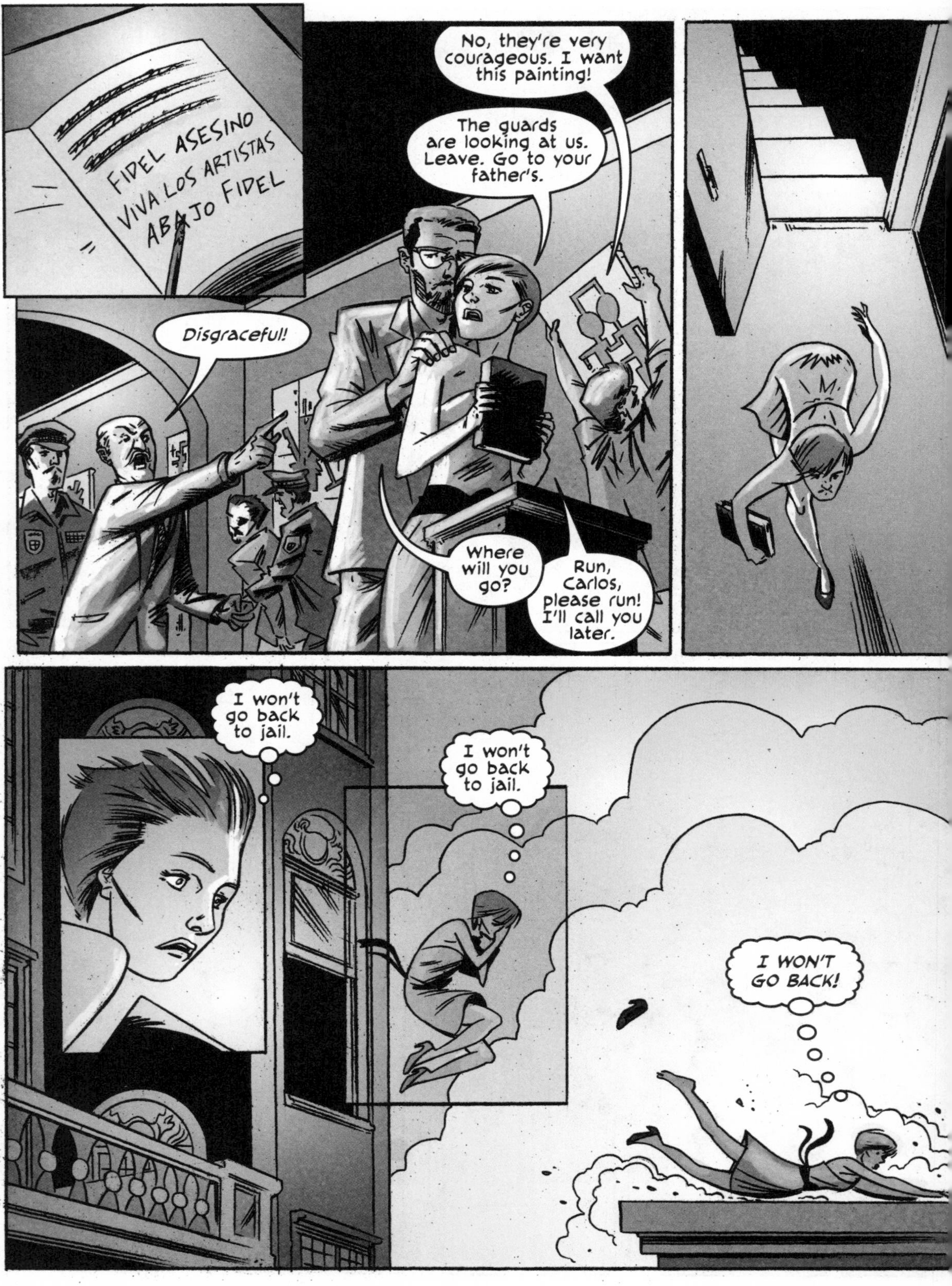
FIDEL ASESINO
VIVA LOS ARTISTAS
ABAJO FIDEL
No, they're very courageous. I want this painting!
The guards are looking at us. Leave. Go to your father's.
Disgraceful!
Where will you go?
Run, Carlos, please run! I'll call you later.
I won't go back to jail.
I won't go back to jail.
I WON'T GO BACK!

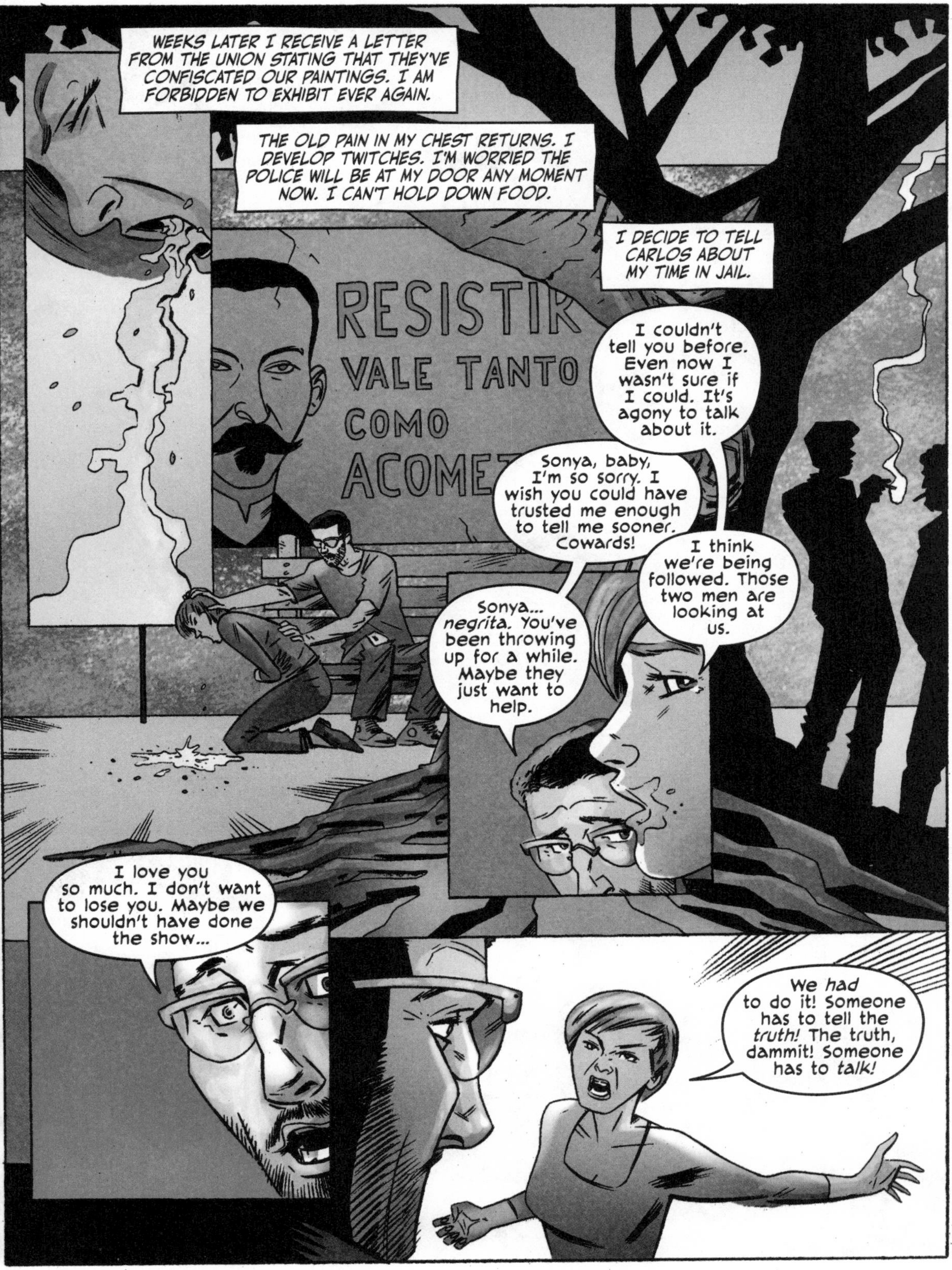
WEEKS LATER I RECEIVE A LETTER FROM THE UNION STATING THAT THEY'VE CONFISCATED OUR PAINTINGS. I AM FORBIDDEN TO EXHIBIT EVER AGAIN.
THE OLD PAIN IN MY CHEST RETURNS. I DEVELOP TWITCHES. I'M WORRIED THE POLICE WILL BE AT MY DOOR ANY MOMENT NOW. I CAN'T HOLD DOWN FOOD.
I DECIDE TO TELL CARLOS ABOUT MY TIME IN JAIL.
RESISTIR VALE TANTO COMO ACOMET
I couldn't tell you before. Even now I wasn't sure if I could. It's agony to talk about it.
Sonya, baby, I'm so sorry. I wish you could have trusted me enough to tell me sooner. Cowards!
I think we're being followed. Those two men are looking at us.
Sonya... *negrita*. You've been throwing up for a while. Maybe they just want to help.
I love you so much. I don't want to lose you. Maybe we shouldn't have done the show...
We *had* to do it! Someone has to tell the *truth!* The truth, dammit! Someone has to *talk!*

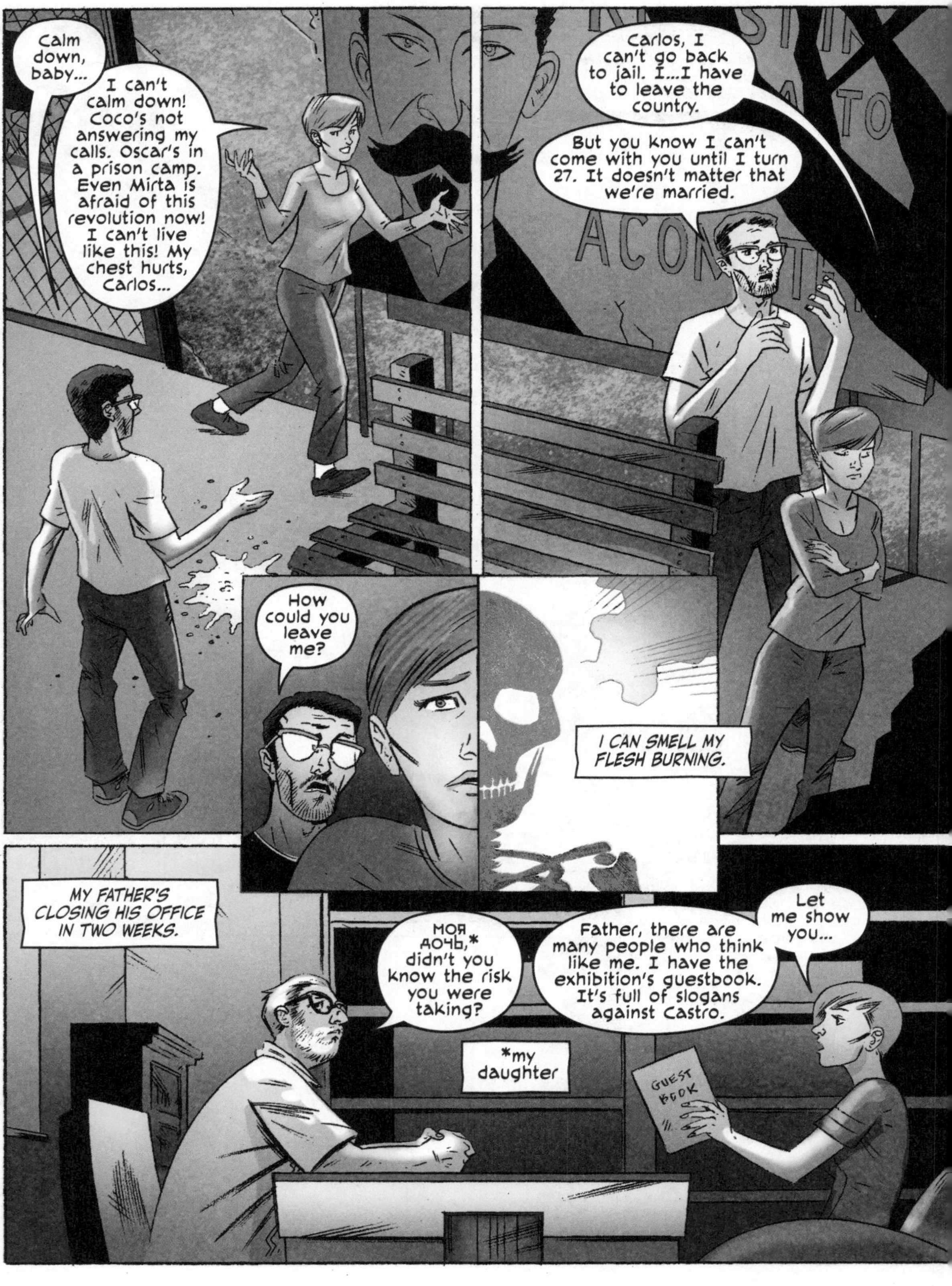

Calm down, baby...
I can't calm down! Coco's not answering my calls. Oscar's in a prison camp. Even Mirta is afraid of this revolution now! I can't live like this! My chest hurts, Carlos...
Carlos, I can't go back to jail. I...I have to leave the country.
But you know I can't come with you until I turn 27. It doesn't matter that we're married.
How could you leave me?
I CAN SMELL MY FLESH BURNING.
MY FATHER'S CLOSING HIS OFFICE IN TWO WEEKS.
МОЯ ДОЧЬ,* didn't you know the risk you were taking?
Father, there are many people who think like me. I have the exhibition's guestbook. It's full of slogans against Castro.
Let me show you...
*my daughter
GUEST BOOK

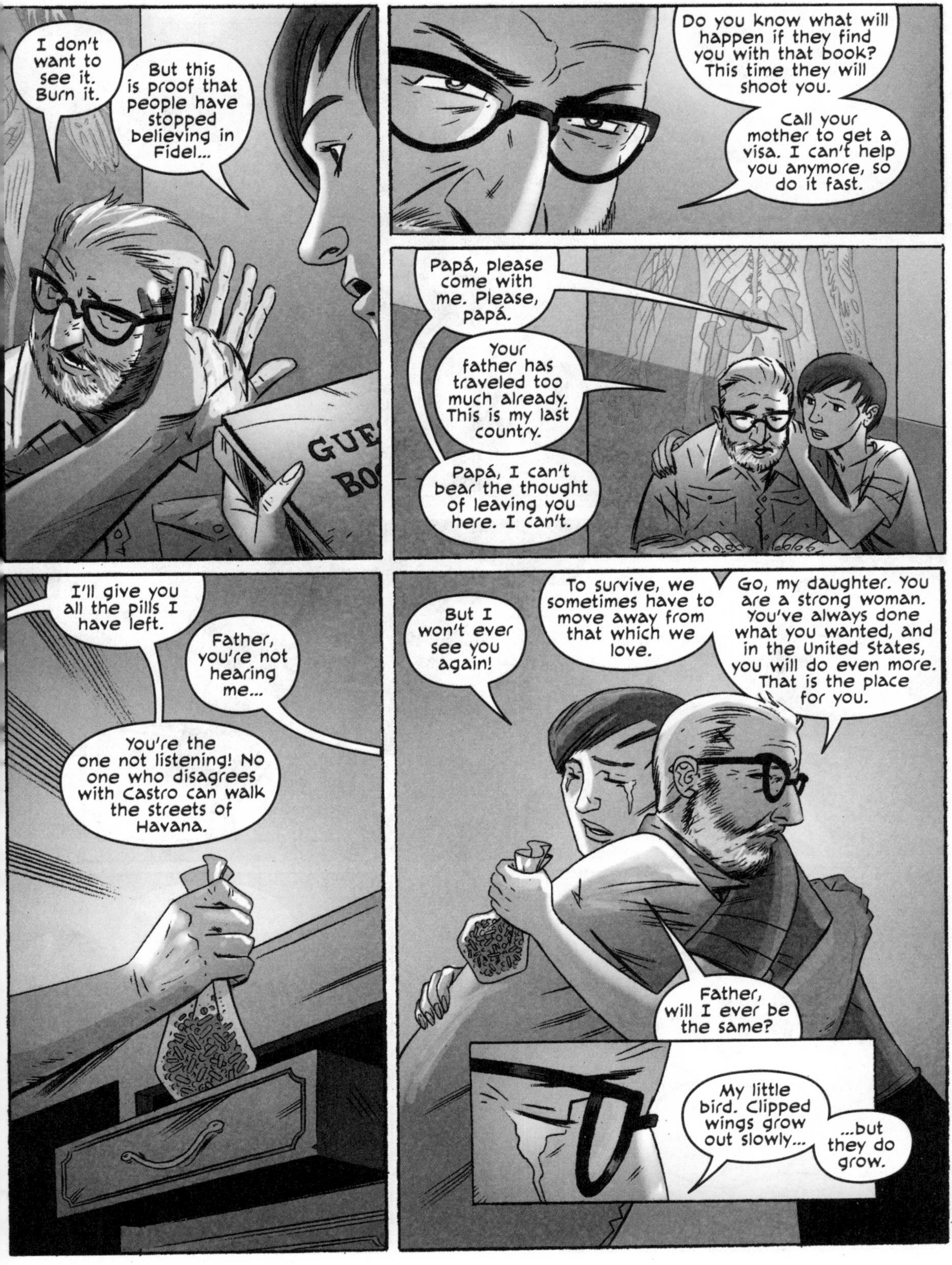

I don't want to see it. Burn it.
But this is proof that people have stopped believing in Fidel...
GUES
BO
Do you know what will happen if they find you with that book? This time they will shoot you.
Call your mother to get a visa. I can't help you anymore, so do it fast.
Papá, please come with me. Please, papá.
Your father has traveled too much already. This is my last country.
Papá, I can't bear the thought of leaving you here. I can't.
I'll give you all the pills I have left.
Father, you're not hearing me...
You're the one not listening! No one who disagrees with Castro can walk the streets of Havana.
But I won't ever see you again!
To survive, we sometimes have to move away from that which we love.
Go, my daughter. You are a strong woman. You've always done what you wanted, and in the United States, you will do even more. That is the place for you.
Father, will I ever be the same?
My little bird. Clipped wings grow out slowly...
...but they do grow.

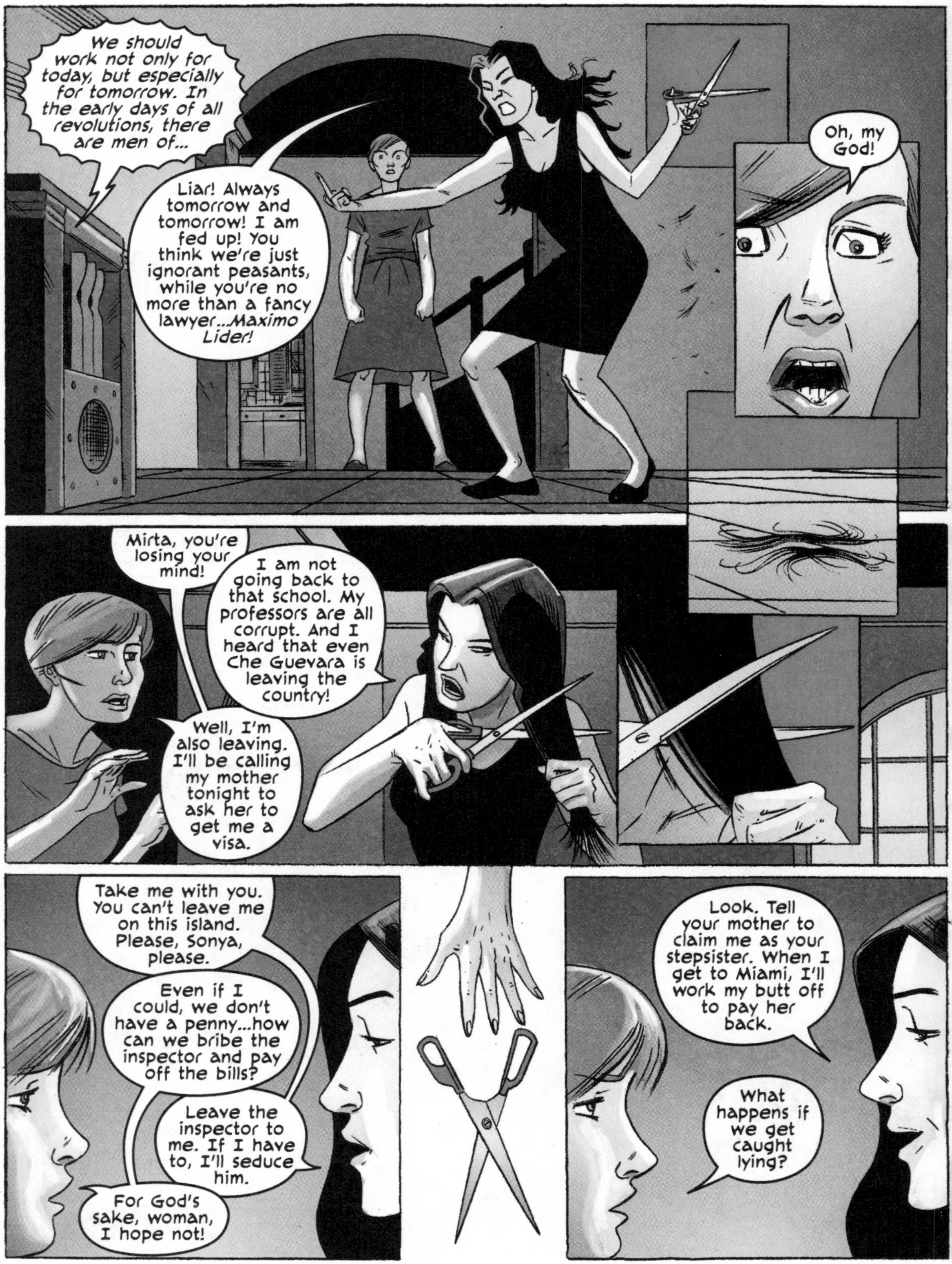
We should work not only for today, but especially for tomorrow. In the early days of all revolutions, there are men of...
Liar! Always tomorrow and tomorrow! I am fed up! You think we're just ignorant peasants, while you're no more than a fancy lawyer...Maximo Lider!
Oh, my God!
Mirta, you're losing your mind!
I am not going back to that school. My professors are all corrupt. And I heard that even Che Guevara is leaving the country!
Well, I'm also leaving. I'll be calling my mother tonight to ask her to get me a visa.
Take me with you. You can't leave me on this island. Please, Sonya, please.
Even if I could, we don't have a penny...how can we bribe the inspector and pay off the bills?
Leave the inspector to me. If I have to, I'll seduce him.
For God's sake, woman, I hope not!
Look. Tell your mother to claim me as your stepsister. When I get to Miami, I'll work my butt off to pay her back.
What happens if we get caught lying?

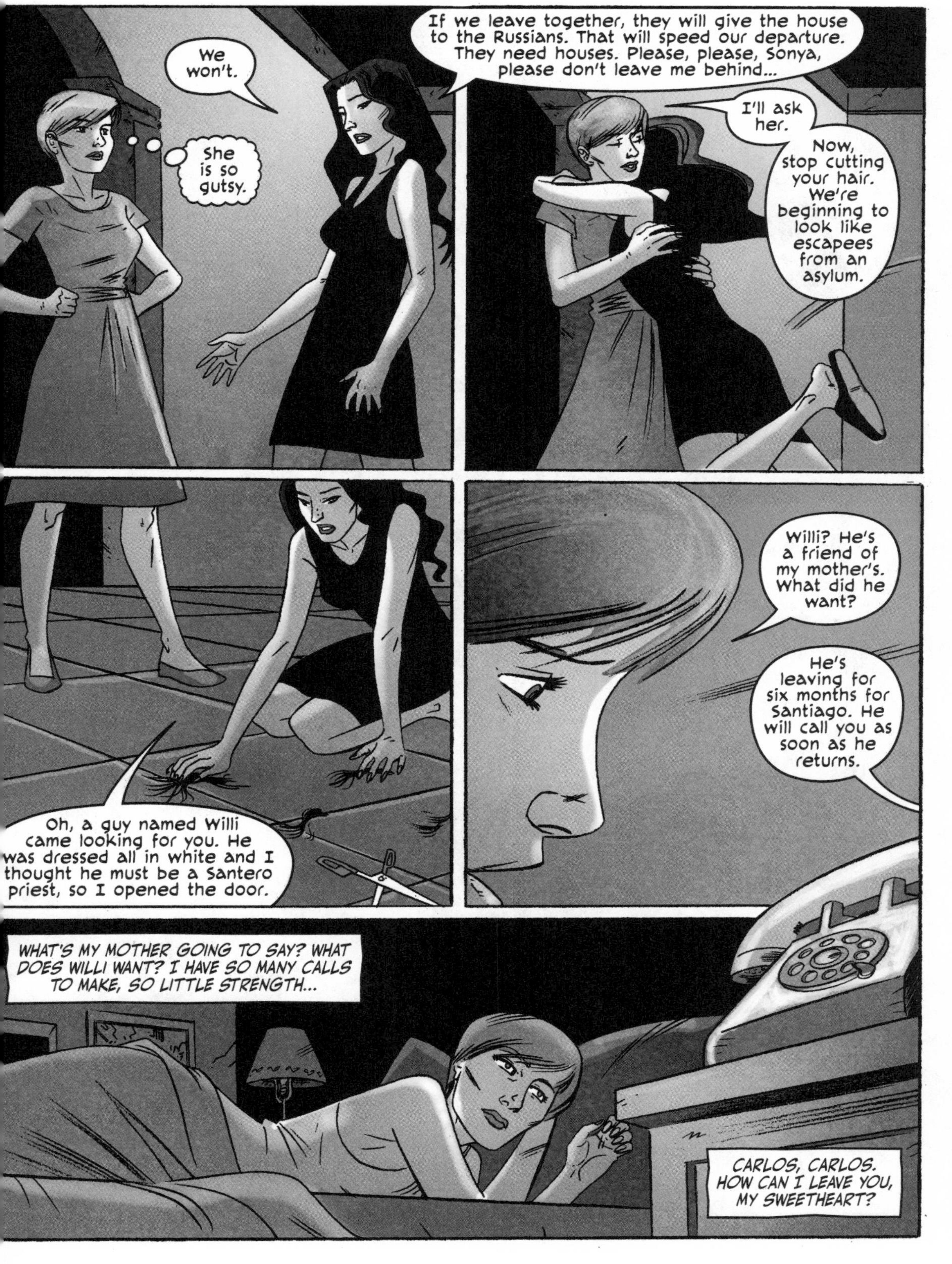

We won't.
She is so gutsy.
If we leave together, they will give the house to the Russians. That will speed our departure. They need houses. Please, please, Sonya, please don't leave me behind...
I'll ask her.
Now, stop cutting your hair. We're beginning to look like escapees from an asylum.
Oh, a guy named Willi came looking for you. He was dressed all in white and I thought he must be a Santero priest, so I opened the door.
Willi? He's a friend of my mother's. What did he want?
He's leaving for six months for Santiago. He will call you as soon as he returns.
WHAT'S MY MOTHER GOING TO SAY? WHAT DOES WILLI WANT? I HAVE SO MANY CALLS TO MAKE, SO LITTLE STRENGTH...
CARLOS, CARLOS. HOW CAN I LEAVE YOU, MY SWEETHEART?

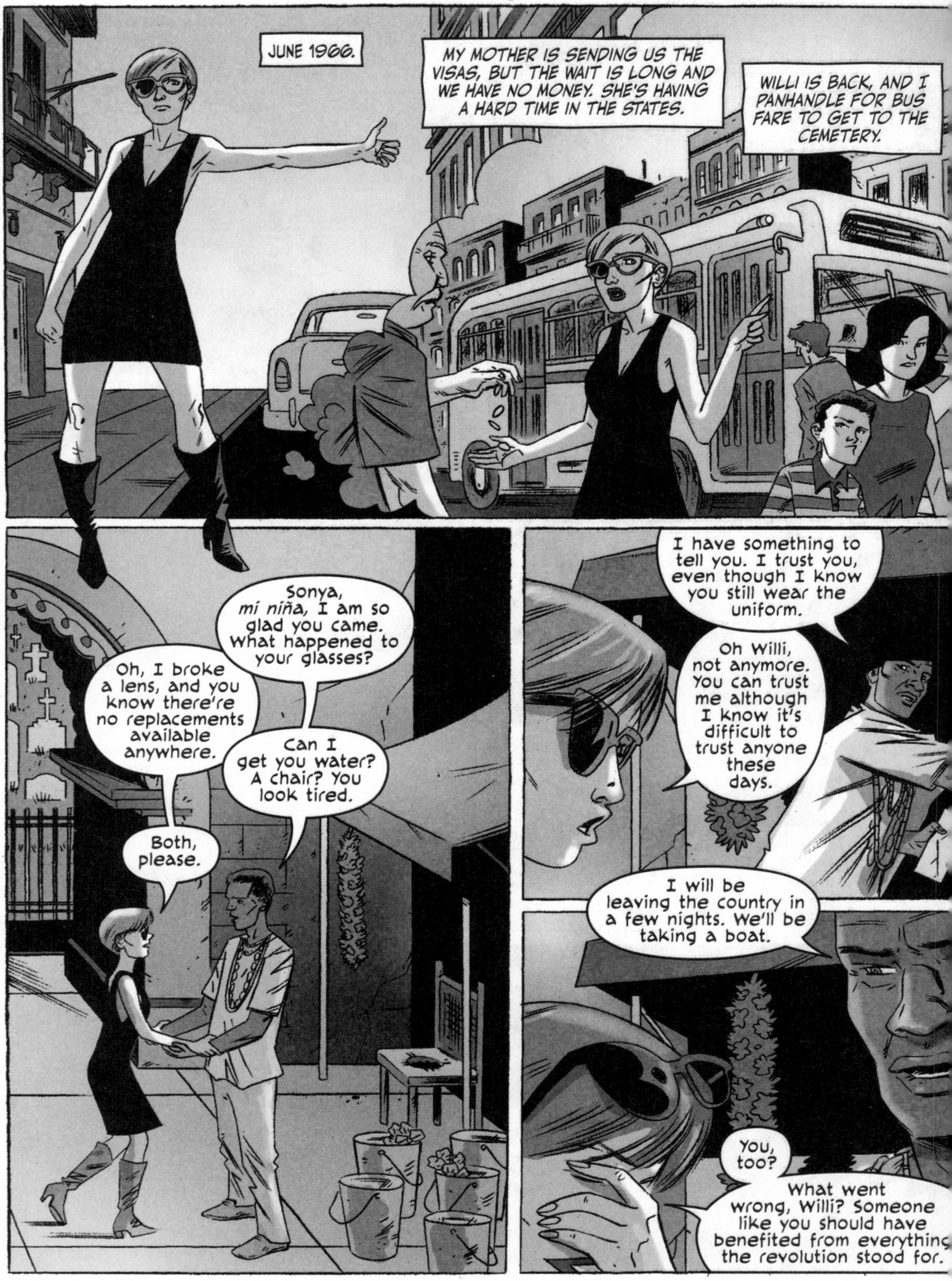
JUNE 1966.
MY MOTHER IS SENDING US THE VISAS, BUT THE WAIT IS LONG AND WE HAVE NO MONEY. SHE'S HAVING A HARD TIME IN THE STATES.
WILLI IS BACK, AND I PANHANDLE FOR BUS FARE TO GET TO THE CEMETERY.
Sonya, mi niña, I am so glad you came. What happened to your glasses?
Oh, I broke a lens, and you know there're no replacements available anywhere.
Can I get you water? A chair? You look tired.
Both, please.
I have something to tell you. I trust you, even though I know you still wear the uniform.
Oh Willi, not anymore. You can trust me although I know it's difficult to trust anyone these days.
I will be leaving the country in a few nights. We'll be taking a boat.
You, too?
What went wrong, Willi? Someone like you should have benefited from everything the revolution stood for.

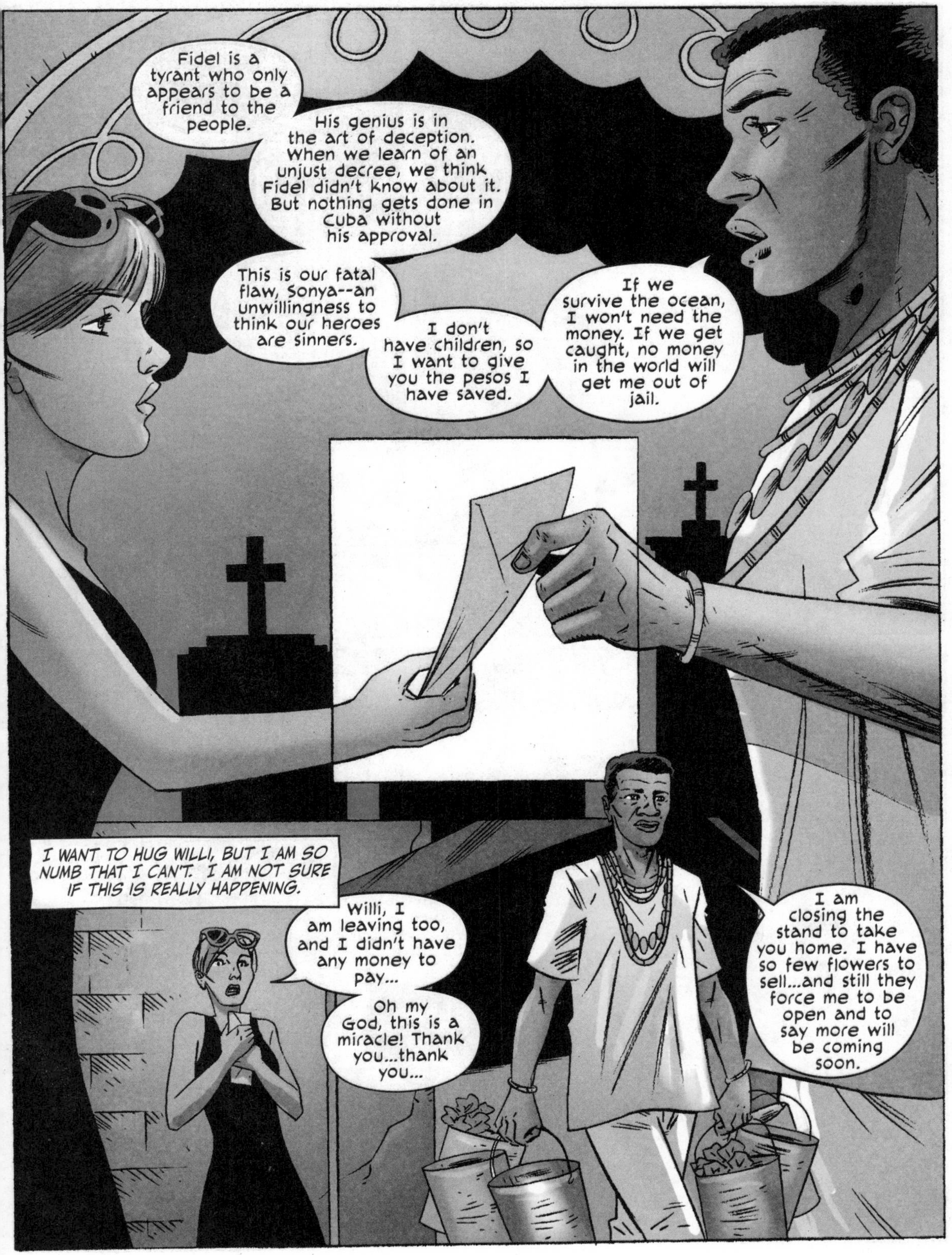
Fidel is a tyrant who only appears to be a friend to the people.
His genius is in the art of deception. When we learn of an unjust decree, we think Fidel didn't know about it. But nothing gets done in Cuba without his approval.
This is our fatal flaw, Sonya--an unwillingness to think our heroes are sinners.
I don't have children, so I want to give you the pesos I have saved.
If we survive the ocean, I won't need the money. If we get caught, no money in the world will get me out of jail.
I WANT TO HUG WILLI, BUT I AM SO NUMB THAT I CAN'T. I AM NOT SURE IF THIS IS REALLY HAPPENING.
Willi, I am leaving too, and I didn't have any money to pay...
Oh my God, this is a miracle! Thank you...thank you...
I am closing the stand to take you home. I have so few flowers to sell...and still they force me to be open and to say more will be coming soon.

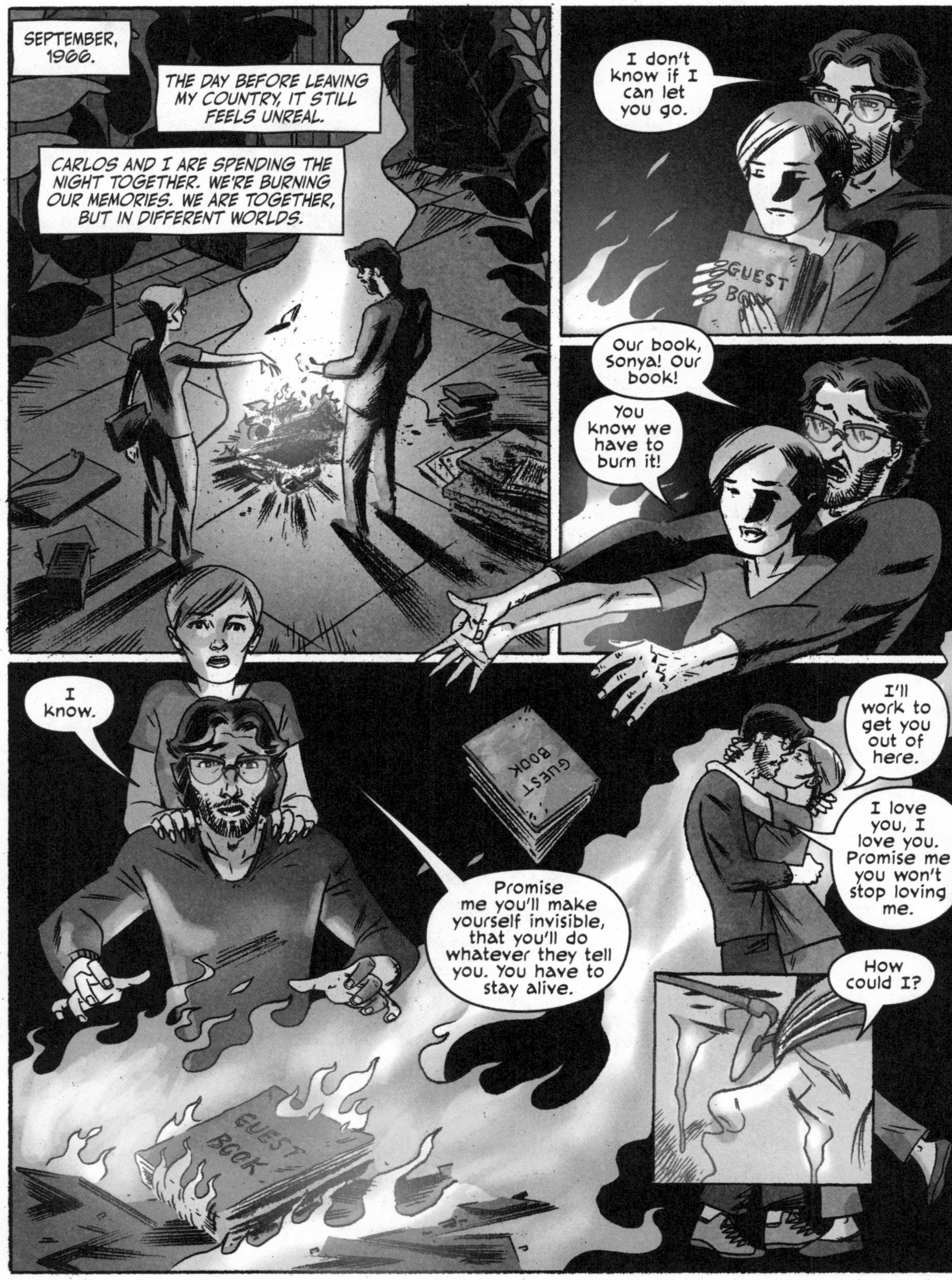
SEPTEMBER, 1966.
THE DAY BEFORE LEAVING MY COUNTRY, IT STILL FEELS UNREAL.
CARLOS AND I ARE SPENDING THE NIGHT TOGETHER. WE'RE BURNING OUR MEMORIES. WE ARE TOGETHER, BUT IN DIFFERENT WORLDS.
I don't know if I can let you go.
GUEST BOOK
Our book, Sonya! Our book!
You know we have to burn it!
I know.
GUEST BOOK
Promise me you'll make yourself invisible, that you'll do whatever they tell you. You have to stay alive.
GUEST BOOK
I'll work to get you out of here.
I love you, I love you. Promise me you won't stop loving me.
How could I?

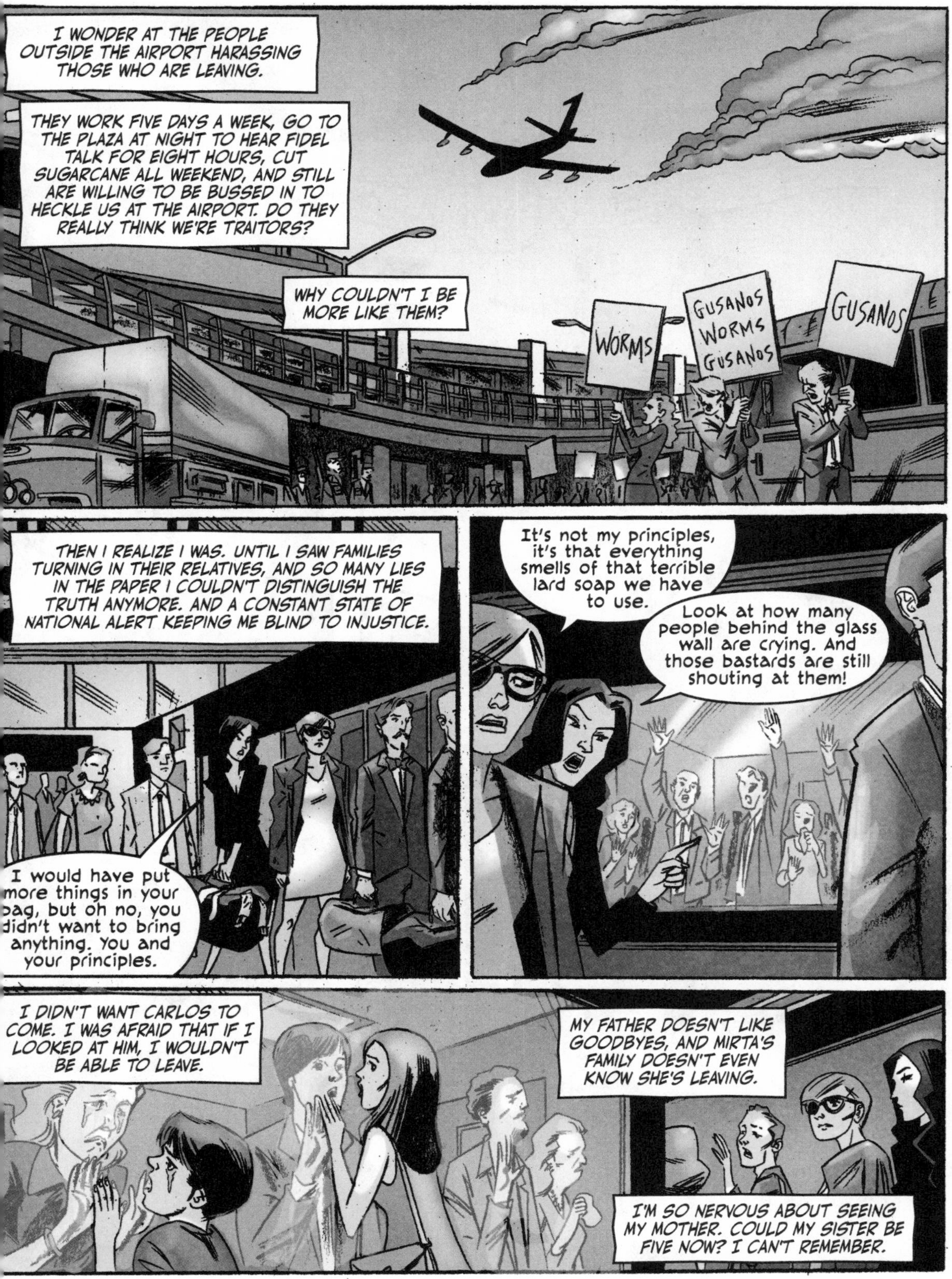
I WONDER AT THE PEOPLE OUTSIDE THE AIRPORT HARASSING THOSE WHO ARE LEAVING.
THEY WORK FIVE DAYS A WEEK, GO TO THE PLAZA AT NIGHT TO HEAR FIDEL TALK FOR EIGHT HOURS, CUT SUGARCANE ALL WEEKEND, AND STILL ARE WILLING TO BE BUSSED IN TO HECKLE US AT THE AIRPORT. DO THEY REALLY THINK WE'RE TRAITORS?
WHY COULDN'T I BE MORE LIKE THEM?
WORMS
GUSANOS WORMS GUSANOS
GUSANOS
THEN I REALIZE I WAS. UNTIL I SAW FAMILIES TURNING IN THEIR RELATIVES, AND SO MANY LIES IN THE PAPER I COULDN'T DISTINGUISH THE TRUTH ANYMORE. AND A CONSTANT STATE OF NATIONAL ALERT KEEPING ME BLIND TO INJUSTICE.
I would have put more things in your bag, but oh no, you didn't want to bring anything. You and your principles.
It's not my principles, it's that everything smells of that terrible lard soap we have to use.
Look at how many people behind the glass wall are crying. And those bastards are still shouting at them!
I DIDN'T WANT CARLOS TO COME. I WAS AFRAID THAT IF I LOOKED AT HIM, I WOULDN'T BE ABLE TO LEAVE.
MY FATHER DOESN'T LIKE GOODBYES, AND MIRTA'S FAMILY DOESN'T EVEN KNOW SHE'S LEAVING.
I'M SO NERVOUS ABOUT SEEING MY MOTHER. COULD MY SISTER BE FIVE NOW? I CAN'T REMEMBER.

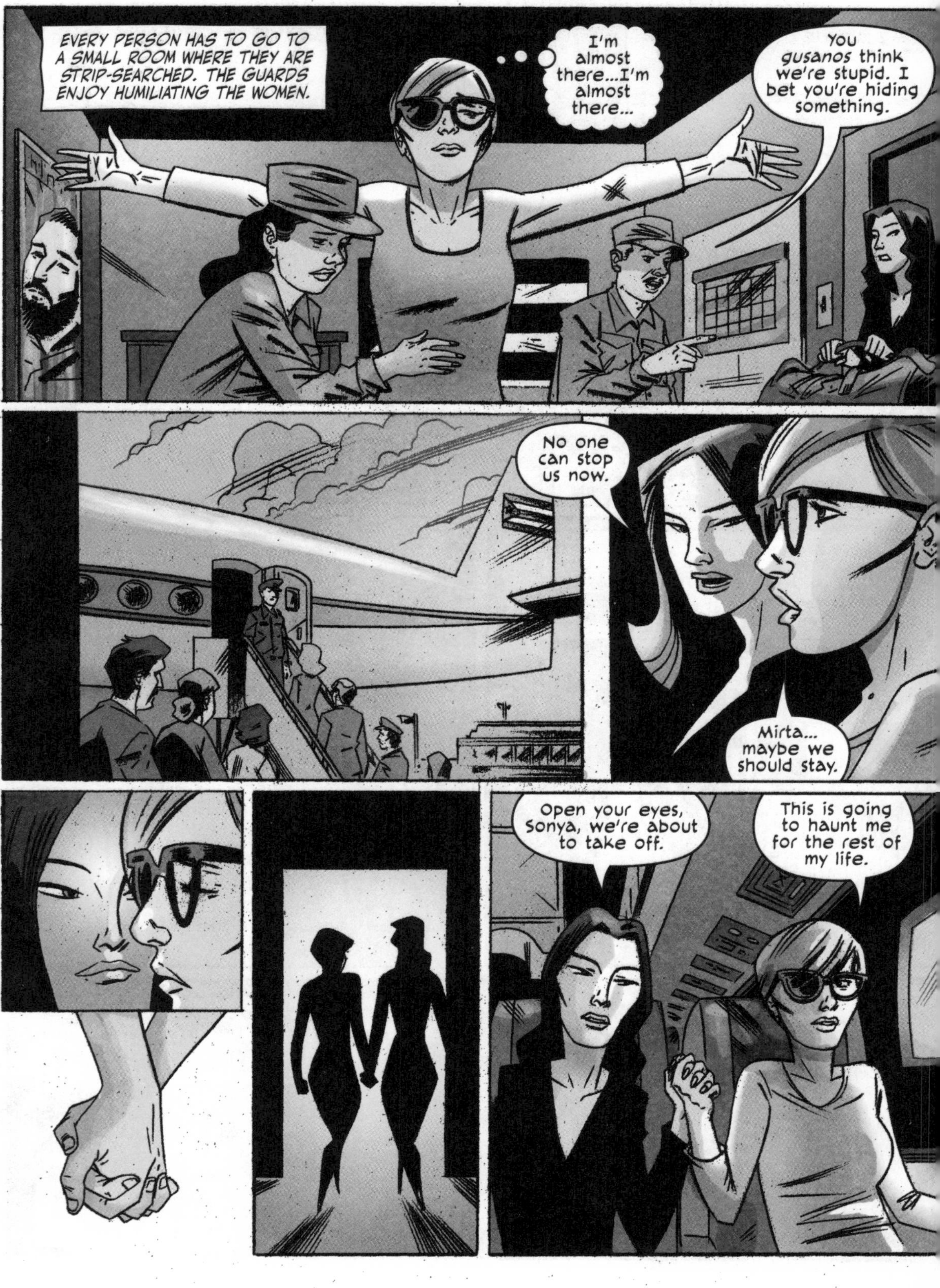
EVERY PERSON HAS TO GO TO A SMALL ROOM WHERE THEY ARE STRIP-SEARCHED. THE GUARDS ENJOY HUMILIATING THE WOMEN.
I'm almost there...I'm almost there...
You gusanos think we're stupid. I bet you're hiding something.
No one can stop us now.
Mirta... maybe we should stay.
Open your eyes, Sonya, we're about to take off.
This is going to haunt me for the rest of my life.

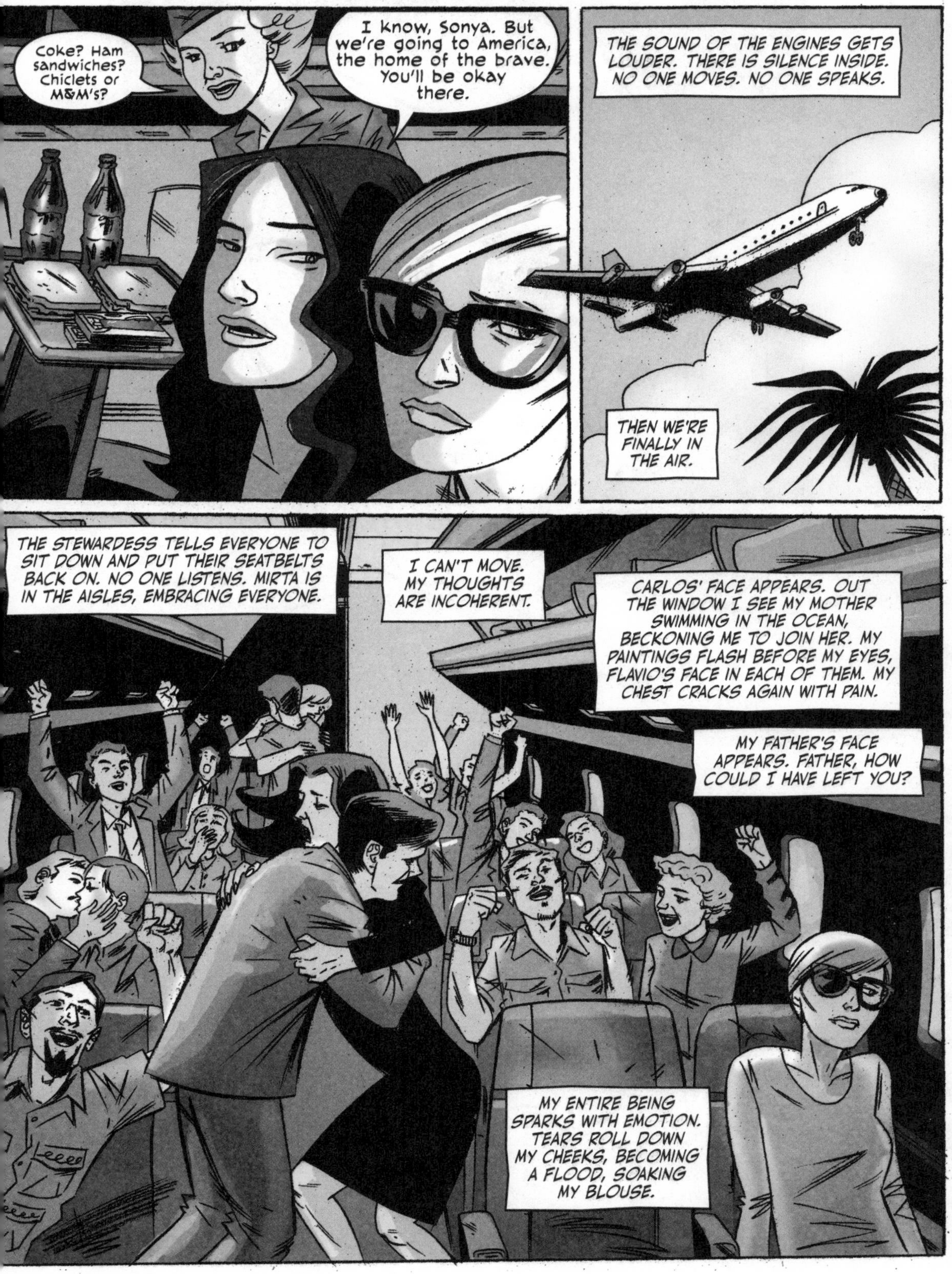
Coke? Ham sandwiches? Chiclets or M&M's?
I know, Sonya. But we're going to America, the home of the brave. You'll be okay there.
THE SOUND OF THE ENGINES GETS LOUDER. THERE IS SILENCE INSIDE. NO ONE MOVES. NO ONE SPEAKS.
THEN WE'RE FINALLY IN THE AIR.
THE STEWARDESS TELLS EVERYONE TO SIT DOWN AND PUT THEIR SEATBELTS BACK ON. NO ONE LISTENS. MIRTA IS IN THE AISLES, EMBRACING EVERYONE.
I CAN'T MOVE. MY THOUGHTS ARE INCOHERENT.
CARLOS' FACE APPEARS. OUT THE WINDOW I SEE MY MOTHER SWIMMING IN THE OCEAN, BECKONING ME TO JOIN HER. MY PAINTINGS FLASH BEFORE MY EYES, FLAVIO'S FACE IN EACH OF THEM. MY CHEST CRACKS AGAIN WITH PAIN.
MY FATHER'S FACE APPEARS. FATHER, HOW COULD I HAVE LEFT YOU?
MY ENTIRE BEING SPARKS WITH EMOTION. TEARS ROLL DOWN MY CHEEKS, BECOMING A FLOOD, SOAKING MY BLOUSE.

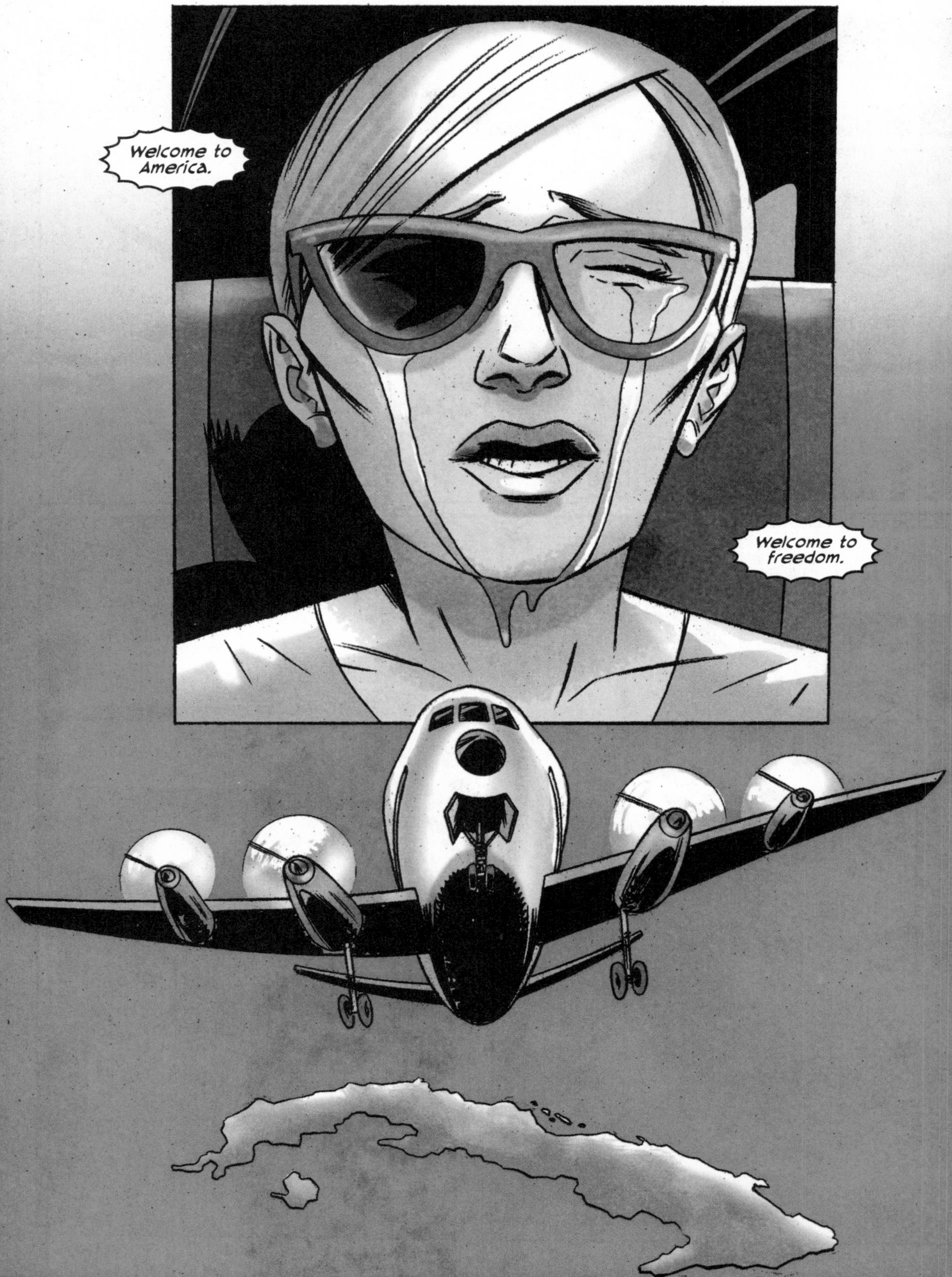
Welcome to America.
Welcome to freedom.